The Growth of Japanese Churches in Brazil

The Growth of Japanese Churches in Brazil

John Mizuki

William Carey Library

533 HERMOSA STREET • SOUTH PASADENA, CALIFORNIA 91030

Library of Congress Cataloging in Publication Data

Mizuki, John, 1922-
    The growth of Japanese churches in Brazil.

    Bibliography: p.
    Includes index.
    1.   Protestant churches--Brazil.   2.   Japanese
in Brazil--Religion.   3.   Church growth--Brazil.
I.   Title.
BX4836.B8M59   280'.4'0981   78-5415
ISBN 0-87808-323-5

Published by the William Carey Library
533 Hermosa Street
South Pasadena, California 91030
Telephone (213) 798-0819

In accord with some of the most recent thinking in the academic
press, the William Carey Library is pleased to present this
scholarly book which has been prepared from an author-edited
and author-prepared camera ready copy.

PRINTED IN THE UNITED STATES OF AMERICA

Dedicated to

THE MISSIONARIES AND PASTORS

WHO HAVE LABORED FOR THE EVANGELIZATION

OF THE JAPANESE IN BRAZIL

Contents

Figures

Tables

xiii

Foreword

The great merit of Dr. Mizuki's book, *The Growth of the Japanese Churches in Brazil*, is that he describes in detail those processes and convictions which must become commonplace in those churches if they are to multiply. He takes church growth seriously. On the basis of a scholarly discussion of the history and sociological background of Japanese churches in Brazil, he courageously tackles the riddle of the little growth and proves that it is not inevitable. He writes from within the movement. He has been there and knows the scene intimately.

Church growth principles, while they differ in detail for each piece of the mosaic of mankind, apply universally. While Dr. Mizuki describes the growth of Japanese churches in Brazil, most of what he says will apply to Japanese churches in other parts of Latin America, and in North America also. Consequently the book ought to be widely read by leaders of Japanese churches. Churchmen in Japan also will rejoice in this book.

Readers will find the book intensely interesting. They will see that church growth in Brazil goes on in many minorities. The same is true of nearly every land. As the Church of Jesus Christ expands across the world, one of the places it grows best is in *newly arrived minorities*. These are important. The Church should grow in ripe pieces of the mosaic. They have been ripened by God. They are frequently the minorities. We can never forget that the Church in the Mediterranean world grew to power during those first fateful years *in the Jewish minority*. From its secure position there, it then spread to the Gentiles.

Readers will do themselves and their churches a favor by studying Japanese Church Growth in Brazil - and putting into practice the procedures Dr. Mizuki advocates.

Donald McGavran
Fuller Theological Seminary
Pasadena, California

Preface

The reason for this research is threefold: to examine the importance of the Japanese in Brazil as a mission field; to recognize the slow growth of the Japanese Christian Churches in Japan, the United States, and Brazil; and to remedy the almost total absence of church growth research on the Christian Churches working among the Japanese immigrants and their descendants in the New World.

At present Brazil has the largest Japanese population outside of Japan. Close to 800,000 Japanese and their descendants live in that country and this number is expected to grow to one million in the coming decade. There are 180,000 in the city of Sao Paulo alone. Yet, Protestant communicant members constitute only 0.6 percent of the total Japanese population. Even when the whole Protestant community is included the ratio will not go beyond 2 percent. To this we should add the practicing Catholics who constitute about 9 percent of the total Japanese population. This means that, even if we combine Protestants and practicing Catholics together, approximately 90 percent of the Japanese in Brazil are people who must yet be discipled. There are still approximately 700,000 Japanese that can be won for Christ. Considering the fact that people who have left their fatherland often become more receptive to the gospel for several reasons, we think that a study of the Japanese in Brazil is missiologically relevant.

When we realize that one hundred seventeen years of Protestant mission in Japan have converted only 0.7 percent of that population, and one hundred years of Christian mission among the

Japanese in the United States, a so-called Protestant country, have been able to disciple only 3 percent of them, and fifty years of Japanese Protestant missionary work have won only 0.6 percent of the Japanese in Brazil, we are compelled to ask "Why has the growth of Christian Churches in Japan and among its emigrants overseas been so slow?" The author, who himself has spent about one-half of his twenty-five years of ministerial life in the evangelization of the Japanese, has been struggling with this problem. He came to feel strongly the need of doing research to find some answers to this crucial question. Brazil was chosen because it is the field of his better acquaintance, having lived and worked there most of his life. To find the whys and hows of the growth and non-growth of the Japanese Churches in Brazil is, we think, vitally important for the present and future work there, and may cast light on the parallel situation in Japan and America.

Up to the present nothing has been written on the growth of the Japanese Churches in Brazil. Much excellent research has been carried out on the general picture of church growth in Brazil, by Davis, Read, Johnson, Monterroso, and Willems, but nothing has been done yet on the ethnic Churches in this country of our study. We feel the need of researching the Churches of this homogeneous unit, whose pattern and rate of growth are different from those of most of the other Brazilian Churches.

The purpose of this research is to investigate the factors of growth and non-growth of the Japanese Churches in Brazil, and to find some principles and methods that could be applied to accelerate their growth. An evangelistic and missionary strategy will then be delineated based on these principles and methods.

The method followed in this study is historical and socio-logical. It is historical because we can not study any church growth without a historical perspective since church growth takes place in time. However, our purpose is not to write a history of the Japanese Churches in Brazil. We used history only as much as it is required to introduce to the readers the very little known Protestant Churches of this segment of Brazilian society, and as much as it is necessary to understand church growth, which is the object of the present study. In describing the history of the Churches, the author has confined himself to mentioning only the first pioneer missionaries, not because they are in every case the first in importance, but because they are the first historically.

The method used in the analysis and interpretation of the data is sociological.

The primary sources of information are the year books, annual reports of the denominations, biographies, correspondence, diaries of the church leaders, questionnaires, and interviews recorded on tapes. In search of data, the author consulted the archives of the Episcopal Church in Austin, Texas, and Porto Alegre, Brazil. He travelled extensively visiting churches and interviewing church leaders in the states of Sao Paulo, Parana, Mato Grosso, and Rio Grande do Sul. He visited eleven Free Methodist churches, five Holiness, one Methodist, one Lutheran, the Sao Paulo Christian Church, and one church of the Hosana Evangelical Mission. He interviewed leaders of eight denominations personally and leaders of two denominations (one Catholic) were interviewed through an assistant. Information on two more denominations were acquired by correspondence with their leaders while data on the three remaining denominations were taken from published literature. Thus the author was able to collect information on 15 out of 16 Christian denominations--including the Catholic Church--working among Japanese in Brazil. There is one independent church whose leader the author was not able to locate and consequently not able to get its data.

The original intention of the author was to study the growth of all the Protestant Churches working among the Japanese in Brazil. But later he decided to limit his research to the three larger and older denominations, that is, Episcopal, Holiness, and Free Methodist. He was not able to collect the essential statistical data for other denominations. But since these three denominations constitute 79.5 percent of the Japanese Protestant total membership in Brazil, the author thought the study of their growth would suffice to understand the rate and pattern of growth of the Japanese Protestant Churches in Brazil in general. A brief historical description of other denominations are given in the appendix.

The word *Church* with a capital letter is used to indicate a denomination or the universal Church; uncapitalized, it indicates a local congregation.

This book has seven chapters. The first is on the Japanese migration to Brazil. This was included to provide the historical and social background of the little known ethnic group of our study. The three following chapters cover the three Churches of our study: Episcopal, Holiness, and Free Methodist, respectively. Chapter 5 is on how Japanese have become Christians. It is based on the data collected through questionnaires. The author collected about 200 questionnaires from eleven churches--eight Free Methodist and three Holiness. Unfortunately over one-half of them were lost by the airline the author used to return from Brazil. Thus, he brought back only 93 questionnaires from the following churches: Apuncarna Free Methodist 11, Saude Free

Methodist 4, Pinheiros Free Methodist 30, Marilia Free Methodist
10, Londrina Holiness 10, Presidente Prudente Holiness 15, Campo
Grande Holiness 13. The questionnaires lost were all from four
other Free Methodist churches. As the sample became so small,
the author was tempted to not use them, but he decided to go
ahead and utilize them because he thought they were too important
to be disregarded. They could at least reveal how the members of
the Holiness and Free Methodist Churches in Brazil have become
Christians. Although the samples are not taken from all the
churches of these denominations, they may be considered pretty
representative of the Japanese Protestant population due to
their great homogeneity, both ethnically and religiously. We
can consider them as all basically the same population group.
He hopes that one day the same questionnaire may be used to find
out the ways of conversion of the members of other denominations.
It may be possible that some denominational differences in conversion patterns become evident. But the author's conviction is
that the differences will not be substantially great due first to
the fact that they all come from the same homogeneous unit and
second to the fact that most of the Churches working with
Japanese in Brazil are evangelical in character. Thus, although
the generalizations we made in this chapter are more for the
Holiness and Free Methodist Churches, we can say without much
fear that they are also valid for most of the denominations
working with the ethnic group of our study. Chapter 6 makes a
comparison of the growth of the three denominations of our
study with their counterparts in the United States. The last
chapter comprises a suggested strategy for the future evangelization of the Japanese in Brazil.

Acknowledgments

The names of the persons to whom I feel indebted in writing this book are listed in the biography. I am grateful for those who have helped me by responding to the questionnaires, interviews, and letters. They provided information without which it would have been impossible to write this work. I am particularly thankful to the Rev. Makoto, pastor of St. Steven's Free Methodist Church, Sao Paulo, who rendered special help in collecting the data from denominations, churches, and individual respondents; to Bishop Elliott Lorenz Sorge of the Episcopal Diocese Sul-Central of Brazil and the Rev. Jun Yuasa, the President of Igreja Evangelica Holiness do Brazil, who made the data of their denominations available to me. The Rev. Andrew Otani and the Rev. Bambi Kishi were very kind in providing information on the Japanese Episcopal Church and the Holiness Church in the United States. The Episcopalian archivists, Dr. V. Nelle Belamy of Austin, Texas, and the Rev. Natanael Durval da Silva of Porto Alegre, Brazil, were most kind in giving me access to the historical and statistical documents.

I also feel much indebted to Dr. Donald A. McGavran and other members of the faculty of the Fuller School of World Mission whose insights and views may be seen in many of the pages of this work. I am particularly thankful to Dr. Ralph Winter for reading the manuscript, correcting and improving my English, and for giving very helpful suggestions; to Mrs. Ralph Winter who corrected and improved my English and other technical parts of this book; and to Dr. Arthur Glasser and Dr. Peter Wagner who read the manuscript and gave many useful suggestions.

I am particularly grateful to the Rev. Dr. Roland Kawano who did the proof reading and editing. I am also thankful to the staff of William Carey Library who helped to publish this book and to Mrs. Ellen Scott who typed the manuscript.

My gratitude is further extended to the Glendale Japanese Free Methodist Church which gave me support and understanding during my years of study and research. My special thanks to my wife, Miyoko, who worked all these past years to make my study possible.

May, 1978   John Mizuki
                                                   Sepulveda, California

1

The Japanese
Immigration to Brazil

HISTORY AND GEOGRAPHICAL DISTRIBUTION

Japanese were not allowed to leave their country during the
period 1639-1854, due to the Tokugawa isolationist policy. In
1854, under the pressure of Commodore Perry, Japan signed a
treaty of friendly relations with the United States. Following
that date, other similar treaties were signed with other
western nations. These treaties were followed by commercial
treaties and the door was now wide open.

With this new era opportunity for immigration arrived. Thus,
in 1868, a group of 153 people emigrated to Hawaii to work in
the pineapple and sugar cane plantations. They were the first
Japanese immigrants to come to the western hemisphere. But this
immigration was not legal for it was not by government agreement.
In 1871 a treaty of friendly relations between Hawaii and Japan
was signed and an officially approved immigration began in 1875.
At the same time there were Japanese immigrants coming to the
mainland United States. By 1910 some 72,157 Japanese were living
in the United States and another 79,675 in Hawaii. Immigration
to the United States was drastically cut, however, with the
"Gentlemen's Agreement" in 1908, and it was terminated with the
Immigration Quota Law of 1924.

However, alternative doors for Japanese immirgrants had been
opened in South America. One was Peru where since 1899 they
could go to work in the cotton *haciendas*, and another was Brazil
after 1908, where they went to work in the coffee plantations in
the State of Sao Paulo. Many of those who emigrated to Peru

were not from rural areas and when they could not find good farm
land, they went to the cities where they became successful
businessmen. As a result of local friction, immigration to Peru
was discouraged after 1935 (Staniford 1973:8).

In 1890 the Japanese government gave private organizations
legal permission to recruit Japanese for emigration overseas.
As a result of this about ten emigration firms were organized.
Some of them, like Kichisa Imin Kaisha, began negotiations with
a similar Brazilian firm, Prado Jordao, in 1894. After 1900,
when Hawaii was annexed to the United States and emigration
there under the auspices of private organizations was no longer
permitted, these firms began to seek other places where they
could send emigrants, and Brazil was one country to which their
attention turned. Due to the lack of official relations between
Brazil and Japan negotiations between Kichisa Imin Kaisha and
Prado Jordao did not commence until 1895, when the two countries
signed a treaty of friendly relations which opened possibilities
for emigration. Thus in 1897 Kichisa Imin Kaisha sent a representative to Sao Paulo to reinitiate negotiations with Prado
Jordao. Kichisa Imin Kaisha was reorganized under the name Toyo
Imin Kaisha, which continued the negotiation with Prado Jordao.
The result of these negotiations was the agreement that Toyo
Imin Kaisha would send a group of 1500 to 2000 farm workers
between the age of twenty and thirty-five. Toyo Imin Kaisha
began immediately and recruited 1500 emigrants, but when they
were about to depart, a crisis in the price of coffee took place,
and Prado Jordao had to inform Toyo Imin Kaisha that it was
unable to receive the immigrants. Thus the first attempt to
send emigrants to Brazil resulted in total failure (Saito 1961:
21-27).

After this failure several other attempts were made. Nippon
Imin Kaisha began negotiations with the firm A Fiorita in 1897,
even to the point of signing an agreement. In 1901, a Brazilian
concessionaire, Marcial Sanz, went to Japan to begin negotiations with Teikoku Shokumin Kaisha of Okayama and with Kosei
Imin Kaisha of Wakayama. He did not succeed due to the inter-
ference of the Ministry of Foreign Affairs which knew the misery
under which European *colonos* (tenant workers) were working on
the *fazendas* (haciendas) in the state of Sao Paulo. The Japanese
government was very cautious, and even suspicious, about sending
emigrants to that state. A few years more would be necessary
before emigration to Brazil could materialize (Saito 1961:27-28).

We notice that in the beginning both Japanese and Brazilians
were cautious about the process of sending and receiving Japanese
migrants. On the Brazilian side, there was a law signed by the
first Brazilian President in 1890 according to which Brazil
would open her door to any people capable to work and not under

criminal lawsuit in their country of origin, excepting the
natives of Africa and Asia. There was also public opinion
against the introduction of Japanese immigrants due to negative
news about the Japanese in the United States, questioning
whether they could be assimilated. Brazil even sent two emis-
saries to the United States to investigate the assimilability of
the Japanese in this country (Rocha Nogueira 1971:41-42).

In spite of this policy against Asiatic immigration, the need
for farm laborers was so great in the State of Sao Paulo that
some *fazendeiros* (landlords) considered trying out Japanese
immigrants. In 1850, Brazil had outlawed the black slave
traffic, and slavery had been abolished in 1888, making it
impossible to get more laborers from that source. But by the
second half of the nineteenth century the coffee business was
booming, and the need of workers in the coffee *fazendas* was
becoming greater and greater. Since new slaves were no longer
available, Brazil began to import workers from Europe, mainly
from Italy, Portugal, Spain, Germany and Austria. But in the
period 1896-1906 there was a coffee crisis due to overproduction.
Coffee had become a very profitable business, and its production
was increased considerably in the years between 1890 and 1900.
The number of coffee-trees, which was 220 million in 1890,
increased to 520 million in 1900. By 1905 the accumulate sur-
plus stock of coffee in Brazil had reached 11 million sacks
which was 70 percent of the total amount consumed in the world.
This brought about an over-production of coffee with a resultant
drastic decline in its price, which dipped to the all-time low
of 3$585 (three thousand-five-hundred-eighty five *reis* - the
rei was the monetary system used in those years, and 2000 *reis*
was equivalent to one dollar). The decline of coffee prices may
be seen in the table below.

TABLE 1

PRICE OF COFFEE PER 22 LBS.

1894	US $7.46	1902	US $2.45
1895	6.73	1903	2.50
1896	6.47	1904	3.18
1897	4.67	1905	3.57
1898	4.18	1906	2.42
1899	4.01	1907	1.88
1900	4.40	1908	1.79
1901	2.80		

Source: (ANDO 1971:21)

This coffee crisis produced a similar crisis in the immigration process. Due to the difficult economic situation many European immigrants left the *fazendas* to work in the cities, or re-emigrated to Argentina, or returned to their countries. This instability of European *colonos* created a shortage of workers on the *fazendas*. In 1900 Brazil faced its first immigrant deficit, for while 22,802 immigrants entered the country, 27,917 left, which meant a deficit of 5115. In the period 1900-1909, 387,698 immigrants entered and 381,228 left, which meant a positive balance of only 6,470 immigrants (Ando 1971:22). Moreover, in 1902 the Italian government prohibited emigration to Brazil in view of the poor situation in which Italian *colonos* were living. The problem was now greatly aggravated since Italy had been once the greatest source of workers for Brazil.

This situation led the Brazilian agencies to look for Japanese immigrants, and in 1901 their representatives went to Japan for that purpose. But the government of Japan, knowing the misery in which Italian *colonos* were living, prohibited the emigration of its citizens, and consequently no contract was signed.

There were, however, some encouraging reports that changed the attitude of the Japanese government. Thus in 1905, Sugimura, the then plenipotentiary minister of Japan to Brazil wrote:

> In consequence of the suspension of the immigration of Italian *colonos*, the State of Sao Paulo is facing a serious shortage of workers. Both the State of Sao Paulo as well as the *fazendeiros* in general, are interested in receiving our workers. I believe, therefore, that the introduction of our immigrants into this State would be more interesting and preferable than to send them to the United States, where persecution is increasing. Of course, the traveling expenses would be higher in comparison to that country, this due to the great distance. Fortunately, the government of the State of Sao Paulo is willing to subsidize in paying totally or partially the traveling expenses, which somehow comes to counterbalance the said disadvantage. Prohibited in Canada, and now restricted also in Hawaii and in the Pacific Islands, our immigrant workers will find in the State of Sao Paulo a rare opportunity and a true paradise (Saito 1961:28-29).

Due to this and other reports, the Japanese government, more or less skeptical in the beginning, began gradually to be more favorable toward emigration to Brazil.

In 1906, Ryu Mizuno, the founder of Kokoku Shokumin Kaisha and a strong advocate of Japanese expansion through emigration, visited Brazil and obtained from the government of the State of

Sao Paulo permission to send 3,000 immigrants, 1,000 a year. According to the contract signed on this occasion, the immigrants were supposed to come in family units. Each family should have at least three members capable of working, that is, to be between twelve and forty-five years of age. Individual entrance would be allowed only to artisans of specialized skills such as masons, carpenters and smiths, but their number should not be more than one fifty of the total number of immigrants. The traveling expenses from Japan to Brazil in those days were 160 yen (US$80.00). Of this the States government would pay a part: $50.00 for the immigrant twelve years of age and up, $15.00 for a child of over three years, $25.00 for children over seven years of age. Part of this government subsidy, however, was charged to the *fazendeiros* who would deduct it from the wages paid to the *colonos*. Thus the actual aid to the immigrants was much less than it might appear. Since the amount paid by the *fazendeiros* was $20.00 for adult, $10.00 for children over seven years, and $5.00 for children over three years of age, the actual total subsidy to an immigrant twelve years old and up was only $30.00.

A serious problem in recruiting emigrants was to find candidates who would meet the requirement of having a family with three members capable of working. Candidates were usually young, and did not have family with three adult members. The solution to this problem was the *kosei kazoku* (artificial family), composed of relatives or friends in order to meet the requirements (Ando and Wakisaka 1971:23-24).

The Japanese immigration in Brazil began when the ship Kasado Maru arrived in the port of Santos on June 18, 1908. The total number of contracted immigrants was 779--593 men and 186 women. In the six following years altogether ten groups of immigrants came, and their number totaled 14,886 persons. In 1914, the government of the State of Sao Paulo rescinded the contract, and that meant a suspension of immigration. This interruption was temporary, however. The three organizations dealing with Japanese immigration--Toyo Imin Kaisha, Morioka Imin Kaisha, and Takemura Shokan Kaisha--began renegotiating with the Sao Paulo State government, and in 1916 a new contract was signed. Under its terms, from 4 to 5 thousand Japanese would enter Brazil yearly for four or five years, beginning in 1917. The Sao Paulo State government agreed to renew the contract because immigrants from Europe were not available during these years due to World War I. In 1917, Kaigai Kogyo Kaisha (K.K.K.), a Japanese government supported agency, was organized and eventually almost monopolized the emigration business to Brazil. From this time on, the emigration policy became more and more state controlled. Organized under the initiative of the cabinet led by the then Prime Minister Terauchi, K.K.K. was the first

step toward a state controlled emigration policy. In 1921 a law
to provide financial aid to K.K.K. passed the Japanese Parlia-
ment, and in 1923 a service to stimulate emigration was created
(Saito 1961:31-32).

In 1920, when the contract expired, the government of the
State of Sao Paulo was undecided about its renewal. Since World
War I was over, immigrants from Europe were not lacking. Following the traditional policy, the Sao Paulo State government gave
preference to the workers from Portugal, Spain and Italy, stating
its reason as being that the Japanese colonos were unstable and
had difficulty in adapting to Brazil in life, language and
culture. Government officials said--with some justification--
that the Japanese stayed in the coffee plantations only for a
very short time, becoming independent as soon as they could.
The government by that time was subsidizing immigration   the
amount of $85.00 per adult, and as the Japanese often stayed on
the coffee plantations only one year (the contract was four or
six years), it was necessary to spend $170.00 in two years to
get a Japanese worker, whereas Portuguese, Spanish and other
European immigrants would work longer for the *fazendeiros* and
were more advantageous even from an economical point of view.
In view of the firm position of the government of Sao Paulo in
not renewing the contract, the Japanese government had to take
some measure to solve the problem. In 1923 the subject was of
highest priority in the discussions of the Japanese government,
and two years later, 1925, it was decided that from that year on
the Japanese government would grant the emigrant the subsidy
that up to that time had been given by the Sao Paulo government.
The year 1925 was a turning point because it marked the shift of
initiative regarding Japanese immigration from the Sao Paulo
State government to the Japanese government (Saito 1961:33).

The period 1926-1941 was one in which emigration to Brazil
was promoted and subsidized by the Japanese government, and
those who entered Brazil numbered 148,975 which was 75 percent
of the total who entered before World War II. From 1926 on the
arrival of Japanese immigrants followed a line of quick ascension, reaching the peak in 1933 and 1934, the year when the
quota bill passed the Congress and immigration began to decline.

The most intensive stage of the Japanese immigration was
1928-1934, in which 108,256 Japanese, or 57.3 percent of the
pre-war immigrants, came to Brazil. One factor that stimulated
Japanese immigration was the work of the K.K.K., which succeeded
in attaining 100 percent subsidy for the transportation of the
immigrants, and in 1932, was granted governmental aid that would
cover the transportation plus other expenses before the trip
(Saito 1961:34).

At this stage, Japan began to consider Brazil not only as a country that would absorb her farming emigrants, but also as a market for investments. The ephemeral prosperity of the post-war period was coming to an end, and world-wide depression was approaching. Labor and capital were devaluating and Japan had to look for investment markets beyond her shores. Thus this period marked the incoming of not only farming immigrants but also proprietors and enterpreneurs. Capital was invested mostly in farming and cattle raising, but in the thirties it was invested in commerce and industry too. These capitalistic organizations that came into Brazil were enterprises owned by the Japanese government or by private companies. A good example of this type of investment was what was done by a company called Bratac, which purchased large estates in the states of Sao Paulo and Parana, divided them into lots of 60 acres each, and sold them to the immigrant families that came with some capital (Saito 1961:35-36).

In 1933 a bill to adopt a quota system in immigration was presented in the Congress and it passed the next year. According to this new law, the entry of immigrants of each nationality would be limited to 2 percent of its total arrival in the previous fifty years. Although the bill did not mention any nationality specifically, it was clear that it was aimed at the Japanese immigrants who were more recent and the largest in number during those years. By this law, the number of the Japanese allowed to enter annually was limited to 2,711. This was taken in Japan as an anti-Japanese law and provoked a variation of hostile reactions (Saito 1961:37).

The decade 1942-1951 may be considered a blank in the history of Japanese immigration in Brazil. Immigration, which was declining after the quota system bill passed, was totally paralyzed with the beginning of the Pacific War. Following the United States, Brazil declared war against Japan in 1942, and consequently the Japanese came to be treated as members of a belligerent nation. Those were hard years for the Japanese in Brazil. They were prohibited from traveling without safe-conduct permits. Thousands of Japanese living on the coast were relocated in the interior. The Brazilian government made a distinction, however, between *Issei* (Japanese born in Japan) and *Nisei* (their children born in Brazil), who, if they were adults and so wished, could remain on the coast. This was different from what happened in the United States where 110,000 Japanese living on the Pacific coast were forced to relocate, regardless of their place of birth or citizenship. If the war brought a bitter experience to the Japanese in Brazil--as it certainly did to those living in the United States--one thing good resulted from it. Isolated completely from their fatherland, the Japanese in Brazil became less dependent on their mother country. Also,

since the result of the war was contrary to what they had
expected--the defeat of Japan--they decided to stay permanently
in Brazil. This was a real turning point which came to change
radically the attitude of the Japanese in Brazil. Before and
during the war, the majority of the Japanese were thinking of
returning to Japan as soon as their economic condition would
permit it, but now they were forced to change completely their
plans concerning their economy, their housing, and the education
of their children. Before this time, their only concern had
been to work, earn, and save enough to go back to Japan. Now,
they began to invest their savings to improve their condition of
living and to provide better education for their children in
Brazilian schools.

During the war, the Japanese in Brazil behaved circumspectly.
Hardly any instance of disorder took place. But after the war,
Japanese went through a very unpleasant experience that eventually compromised their reputation. This arose because a group
of the immigrants would not believe in the defeat of Japan and
began to brand as traitors those who did. They organized groups
of terrorists (*shindoremmei*) in order to eliminate the leaders
of those who believed in Japan's defeat. Over forty leaders of
the Japanese community were killed and many wounded. The
Japanese community divided in two factions, *makegumi* (defeatists)
and *kachigumi* (victorists). There was tension, unrest, and fear,
even worse than during the war. As a consequence of this and
the animosity developed during the war, the reputation of the
Japanese in the Brazilian society fell dramatically. In 1946,
a bill to prohibit the immigration of Orientals was presented to
the Congress. After a prolonged discussion votes were cast
resulting in a tie. The chairman, saying that to create such a
discriminatory law was contrary to the Brazilian tradition, used
his casting vote to break the tie, and the bill did not pass
(Saito 1961:39).

Post-war Japanese immigration to Brazil was resumed in 1953.
According to the Instituto Brasileiro de Estatistica, the number
of the pre-war immigrants was 180,031 while more than 69,685
immigrants from Japan entered in the post-war period. Thus,
between 1908 and 1973 a total of 249,716 Japanese immigrants
entered Brazil. The number of immigrants in the past ten years
has decreased considerably due to the economic prosperity of
Japan which required all the man power possible in the homeland.
Also, Brazil has become highly selective recently in the choice
of new immigrants, giving priority to those who have skills
essential to her economy.

FIGURE 1
JAPANESE IMMIGRANTS ENTERING BRAZIL

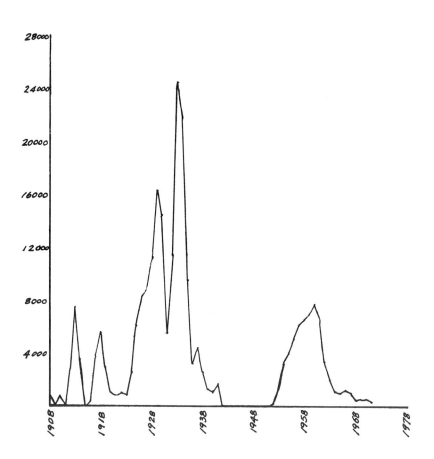

The geographical distribution of the Japanese population by the Brazilian states in the period 1923-1974 is given in Table 2.

TABLE 2

DISTRIBUTION OF JAPANESE POPULATION BY STATES
(1923-1974)

States	1923	1932	1940	1958	1974
Sao Paulo	34,707	120,285	193,364	325,899	535,356
Parana	2,126	3,967	4,300	77,846	133,368
Minas Gerais	1,012	1,997	1,922	2,885	4,799
Mato Grosso	1,143	2,337	3,710	8,926	13,855
Goias		874	297	1,797	2,703
Rio de Janeiro	261	389	1,191	5,805	5,356
Para, Amazonas		1,461	845	5,249	8,141
Other States		1,868		1,744	5,969
TOTAL	39,249	133,358	205,850	430,151	712,900

Source: Saito 1961:159
Consulado Geral do Japao 1974:7.

According to Table 2, in 1974, 76 percent of the Japanese were living in the state of Sao Paulo and 18 percent in the state of Parana, whereas 6 percent were scattered in other states.

Up to the Second World War, 90 percent of the Japanese lived in the rural areas along the four major railroads in the interior of the state of Sao Paulo. These railroads were Mogiana, Noroeste, Paulista, and Sorocabana. Beside these areas, there were large concentrations of Japanese in the city of Sao Paulo and its vicinities and along the railroad Santos Juquia on the southern coast of the state of Sao Paulo. A large concentration was also found in the northern part of the state of Parana. Up to 1922 the old zone of coffee (Zona Velha do Cafe), Mogiana, had the largest concentration, in the period 1923-1947 the primacy shifted to Noroeste, and then since 1948 the largest concentration of Japanese has been in the city of Sao Paulo and its vicinities (Suzuki 1971:92-99). Most of the Japanese immigrants went initially to Mogiana where they worked in the coffee planatations as wage laborers. After finishing their contract of four or six years many of them moved to the new frontier of Noroeste where they worked also in coffee plantations as sharecroppers, tenant-farmers, or small landowners.

During the depression of 1929 the coffee business faced a great crisis, and consequently the government prohibited the planting of new coffee trees. An alternative to coffee was cotton, and the cotton economy began to boom after 1930, especially in Sorocabana and Alta Paulista, attracting many Japanese. In 1938 32,000 Japanese families were engaged in the cotton industry producing 26 million *arrobas* (one arroba is about 32 pounds). This was 50 percent of the total production of the state of San Paulo in that year (Saito 1961:142).

The thirties also marked the migration of people from many nationalities, including Japanese, to the northern Parana. Fertile soil (*terra roxa*), the non-prohibition of coffee planting, and the building of the Sao Paulo-Parana Railroad were the main stimuli to this great migration.

The Industrial revolution that started in Brazil in 1930 began to attract people in the metropolis of Sao Paulo following that date. In the late thirties some Japanese moved into that city. But since during the War Japanese were not allowed to move, the real migration of Japanese to the city of Sao Paulo did not gain momentum until after the end of the War. A research of 1,579 Japanese families which had moved to the city of Sao Paulo in the period 1936-1948 illustrates this fact, as we can see in Table 3.

TABLE 3

MIGRATION OF JAPANESE TO THE CITY OF SAO PAULO
(1935-1948)

Year	Percentage
1935	0.46%
1936	0.93
1937	0.93
1938	0.93
1939	3.24
1940	3.70
1941	7.41
1942	6.94
1943	5.09
1944	6.94
1945	7.41
1946	9.72
1947	22.22
1948	22.22
Unknown	1.85
TOTAL	99.99%

Source: Saito 1961:145

Note that of those 1,579 families, 54.16 percent moved in the years 1946-1948.

As a result of industrialization and urbanization, the number of Japanese living in the cities has increased from 10 percent of all Japanese in the pre-war period to 50 percent in 1974. About a half of the urban Japanese live in one single city of Sao Paulo. The number of the Japanese living in the city of Sao Paulo increased from 3,467 in 1939 to 180,000 in 1974 (Consulado Geral do Japan 1974:7).

The influx of the Japanese was not only in the city of Sao Paulo, but to its surrounding countryside. Thus, the Japanese settlements which up to 1939 were located in areas whose radii did not go beyond 50 kilometers from the city of Sao Paulo, today there are many settlements in the surrounding areas of 100, 150 and even 200 kilometers from that same center.

Parallel to the mass migration of Japanese to Sao Paulo and its vicinities was a migration in the opposite directions to the farther new frontiers of the states of Parana, Sao Paulo, Mato Grosso, Brasilia, Rio Grande do Sul. Thus in the thirties the inland settlements that were located between 500 and 700 kilometers from Sao Paulo were extended as far as 1,500 kilometers from the city in the post-war period (Saito 1961:151).

ECONOMY

Wage-laborer, tenant-farmer and landowner are the three steps of the social ladder most of the Japanese have gone through. They started from the bottom as wage workers in the *fazendas*. After having finished their four or six years contract, many times even before that they moved from the *fazendas* to the frontiers where they became tenant-farmers. Then after they had saved some money, they would purchase a piece of land. This change of status of the Japanese farmers becomes evident when we note that while 87.9 percent of them were tenant farmers in the early period of Japanese immigration history, only 2.9 percent of them were in the same status in 1958. And while only 5.1 percent of them owned land in the early period, the number of landholders increased to 64 percent by 1958 (Comissao de Recenseamento da Colonia Japonesa 1964:716) and to 75.1 percent by 1974 (Consulado Geral 1974:7).

The greatest economic contribution of the Japanese has been in the area of agriculture, mainly in the introduction of improved technology, new kinds of vegetables and fruits, quality control of all products, increased productivity, and in the creation of cooperatives.

The Japanese were the first in Brazil to use fertilizers, the bordeaux mixture, and the Japanese plow, which in the tens and twenties were revolutionary technological innovations (Ando 1973:173). Besides using modern machinery to mechanize agriculture, they have contributed substantially with agricultural know-how brought from Japan.

The Japanese have introduced at least fifteen new varieties of vegetables and fruits, although many of them have not diffused among non-Japanese; *nira* (a leek), *shungiku* (chysanthemum coronarium), *udo* (an asparagus), *fuki* (a butter bur), *myoga* (zingiber mioga), *shisho* (a beefsteak plant), *gobo* (a burdock), *konyaku* (devil's tongue), *kuai* (an arrowhead), *azuki* (a red bean), *hakusai* (a Chinese cabbage), *daikon* (a garden radish), *rakkyo* (a scallion), *ponkan* (a shaddok), and *kinkan* (a kumquat) (Saito 1973:192-193).

But the contribution of Japanese has been more in productivity than in the introduction of new kinds of plants. There are some products that Brazil used to import but now is exporting due to the contribution of Japanese. For example, tea, black pepper and jute which are almost one hundred percent produced by Japanese (Teixeira Mendes Sobrinho 1971:143).

TABLE 4

PARTICIPATION OF THE JAPANESE FARMERS IN THE
BRAZILIAN AGRICULTURAL PRODUCTION

Products	Participation in Percentage
Tea	92.1%
Ramie	91.7
Mint	90.0
Strawberry	90.0
Black pepper	82.0
Cocoon	80.0
Paulownia	80.0
Soybean	60.0
Tomatoes	58.1
Peach	50.0
Eggs	43.8
Potatoes	41.0
Peanuts	21.1
Cotton	13.7
Coffee	8.8
Rice	4.2
Corn	3.2

Source: Consulado Geral Do Japao 1974:8

Considering that the Japanese are only 0.7 percent of the
Brazilian total population, we may say that their contribution
to the Brazilian agriculture as it is seen in Table 4 is significant.

Japanese were also pioneers in the organization of cooperatives, of which the two largest are Cooperativa Agricola de
Cotia founded in 1927, and Cooperativa Central Agricola Sul
Brasil founded in 1928. These cooperatives have given financial
and technical assistance to their members and have made a remarkable contribution to the advancement of agriculture in Brazil.

TABLE 5

OCCUPATIONAL DIVERSIFICATION OF THE JAPANESE

Occupation	1932	1958	1967
Agriculture	93.6%	57.3%	50.0%
Industry	2.2	7.8	12.0
Commerce	4.2	34.9	38.0

Source: Nogueira Martins 1971:130

Table 5 indicates that the Japanese, who were mostly engaged
in agriculture in the pre-war period, have changed to more diver-
sified occupations in industry and commerce. Their participation
in industry is growing rather slowly but steadily while their
participation in commerce has grown substantially.

Although we may see Japanese involved practically in all
kinds of activities today, there are some occupations in the
city of Sao Paulo which are very common among them: *tinturaria*
(laundry), *feirante* (seller at an open market), *quitanda* (green
grocery), *emporio* (grocery store), and *cabeleireira* (hairdresser
or beauty salon). As we can note, these are the businesses that
require a relatively small capital and most of them have some
relation to the former occupation of the Japanese, namely
agriculture.

The Japanese who have started from the bottom--from *hadaka-
ikkan* (nothing) as they say--have moved up in Brazilian society,
and as early as 1958, 83 percent of their urban population
belonged to the middle class (Maeyama 1970:8). Today that
percentage must be much higher.

EDUCATION AND SOCIAL ASCENSION

The schooling of the Japanese in Brazil is low in comparison to that of the Japanese in Japan or the United States. But their literacy rate, 99.1 percent, is very high when it is compared with that of the general Brazilian population whose literacy rate is 60.7 percent (Lopes Cowles 1971:89).

TABLE 6

PERCENTAGE OF NISEI ENROLLED IN HIGHER EDUCATION (CITY OF SAO PAULO, 1967)

Schools	Total Enrolled	Nisei	% of Nisei
Medicine, Dentistry, Veterinarian, Pharmacy and Public health	2,231	312	13.9%
Engineering, Architecture and city planning	4,632	605	13.1
Law	4,195	148	3.5
Economic and Business administration	3,181	563	17.7
Philosophy, Letters, Social Service, Journalism, Arts...	13,203	1,143	8.7
TOTAL	27,442	2,771	10.1%

Source: Martins 1971:131

Considering that in the State of Sao Paulo the percentage of the Japanese is only 3 percent of the total population, we may say that they are comparatively speaking highly educated. There is no doubt that the relatively rapid social ascension of the Japanese is due in part to their degree of education.

Tables 7 and 8 on the following page show the social ascension of the Japanese in Brazil.

TABLE 7

NISEI IN PUBLIC LIFE

Congressmen	3
Assemblymen to State congress	4
Mayor	11
Councilmen	200

TABLE 8

NISEI PROFESSIONAL MEN

College and university professor	40
Primary and secondary teacher	1,200
Judge	5
Public prosecutor	5
Lawyer	450
Physician, dentist, pharmacist	1,300
Other college and university graduate	2,910
TOTAL	6,520

Source: O Cruzeiro 1970:62-63

For an ethnic group which had been in Brazil only for a little over sixty years, we must say that the achievements revealed on Tables 7 and 8 are remarkable.

RELIGION

Ninety-eight percent of the 176,775 immigrants who entered Brazil between 1908 and 1936 were non-Catholics--that is, they were Buddhists and Shintoists. But according to the census taken in 1958, the religious distribution of the Japanese population in Brazil was 44.5 percent Buddhists, 42.8 percent Catholics, and 12.7 percent practiced other religions (Comissao de Recenseamento 1964:280). This change is due to the acculturative trend of Sansei (third generation), Nisei, and even some Issei to adopt the religion of the receiving country as Table 9 on the following page clearly shows. According to this table while Buddhism decreases Catholicism increases.

TABLE 9

RELIGIOUS AFFILIATION OF THE JAPANESE BY GENERATIONS
(For People Seven Years of Age and Up in 1958)

Religion	Issei	Nisei	Sansei/ Yonsei*
Buddhism	70.6%	29.2%	19.0%
Catholicism	15.5	58.7	70.0
Other	13.9	12.1	11.1
Total	100.0%	100.0%	100.0%
Number	136,694	184,510	29,383

Source: Comissao de Recenseamento 1964:283

If the trend of the above table will continue--all indicates
that it will--there will be no Buddhists among *Gosei* (fifth
generation) and practically all of them will have become
Catholics. But one question that should be raised is how many
of the Japanese who have declared themselves Catholics are
practicing Catholics. According to Father Takeuchi, S.J., about
10 to 20 percent of them are practicing Catholics. This low
percentage of practicing Catholics is due in part to the motiva-
tion of the Japanese parents when they baptize their children in
the Catholic Church. Many Japanese baptize their children
because of social convenience or social pressure. They think it
is good for them to have *compadres* or *comadres* (godfathers or
godmothers) to their children who have a certain social prestige,
for they may help them and their children in time of need. There
has also been social pressure for Japanese children to be
baptized. There have been several instances when elementary
school teachers who are Catholics may, under the direction of
the local priests, force the Japanese children to be baptized.
This way thousands of them have been baptized without knowing
anything about what they were doing. In more specific terms
Maeyama gives the motives of the Japanese parents who have
their children baptized in the Catholic Church. They do it:
1) in order to prevent any possible future difficulty for their
children in the Brazilian context, 2) to respond as good neighbors to social pressure by the host society, 3) to get better
opportunities and give social prestige by means of the traditional co-parenthood (*compadresco*), 4) because teachers suggest
that they do so, 5) because their children have frequently been
told by their peers that a pagan is a *pecador* (sinner) and no

*Yonsei (Fourth generation)

more than a *bicho* (worm or beast), and 6) because Brazilian
friends or neighbors have volunteered to become *padrinhos* (godfathers) to their children, and they have been reluctant to
refuse any "kind" offer (Maeyama 1973:250).

As we have seen, practically all Japanese who came to Brazil
were Buddhists. Their number did not grow in the past and at
present is in decline. The reason for this is that since 1918
to the end of World War II, the Ministry of Foreign Relations of
Japan forbade the emigration to Brazil of any religious missionaries, except Catholic missionaries. It is reported that even
some immigrants were required to commit themselves, in writing,
not to do any religious propagation in Brazil. The Japanese
government took this measure in order to avoid any anti-Japanese
climate which would arise from religious motives (Maeyama 1973:
250). It was only after the War that Buddhist priests and other
religious missionaries came to Brazil. Buddhism is in decline
among the Japanese, but this trend may change if the Buddhists
in Brazil begin missionary work among Brazilians. Right now
they are limited in this mission because their priests (being
from Japan) do not have command of Portuguese and consequently
are unable to propagate their faith among Brazilians. Their
work right now is confined to the Japanese, particularly those
of older generations.

Of the new religions of Japan that have come to Brazil, we
have some data in our hands only of *Seicho no Ie*, which has been
pretty successful in converting Japanese. In 1966 they had 553
associations divided between men, women, young people, and their
total membership in Brazil was 15,630. The young people's
association had 4,500 members, composed almost entirely of those
born in Brazil (Maeyama 1973:255). This religion, being a
syncretism of Buddhism, Shintoism and Christianity with its
stress on the old Japanese values, has attracted the old immigrants and the segment of the Japanese community attached to the
old values. Its members belong to the old middle class, and
Maeyama says that when he did his research in 1966, he noted
that very few of them were college graduates. In an association
of 31 youth there was not one college graduate nor one enrolled
in college. They were mostly people who had completed elementary
or junior high education, or were graduates of technical schools.
Asked why they were attending the association, they said they
were doing so because of their parents' pressure. Many of them
did not know what their religion really meant. A good number of
these young people participated in the youth activities because
this gave them a chance to meet their girl or boy friends and to
be engaged in sports (Maeyama 1973:256).

Protestants constituted 1.8 percent of the total Japanese
population in 1958 and this ratio has not improved in the years

up to the present. There are at present 59 churches, 70 pastors
and missionaries, and approximately 5,000 communicants. Since
we shall be dealing with them in detail in the following
chapters, we will not here give any further description of them.

ACCULTURATION AND ASSIMILATION

There are a few factors that have contributed to accelerate
the acculturation and assimilation of the Japanese: the War,
industrialization and urbanization, education, and the Nisei
youth association. The effect of the War on the acculturative
process can hardly be exaggerated. Up to the War the Japanese
were under the influence of the militaristic and nationalistic
mood of their country of origin. They had Japanese language
schools where not only the language but Japanese values were
taught. Practically all sources of information were Japanese
newspapers and magazines. And, as the great majority lived in
the Japanese nucleus of rural areas, they formed a closed
society where social cohesion and control were strong. Their
contact with Brazilians was through *caboclos* or *nordestinos*, who
belonged to the Brazilian lower class and who worked for them.
This type of contact would work against acculturation.

But with the outbreak of the War, the Japanese language
schools were closed, all Japanese newspapers were forbidden to
circulate, and the use of Japanese in public or on the streets
was forbidden. In a circumstance like this, those who wanted to
read the news had to learn Portuguese to be able to read Brazilian newspapers. Many Japanese felt the need of Portuguese in
this period and began to study the language and to read
Portuguese newspapers. As a result many came to know not only
what was happening but to know the Brazilian culture too. Thus
they became more acculturated.

Another important factor of acculturation was the rapid
industrialization and urbanization of post-War Brazil. Many
people migrated to the cities and particularly to the metropolis
of Sao Paulo. Japanese also followed this general trend and
migrated from the country to the cities. Here their contact
with Brazilians was more frequent, continuous and total, and
they were less bound by Japanese group control. In contact
with middle class Brazilians they began to appreciate the values
of the host country, their image of Brazilian changed, and this
helped in the acculturation process.

Education has also helped the Japanese to acculturate to
Brazil. The absence of secondary schools and colleges in
Japanese forced them to send their children to Brazilian schools.
Even for elementary education, they had to send their children
to the public school as well as to a Japanese language school.

Although they were deeply committed to preserving Japanese
values, at the same time they could see that the success of
their children in Brazilian society would bring prestige to the
family. So they became interested in sending their children to
Brazilian schools where their children are taught not only
Portuguese but Brazilian history and culture, and brought into
contact with their non-Japanese peers. Inevitably these children gradually became acculturated to Brazilian life.

Youth associations (*seinenkai*) have contributed to the
acculturation of the Japanese for they have exposed Nisei to
certain practices that do not exist among Japanese--such as
dancing and dating, the use of Portuguese in their meetings, and
participation in Western festivals, beauty contests, etc.
(Cardoso 1973:317-345).

One can notice the degree to which the Japanese have
acculturated by looking at the change in their food habits, the
use of the Japanese language, the marriage system, and their
religious affiliations, etc. This is also observable among the
Japanese in the United States where old food habits have per-
sisted longer than any cultural elements. Nisei in the United
States say that in food they are Japanese. Even Sansei or
Yonsei still eat Japanese food although not as frequently as
their parents or grandparents. In Brazil they have been eating
Japanese food for nearly seventy years. At the initial stage
of their life as immigrants they ate what was available where
they settled, of course with Japanese seasoning. When they
arrived on the coffee plantations they were usually provided
rice, brans, flour, dry jerky, dried cod, grease or pork fat,
vegatable oil, manioka flour, dough, coffee, salt and sugar.
Japanese had a hard time getting used to Brazilian greasy food
seasoned with garlic. In the state of Sao Paulo where rice was
a part of Brazilian daily diet, the Japanese had no problem,
but the immigrants who went to the North or Northeast of Brazil
faced difficulty, for rice was not available in those areas and
they had to grow it for themselves.

When the Japanese became better off economically and were
able to afford buying Japanese food, they shifted from Brazilian
to Japanese food. Later, when they became more adjusted to the
new environment, their diet became a mixture of Japanese and
Brazilian elements.

In 1953, 448 people were interviewed by Saito who asked about
their food preferences, and the result indicates that there was
a duality of food in the Japanese diet as we can see in
Table 10 on the following page.

TABLE 10

FOOD PREFERENCE OF THE JAPANESE

a. I would rather have Brazilian food	14.1%
b. I would rather have Brazilian food but some-times I alternate it with Japanese food	33.5
c. I like both	4.4
d. I would rather have Japanese food but some-times I alternate it with Brazilian food	46.4
e. I would rather have Japanese food	1.1
f. I don't know	0.5
Total	100.0%

Number = 448

Source: Saito 1961:97

Table 10 indicates that in matter of food preferences, Japanese are equally divided--47.6 percent preferring Brazilian food and 47.5 preferring Japanese. Thus, as far as food is concerned, we may say that the acculturation of the Japanese has come half way.

Thirty-six percent of Nisei reported in 1958 that they read Japanese newspapers as their source of information. This percentage is high compared to the Nisei in the United States where not many speak or read Japanese fluently. This may be due to the intensive Japanese study to which at least the older Nisei in Brazil were subjected. The author has some Nisei friends who, when they write to him, do so in Japanese. Although this is true with the older Nisei, the tendency is that the younger the person, the less Japanese he knows. Nisei who are in their twenties, and even those in their thirties, speak, read, and write Japanese less than those who are forty or over. When the author was growing up practically every Issei parent thought Japanese was more important than Portuguese, and 90 percent of the pre-War Japanese were planning to return to their country as soon as their economic situation permitted. But the research conducted by Izumi in 1957 shows that while 98.4 percent of Issei parents still thought that Japanese was necessary for their children, when asked which language--Japanese or Portuguese --would they prefer to be formally taught to their children, 53.4 percent responded "Portuguese" against 19.6 percent that answered they would rather have Japanese taught them (Izumi 1973: 377). This indicates that a substantial change of attitude regarding the teaching of Japanese is taking place.

The Japanese who migrated to Brazil had arranged marriages and those who married in Brazil followed the same custom. Even some older Nisei have had arranged marriages, but as Nisei become more acculturated the trend was for each one to choose his or her own mate. The research conducted by Izumi reveals that even in Issei parents a change of attitude regarding the marriage of their children is occurring. Table 11 indicates that there is a certain difference in their attitude toward their sons and their daughters in this sense, since they are usually more strict in relation to the latter. While 26.4 percent of parents do not permit their sons to choose their mates freely, 39.3 percent of them do not permit their daughters to do the same. Also, while 31.8 percent of the parents think their sons are free to choose their mates, only 18.0 percent give the same freedom to their daughters.

TABLE 11

ATTITUDE OF PARENTS TOWARD THE CHOICE OF MATES
FOR THEIR SONS AND DAUGHTERS

For son:

My son is free to choose	31.8%
I want to be consulted before he decides	32.8
I do not permit a free choice	26.4

For daughter:

My daughter is free to choose	18.0
I want to be consulted before she decides	37.8
I do not permit a free choice	39.3
I don't know	4.9

Source: Izumi 1973:372

Unfortunately we do not have recent data on the marriage between Japanese and non-Japanese in Brazil. But the dates that are available to us can show what the trend is with regard to the interracial marriage of Japanese and non-Japanese. Table 12 shows that the percentage of intermarriages grew in the quinquennium 1958-1962 to 14.1 percent from 6.1 percent in the previous quinquennium. We note also that it remained low throughout the quinquennia preceding 1958. Now when we compare the intermarriage of the Japanese in Brazil with that of the Japanese in the United States, we realize that its percentage is low. But we note also that the percentage of intermarriage in the United States is also low up to the end of the fifties, that is below

30 percent. It is only in the sixties and seventies that it goes above 40 percent. Thus we may say that intermarriage in the United States is a phenomenon of the sixties and seventies and of the third generation (Sansei).

TABLE 12

RATE OF JAPANESE INTERMARRIAGE IN BRAZIL AND U.S.

Year	Percent Intermarriages	Year	Percent Intermarriages
Brazil		Hawaii	
1908-22	1.5%	1912-16	7%
1923-27	4.3	1920-24-	3
1928-32	2.0	1924-28	7
1933-37	1.9	1928-30	8
1938-42	2.3	1930-34	9
1943-47	2.8	1945-54	22
1948-52	4.7	1970	47
1953-58	6.1		
1958-62	14.1		
Fresno		Los Angeles	
1958	18%	1924-33	2%
1959	7	1948-51	12
1960	13	1949	11
1961	7	1950	11
1962	14	1951	14
1963	8	1952	14
1964	38	1953	17
1965	36	1954	16
1966	36	1955	21
1967	39	1956	22
1968	38	1957	24
1969	56	1958	20
1970	48	1959	23
1971	49	1971	47
		1972	49

Source: (Suzuki 1969:159) and (*The Journal of Social Issues*, Vol. 29, No. 2, 1973)

It has taken over eighty years for the rate of intermarriage to go above 40 percent. The Japanese of Brazil have another twelve years to reach eighty years of history and by 1988 it is very

likely that their intermarriage rate will be as high as of their
counterparts in the United States. In Brazil's case it took fifty
years for the intermarriage rate to go above 10 percent, while in
Hawaii it took sixty years and in Los Angeles and Fresno it seems
that it took even longer, if we count the history of the Japanese
immigration in this country from 1875. The lack of recent data
makes a better comparison impossible, but we think that it is
possible to assume that the intermarriage rate of the Japanese in
Brazil has increased since 1962. The data collected by Cornell,
Smith and Yutaka in 1966-67 indicates that 28.7 percent of Nisei
had had their last dates with non-Nisei, whereas 71.3 percent had
dated Nisei (Shimidu 1973:480). Vieira, who did a research on
the life style of the Japanese in the city of Marilia, says that
Japanese who intermarried are those who, in contact with Brazilian
society, become more emancipated from their ethnic communal life
and consequently more individualistic (Vieira 1973:302-316).

   With regard to the degree of acculturation of Nisei we may
say that there are at least three categories of Nisei: 1) those
who are so acculturated that they are Brazilian except in their
appearance; 2) those who are born and reared in Brazil yet have
retained to their parents' culture so well that they are as
Japanese as their parents; and 3) the great majority who belong
somewhere between these two extremes. These are bilingual and
bicultural. John B. Cornell, who has done research on this point,
says that Nisei do not have a culture of their own but have elements of the two cultures in themselves. This fact creates a
problem, for these elements are sometimes contradictory. Some
statements made by Nisei whom he interviewed reveal the contradictory nature of Nisei personality. The difficulty *Nisei* face
in relating to Brazilians is witnessed by the comment by a
Nisei girl of Getulina in the interior of Sao Paulo:

   In what ways are nisei different from Brazilians? For
   example, at a festival or a meeting, Brazilians always
   stand out. They know how to relate to others, how to be
   ingratiating, are much more sociable than nisei. *Nisei*
   ...can't have the social grace of Brazilians. Brazilians
   are more calm, nisei are less natural, thinking of what
   to do next (Cornell 1970:28).

A Nisei male in Mackenzie University remarks:

   I believe that a nisei is almost a Brazilian. All
   immigrants preserve something of their land; and the
   nisei have customs from their parents... The *nisei* is
   different from a Brazilian in that: he looks different
   physically; he generally doesn't feel at ease with a
   Brazilian, but neither does he among issei -- he feels
   comfortable only with other nisei. I think that the

nisei is a more limited person -- for example at home if
his parents speak ill of Brazilians he is offended, but
if Brazilians speak ill of Japanese, he is also offended
-- A majority of *nisei* are timid -- I don't know how to
explain it; and *nisei* show a lot of courage (Cornell 1970:
29).

Although these remarks do not describe the situation of all
Nisei, we think this is the situation for most of them. Their
enculturation has come from both sides. From home and from
Brazilian society. At home they are too Brazilian, but outside
they are too Japanese. When contradictory elements come
together, conflict in their personality becomes inevitable. We
should also say that, in a limited number, there is a fourth
type of *Nisei*, those who have mastered both Portuguese and
Japanese, and who feel at home in both ambients.

2

The Episcopal Church
of Brazil

Yasoji Ito was born to a farmer family in the prefecture of
Nagano, Japan, on December 3, 1888. He was the second son of
the Ito family. He finished his eight years of formal education
in 1904 and then moved to Tokyo where he was enrolled in the
Tokyo Mercantile Marine School. After graduating in 1909, he
became an apprentice on board the ocean ship Koun-Maru. His
dream was to become a captain one day. As an apprentice he was
subjected to all sorts of work--like cleaning the bathrooms,
washing the decks, and painting the masts (Ito Yasoji Sensei
Tsuioku-Jikko Iinkai 1970:4).

On September 14 of 1910, on the way from Shang Hai to
Hokkaido, the ship was hit by a violent storm and sank. Only
three men, the captain, the head of seamen, and Ito survived
because they were rescued by fisherman. While recovering from
the shock at the home of a shipping agent in Osaka, Ito began to
attend the Saint Savior Church in that city. He was baptized by
the pastor Kawaoi and under his recommendation entered Trinity
Seminary in Osaka in 1911. No doubt that traumatic experience
was the major reason for the change of the entire course of his
life. "If God spared me out of so many lives, He must have some
mission for me," he thought. Three years after his enrollment,
Trinity Seminary merged with Ikebukuro Seminary in Tokyo, and
Ito moved to Tokyo where he spent another three years in the
seminary. Because of his health he had to take a leave of
absence for two years, which delayed his graduation until 1919
(Ito...1970:4).

In that same year his younger brother emigrated to Brazil, and Ito went to the port of Kobe to see him off. Here he met his former teacher, Kuniho Nakamura, who spoke about the poor conditions of the Japanese immigrants in Brazil and of the need for spiritual guidance there. He also appealed to Ito to give his life to the evangelization of the Japanese in Brazil. While attending seminary, Ito recognized the missionary call to go with the emigrants, and to live with them and help them in their spiritual life. "Lord, if it is your will, send me," was his prayer. The appeal of his former teacher reinforced his conviction of the need for religious workers in Brazil. He felt strongly that Brazil was the land where God wanted him to work. So he entered Rikkokai, an association of Christian orientation whose purpose was to prepare and train young people to live in a country of Western culture and Christian religion. "Thus making it my ambition to preach the gospel, not where Christ has already been named, lest I build on another man's foundation" (Rom. 10:20) was Ito's ambition and conviction. His ambition was to be a pioneer missionary (Ito...1970:52-54).

Before going to Brazil, he decided to stop in the United States. He left Japan in December of 1919 on Siberia Maru and came to San Francisco. There he met Junkichi Mori, the pastor of the Dutch Reformed Church in San Francisco, who advised him to stay and help him for awhile, for it would be very difficult to go and start a work alone. So he worked there as an assistant pastor for six months. He came to realize that, in order to do pioneer work in Brazil he would need some money to support himself, so he decided to work on a farm as a laborer in order to earn and save some money before going on to Brazil. He went first to Stockton where he worked for a year and was able to save one thousand dollars (Ito...1970:55).

From there he went to Fresno where he was less fortunate. He earned a few hundred dollars but his employer did not pay him. He promised Ito that he would send him the money later but that money never arrived. Disappointed, he left Fresno for Los Angeles. Here, in Chinatown, he went into a church where he saw a lady weeping and praying and was reminded of the experience of Jacob at Bethel: "Indeed God was here and I did not know it." He left the church with new courage and hope, went to the railroad station and boarded the train that took him to the Imperial Valley. Here he worked for half a year and saved $500.00 more (Ito...1970:56).   th

From the Imperial Valley he went back to Los Angeles, where he worked sometimes on the farm and sometimes as a servant for fishermen at the San Pedro Port. After half a year he was praised for his diligence and was given a hundred dollar bonus in addition to his wages (Ito...1970:56).

Finally he went to Turlock where he worked on a watermelon
farm. Thus, from the end of 1919 to the beginning of 1923, he
was able to save $2,500.00 in a missionary fund for himself.
But that was not all he gained. In those years he came to
experience a real sense of God's omniscience, omnipresence and
goodness. It was a real school of training for the missionary
work he was to begin. How could a higher education diploma
holder endure that time of hard work? His answer is that he
could because he had been born and reared on the farm and
because he had been taught from boyhood to do any work with
gladness, an experience which was the way to please both parents
and God (Ito...1970:57).

On the last day of 1922, he changed from work clothes to his
suit, intending to end his life as a farm-worker. He took a
Western Pacific train in the San Joaquin Valley to go back to
San Francisco where he arrived on New Year's Day, 1923. At
Gery Street he was received by Sadaji Nakajima and his family
who had been very gracious to him in earlier years. He could
not recall the kindness of that family without tears even after
thirty-five years when he retired from his missionary labors
(Ito...1970:58).

Those were the years of strong prejudices against Japanese in
California, and many of them were concerned about the future of
their children. Some were looking for a new land. Ito proposed
holding a meeting at the Dutch Reformed Church in order to talk
about the evangelization of the Japanese in Brazil. After Ito
talked, Junkichi Mori responded by saying: "I will go with you."
So did Toko Yamada, a member of that church and a businessman
who was running an Oriental art shop on Gery Street. He decided
to sell his store and accompany Ito and Mori. The three left
San Francisco on January 10, 1923. "You shall not do as they in
the land of Egypt, where you dwelt, and you shall not do as they
do in the land of Canaan, to which I am bringing you. You shall
not walk in their statutes," (Leviticus 18:3). These were the
words given to Ito at that time, which he interpreted as
America being Egypt and Brazil being Canaan. He was not to walk
according to the ways of the United States nor of Brazil, but to
do "my ordinances and keep my statutes and walk in them"
(Leviticus 18:4). On the way to New York they stopped in Salt
Lake City, Denver, Chicago, Philadelphia, and Washington, D.C.
(Ito...1970:56-62).

On February 1, 1923, at 10:00 a.m., a British ship carried
the three men from New York for South America. "Come over and
help us"--this Macedonian appeal was sounding constantly in
Ito's ears. This appeal had moved Paul, John Elliot, William
Carey, and now was moving Ito. On the deck he prayed:
"Heavenly Father, guide every step of my way and help me to

approach my fellow countrymen with a holy love, and render then an unselfish service. In Christ's name. Amen."

The ship arrived in Rio de Janeiro on March 11, at 9:00 a.m. It was a Sunday and they went to the Episcopal Church on Rio Branco Avenue for worship, and there they thanked God for the safe arrival in the long-awaited land (Ito...1970:63).

On March 13, 1923, at 8:00 a.m., the first Protestant worship service in Japanese in Brazil was held at the dental office of Shinichiro Murakami, on 11 Conde de Sarzedas Street, Sao Paulo. Ito spoke on the mission of a missionary to Brazil. There were seven present at the meeting: Junkichi Mori, pastor of the Dutch Reformed Church in San Francisco, Toko Yamada, a member of that same church, Shinichiro Murakami (dentist), Takesaburo Honda, Matagoro Moriya, and Isoji Ito (Ito...1970:63).

Ito rented a room on 23 Conde de Sarzedas Street and held regular Christian services there. But the owner stopped renting him that place one month later, when he found out that Ito was a Protestant minister. So Ito moved to another building on 71 of the same street where he continued his Sunday services. At that room Ito would receive people who came for counselling and these people would go home to be witnesses to their neighbors (Ito... 1970:65).

A significant event for the Episcopal work among the Japanese in Brazil was its connection with the Brazilian Episcopal Church and the American Episcopal mission in Brazil. Bishop John Mackim, chairman of the board of bishops of Japan, and Bishop Sakunoshin Motoda, of the Tokyo Diocese, wrote letters of recommendation to the bishop of the Brazilian Episcopal Church, Lucien Lee Kinsolving. About the same time, Shinji Sasaki, professor of the Episcopal seminary in Japan, who was then attending Oxford University, met the Anglican bishop of South America, the Rt. Reverend Ebery, and requested his cooperation with the Japanese mission in Brazil. Thus, from the beginning of the Christian mission among the Japanese in Brazil, there was cooperation from the Anglican Church, the American Episcopal Mission, the Brazilian Episcopal Church, and the Japanese Episcopal Church. On October 23, 1923, Ito officially became a lay minister of the Brazilian Episcopal Church, supported by the American Episcopal Mission. He would be in charge of the Japanese Mission, which was organized on November 25, 1923, a Sunday, at the Anglican Church in Sao Paulo. On April 18, 1926, he was ordained deacon at the Redentor Church in Santa Maria, Rio Grande do Sul, and on April 22, 1928, he was ordained to the priesthood at the Salvador Church, Rio Grande do Sul (Ito... 1970:19).

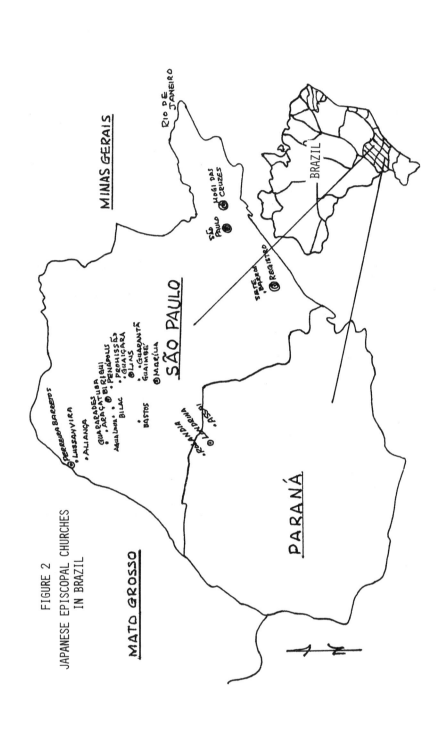

FIGURE 2
JAPANESE EPISCOPAL CHURCHES
IN BRAZIL

Besides his regular work in Sao Paulo, Ito travelled extensively between Registro and Lussanvira, a distance of 600 miles,
visiting cities, villages, and colonies, by ship, canoe, train,
bus, truck, horseback, and on foot. Besides laboring in these
two extremes, he planted churches in Sao Paulo, his base,
Guaimbe, Nipolandia, Birigui, Guararapes, Aracatuba, Alianca,
and later in Londrina, plus dozens of preaching stations. Five
years after his arrival he had 74 people baptized and had
established 11 preaching stations (Ito...1970:12).

His first ministerial candidate was Kiyoshi Iso, a Japanese
language school teacher in Bilac. He was touched by the love
Ito had for their people and came to want to be like Ito. When
he was asked by Ito whether he would like to be a minister, he
was ready to answer yes. He was sent to Japan in June, 1924,
entered the Episcopal Seminary in September, and spent three
years there studying theology. After he graduated he worked for
a year for the Nikko Episcopal Church, married and then returned
to Brazil in December, 1928. In January of the following year
he became the pastor of the Registro Episcopal Church (Ito...
1970:131).

In December of 1929, Ito returned to Japan and on April 15,
1930, he was married to the second daughter of the Bishop Hotaro
Nade of the Osaka Diocese, Fumiko, returning to Brazil in
October of the same year (Ito...1970:5).

In January of 1931 he moved his regular meeting place in Sao
Paulo to Capela do Salvador on 452 Consolacao Street. Here he
remained until 1933, when in January, he purchased a property at
10 Corope Street, Pinheiros, which would become his permanent
base for his missionary work (Ito...1970:5).

In order to show the type of meetings Ito used to hold in his
missionary journeys and the type of his messages, we shall
mention what he has recorded:

TABLE 13

MEETINGS HELD BY ITO

REGISTRO AREA

Date	Place	Sermon	Attendance
1925			
August			
1	Registro El School	Cultivation of heart	80
2	2nd Section School	Cultivation of heart	25
3	Horikawas	Christ's gift	18
4	4th Section School	Cultivation of heart	15
5	Boa Vista (Nakajimas)	Cultivation of heart	12
6	Otaki Cooperative	Cultivation of heart	18
7	Otaki Cooperative	Faith supplies 2nd chance	5
1926			
January			
12	Sete Barras (Youth)	The cardinal principles of faith	18
14	Ishikawas	Cultivation of sentiment and faith	12
17	Nagais	God the Creator	4
17	Okawas	The art of living	5
18	Otakis	Christ's gift	10
19	3rd School	Cultivation of heart	18
19	Quilombo (Yoshikawas)	Cultivation of heart	18
27	4th School	Building on the rock	20
27	4th School	The religious migration of Mormons	20
27	4th School	The migration of Abraham	20
27	4th School	The practice of benevolence	20
27	4th School	Story of Yuriko	30
28	4th Section (Women)	Life with God	16
29	2nd Section School	The Art of Living	60
30	Registro School	The Art of Living	90
30	Amatanis	Life with God	20

NOROESTE AREA

Date	Place	Sermon	Attendance
1924			
January			
3	Corrego School (parents)	Cultivation of heart	60
4	Colonia Feijao	The success of a failure	40

TABLE 13 CONT'D (NOROESTE AREA)

Date	Place	Sermon	Atten-dance
1924			
January			
4	Youth and Women Asso-ciation (Joint)	I have overcome the world	
4	Youth hall	God is love	13
4	Colonia Asano School	The ten virgins	15
5	Iruujo Club	Remembering the father-land	30
5	Salto Coutinho	The past of the Chris-tian is in his future	25
6	Corrego Liza	Christ's gift	10
6	Corrego Liza (Children)	Love your enemy	10
7	Roberto Youth Association	Cultivation of heart	35
7	Iruujo	Cultivation of heart	
7	Yoshizumis	The central problem of Christianity	18
8	Iruujo (Kosohos)	The central problem of Christianity	25
8	Truujo Youth Association	Cultivation of heart	15
9	Agua Limpa (Kurohas)	Cultivation of heart	14
10	Agua Limpa (Yamadas)	Cultivation of heart	40
10	Agua Limpa (Yamadas)	Christ's gift	45
11	Agua Limpa (Maruichis)	Cultivation of heart	13
11	Agua Limpa (Katais)	Central problem of Christianity	35
11	Agua Limpa (Kajimotos)	Religious life and family	10
11	Tupi (Ujinos)	Cultivation of heart	15
12	Tupi (Inashiros)	Cultivation of heart	27
13	Jangada, Rio Feio (Hondas)	Christ's gift	16
14	Birigui (Nakamura hotel)	Lesson from suffering	17
15	Penapolis (Umemotos)	Cultivation of heart	15
16	Correo de Unca (Miyamotos)	Christ's gift	10
17	Corrego de Onca	Cultivation of heart	20
17	Corrego de Onca	Christ's gift	20
18	Sitio Americano	Cultivation of heart	15
19	Barra Mansa	Cultivation of heart	20
20	Gonzago Club	Cultivation of heart	20
21	Bom Sucesso	Cultivation of heart	15
21	Pinto	Cultivation of heart	15
21	Gonzago	God is love	60
22	Corrego Azul	Cultivation of heart	15

Source: Ito...1970:152-153

The above table reveals a few things about the method used by
Ito in reaching his fellow countrymen. We will refer below to
his favorite theme, "Cultivation of Heart." For his meetings he
used school buildings, youth and women association halls, hotels,
cottages of the families that would welcome Christian work. In
those pioneer days, Japanese language schools were the most
important meeting places for the Japanese immigrants. Ito was
right in his strategy when he went to the settlements of heavy
concentration of Japanese and used the places where they most
often gathered. It was similar to Paul who went to the Jewish
synagogues in each city.

Another point that attracts our attention is the size of
these meetings. The average attendance was 24 in the Registro
area and 23 in the Noroeste Zone. In those days when Japanese
lived in rural areas, it was difficult to have a large gathering.
Small meetings were easier to hold and perhaps more effective
for evangelization. Ito was alone and that type of meeting was
the only possible kind in his situation. He could devote more
personal attention to each attendant according to each one's
needs.

One more noteworthy fact is the number of times he preached.
There were days when he preached four to five times a day and
this indicates his zeal for preaching the gospel. Souls can not
be won without earnest preaching.

His favorite sermon was "Cultivation of Heart." Twenty-four
times out of fifty, that is, 41 percent of the time, he preached
that sermon. The literal translation of the sermon's title is
"Cultivation of the Spiritual Ricefield" and we can understand
how this sermon appealed to the Japanese farmers. The sermon
was on the parable of the sower, Luke 8:8,15, and its main
thoughts follow:

> The cultivation of soil is essential to supply food for
> the hungry world. But there is a problem which is more
> important than the cultivation of soil, that is, the
> cultivation of the soil which is inside each human heart.
> Jesus Christ said that the soil is the human heart and
> the word of God is the seed. What he is saying is that
> if we cultivate our heart and sow in it the good seed of
> the word of God and grow it with patience, we will har-
> vest a hundredfold, two-hundredfold and can begin a
> truly happy life. Jesus is teaching the secret of
> getting into a happy life in Luke 8:4-15.
>
> *The substance of activity.* There are people who have
> status, wealth, education and who are apparently happy,
> and yet are to be pitied. What is the cause of this?

These people forget to cultivate their hearts. What makes man important is his soul. Happiness or unhappiness depend on whether one cultivates his heart or not. Heart is the substance of activity. If you cultivate your heart according to the teaching of Jesus, and receive the word of God, you will have a happy life.

Spiritual harvest. The social problems to be featured by the newspapers are, in final analysis, due to how each one cultivates his heart. We have the conflict between "haves" and "have nots," between laborers and capitalists, between the employees and employers, and if we do not keep calm we may be pulled into the whirlpool of debates. The cause of these problems is in the human greed that does not know how to be satisfied. The antagonists may come to some sort of compromise, but never to a permanent solution. But if they of both sides cultivate their hearts, and receive the word of God, they surely will find a satisfactory solution. And even living in this unsatisfactory world, they may find meaning in their lives, and will harvest thanks, joy and peace which are spiritual blessings.

Religious education. Parents who live in colonies are concerned about the education of their children. They are often surprised with the result of their children's education which does not meet their expectation. Why does this happen? The answer is that although our educational system is based on the philosophy of many God-fearing educators of the past, today education is divorced from religion and professionalism has replaced humanistic person-centered education. This is why awful crimes are practiced by educated people. The decline of the character of those engaged in education is also lamentable fact. In order to correct this shortcoming, parents must kneel and pray to the great spiritual Master, Jesus Christ, cultivate their hearts and those of their children, sow the seed of word there, care for the family's religious education, expecting a good harvest. Then they will for sure have a good and abundant harvest.

Social reform. Today the world is divided between democracy and communism. Like it or not we are under the influence of these ideologies. The social reform advocated by the followers of these ideologies sound reasonable, but a real social reform cannot be attained by the use of violence and we must be aware of the danger of this way of thinking and be cautious about it. A real social reform comes when each and every individual

comes to know that he is a sinner and repents before God.
Then the cultivation of heart is done and the seed of
the word of God is sowed there and thus the first step
of social reform begins. And when this individual conversion extends to each one's surrounding neighbors, the
world-wide coexistence and coprosperity, that is, the
kingdom of God, will finally come (Ito...1970:47-49).

There is no doubt this message appealed to the newly arrived
Japanese farmers who were struggling for their survival, for it
pointed out the other need--the spiritual--that they so often
tended to forget or neglect. In those days when over 90 percent
of the Japanese people were engaged in farming, we can imagine
the timeliness and appropriateness of this message. He related
his Christian message with the experience of daily life of the
people who were concerned with cultivating soil and getting
material harvest. To cultivate soil is not enough. People
must cultivate their hearts through repentance and receive the
word of God. When human heart changes under the influence of
the word of God, then everything else will change. Transforma-
tion of heart is the key to the individual happiness, to the
solution of economic, social, educational, and political
problems. What he was saying, in other words, was that the
Christian gospel was the answer to all human needs. For the
people who had many needs and also many frustrations, this
message was good news.

Now let us turn to Ito's missionary itinerary to see the
extension and places of his missionary action.

TABLE 14

MISSIONARY ITINERARY OF ITO

Date   Place

1923
   March 27-28   Registro
   May 10   Guaimbe

1924
   January 3-22   Birigui, Penapolis
   May 13-25   Birigui
   September 18-21
   (With Kinsolving)   Birigui

1925
    March 7–May 22   Guarantan, Birigui, Lussanvira,
                                    Alianca, Guaicara
    July 7–14   Guarantan, Birigui, Promissao
    July 18
    (With Kinsolving)   Registro
    August 1–8   Registro
    August 24–   Quilombo
    August 31–
    October 24   Birigui, Guaimbe, Guaicara

1926
    January 12–30   Registro
    March 1–22   Guarantan, Birigui
    June 18–20   Agua Limpa, Promissao, Guaimbe,
                                    Lins, Guarantan
    July 28–30
    (With Kinsolving)   Birigui
    September 19–
    November 15   Registro, Sets Barras
    September 17–29   Penapolis

1927
    January 1–5   Registro
    February 18–
    March 22   Registro
    March 25–30   Sete Barras, Ribeira
    May 18–
    July 14   Guaimbe, Lins, Guaicara, Birigui,
                                    Penapolis, Guarantan
    November 13–
    December 25   Promissao, Alianca, Birigui,
                                    Guaicara

1928
    January 7–20   Guaimbe, Lins, Guaranta
    February 15–
    March 26   Registro, Quilombo, Sete Barras
    June 5–
    August 5   Guarantan, Birigui
    September 16–
    October 29   Birigui, Promissao, Guicara,
                                    Penapolis, Guarantan
    November 18–
    December 30   Nipolandia (working for fund rais-
                                    ing and building of Sao Mateus
                                    church)

1929
January 1-6	Nipolandia
January 19-20	Registro
February 11-12	Promissao
February 21– March 27	Alianca, Birigui, Guaimbe
April 10-15	Guaicara, Penapolis
May 1– June 29	Registro, Quilombo, Sete Barras Guarantan, Penapolis, Guaimbe, Guaicara, Birigui, Alianca
July 29– September 24	Registro

1930
November 1	Registro (dedication of the church)

1931
January 27-31	Registro
March 27– April 9	Alianca, Frutal, Agus Limpa, Birigui, Guaimbe, Guaicara
June 14– July 5	Registro
July 21-29	Guarantan, Guaimbe, Guaicara, Promissao, Birigui, Agua Limpa, Frutal, Alianca
September 21-23	Registro
October 18-27	Guarantan, Guaimbe, Guaicara
November 18-26	Alianca
December 20	Registro

1932
January 18-20	Birigui
April 20-24	Registro
May 14-28	Birigui, Agua Limpa, Perobal, Aracatuba, Guaicara
June 19-July 3	Nipolandia
October 19	Registro, Quilombo
October 27– November 1 (With Thomas)	Lins, Guaimbe, Guaicara, Birigui, Agus Limpa, Aracatuba, Alianca Alianca, Birigui, Agua Limpa, Guaimbe, Promissao

1933
    April 16   Registro
    May 17-23   Birigui
    June 6-25   Guarantan, Guaicara, Guaimbe,
                              Birigui, Registro
    August 27-28   Registro
    September 5-13
    (With Thomas)   Birigui, Aracatuba, Guararapes
                              (former Frutal) Alianca
    November 19   Birigui
    December 1   Brejo Alegre (dedication of Sao
                              Luas church)

1934
    February 28-March 4   Nipolandia
    June 15-July 10   Novo Oriente, Birigui, Guaimbe
    October 13-
    November 4   Birigui, Guaimbe
    December 3-12   Alianca, Guaimbe

1935
    April 25-May 13   Aliance, Birigui, Guaimbe
    July 18-20
    (With Thomas)   Guarantan, Guaimbe, Lins, Guaicara,
                              Birigui, Agua Limpa, Perobal,
                              Guararapes, Aliance, Tiete, Colonia
                              Tiete
    November 17-24   Guaimbe, Nipolandia

1936
    April 19-May 5   Birigui, Alianca
    June 19-23   Registro
    August 4-20
    (With Thomas)   Bastos, Marilia, Guaimbe, Lins,
                              Guaicara, Birigui, Agua Limpa,
                              Guararapes, Alianca, Tiete
    October 18-27   Tiete
    November 29-30   Guararapes

1937
    April 24-May 20   Alianca, Formosa, Promissao,
                              Nipolandia

    July 21-
    August 14
    (With Thomas)   Tres Barras, Cafezal, Rolandia,
                              Londrina, Alta Sorocabana, Bastos,
                              Marilia, Guaimbe, Lins, Guaicara,
                              Promissao, Birigui, Brejo Alegre,
                              Nipolandia, Agua Limpa, Aracatuba,
                              Alianca, Tiete, Guarantan

1937
   August 20–
   September 8   Nipolandia, Birigui, Aracatuba,
                                  Alianca

1938
   June 10-19   Marilia, Aracatuba, Alianca, Guara-
                                  rapes, Birigui, Guarantan

   July 21-August 23
   (With Thomas)   Tres Barras, Londrina, Alta
                                  Sorocabana, Bastos, Marilia, Guaimbe,
                                  Promissao, Birigui, Agua Limpa,
                                  Aracatuba, Alianca, Guarantan,
                                  Registro, Quilombo

1939
   July 14-28   Marilia, Guaimbe, Bilac (former
                                  Nipolandia), Agua Limpa, Aracatuba,
                                  Tiete, Alianca, Guararapes,
                                  Registro, Sete Barras

   November 9-25
   (With Thomas)   Tres Barras, Londrina, Rolandia,
                                  Alta Sorocabana, Bomfim, Bastos,
                                  Registro, Quilombo, Guarulhos

1940
   October 1-14
   (With Pitan)   Marilia, Bilac, Aracatuba, Tiete,
                                  Alianca, Formosa, Registro, Sete
                                  Barras, Itariri, Pedro Ana Jaz

   Source: Ito...1970:153-159

Let us note first the place of Ito's missionary work. We
note that he concentrated his work in three areas: Sao Paulo
which was his base, Registro area, and Noroeste zone. In
Registro area he had as his visiting points Quilombo, Sete
Barras, Ribeira, Itariri. In Noroeste zone his traveling
places were Guarantan, Lins, Guaimbe, Guaicara, Promissao,
Penapolis, Birigui, Bilac, Agua Limpa, Aracatuba, Guararapes,
Alianca, Lussanvira. Strategically he was right, for these were
the places of larger concentrations of Japanese; particularly
Zona Noroeste was where the largest number of Japanese were
living in the decades of the twenties and thirties (Suzuki 1969:
200).

Another point that compels our attention is the extent of
his itinerant ministry which is amazing when we consider not
only its distance but the difficulties of the means of

transportation of those days. It is 600 miles from Registro to
Lussanvira. With the distance he traveled each time he stopped
in the cities and settlements, we know that each time Ito
visited his missionary field he would travel 1200 miles. There
is a record of the mileage of his trip in some years. For
instance in 1925 he traveled 3729 miles; in 1926, 3107 miles;
in 1939, 3107 miles; and in 1940, 2796 miles. Now when we
consider that in those days it took three days to go from Sao
Paulo to Registro (because one had to go to Santos and from
Santos to Juquia by train, then from Juquia he had to take a
boat to Registro) we realize how difficult so much traveling
must have been. Today there is a highway, and it is possible
to in three hours get from Sao Paulo to Registro. Also in
those days it would take seventeen hours to go to Lins from Sao
Paulo, while today one makes it in six hours by bus. From Lins
to Guaimbe (which is only twenty-two miles) it would take from
three to five hours in those days, while today it is only a
half-hour trip. When we consider these difficulties we may
understand how hard it was to travel over 3000 miles a year on
those poor roads and paths. It was a work of real sacrifice.
And when we add to this Ito's parish responsibility in Sao Paulo
we can not but admire his dedication and capacity for personal
sacrifice.

Up to 1935 Ito had concentrated his work in Sao Paulo,
Registro and Zona Noroeste. But in 1936 we see him in Bastos
and Marilia, a new frontier in Alta Paulista. From 1937 on,
however, his itinerary is extended to the North of Parana State
covering Tres Barras (now Assai), Cafezal, Rolandia, and
Londrina. At this time he began to visit Alta Sorocabana
which, with Alta Paulista and Norte do Parana, was becoming a
zone of Japanese concentration. The concentration of the
Japanese was shifting from Zona Noroeste to Alta Paulista,
Alta Sorocabana, and Norte do Parana. Ito did not, however,
plant any churches in Alta Paulista and Alta Sorocabana. In
Norte do Parana he planted a church in Londrina.

The time Ito spent in his missionary journeys is noteworthy,
too. Table 15 indicates that in his first term (1923-1929),
almost half of his time was spent in traveling and church planting). Ito spent a great deal of his time on missionary
journeys. On the average he spent 155.8 days a year traveling
throughout his 600 mile long parish. After he came back from
furlough the time he spent on missionary journeys was much less
(47.8 days per year), but this we can understand when we note
that by that time he had pastors to take care of the churches he
had planted. He had one pastor in 1929, three by 1933, and five
by 1938, who could take care of the churches. The Sao Joao
Church in Sao Paulo was growing and required more of his time;
besides, now, he had a family to which he had an obligation as
the head of the household.

TABLE 15

TIME SPENT BY ITO ON HIS MISSIONARY JOURNEYS

Year	Days	Year	Days
1923	3	1932	48
1924	34	1933	41
1925	146	1934	64
1926	113	1935	46
1927	146	1936	50
1928	203	1937	72
1929	171	1938	44
1930(furlough)		1939	32
1931	67	1940	14

Source: Ito...1970:153-160

In order to show how his missionary trips were carried out I will transcribe part of the episcopal diary of 1939 of the Bishop William M. M. Thomas whom Ito accompanied.

July 20.   I left Rio by the night train for Sao Paulo.

21.   I arrived in Sao Paulo. At 7:00 p.m., in company of The Ven. John Y. Ito, I embarked for Ourinhos.

22.   In Ourinhos we changed trains to the Sao Paulo-Parana Company. We arrived in Jatai at 3:00 p.m. We took an auto for Tres Barras, one hour away from the station. Still by auto, we went to the house of the parishioner Mr. Katow. After dinner, Rev. Ito baptized a lady and her child and presented 3 candidates for confirmation. I preached and celebrated the Communion for nine members.

23.   In the morning, we went, by foot, to the house of the parishioner Mr. Arata Saezawa. There after 2 were baptized, I confirmed 3 persons, the couple and the daughter. I preached and celebrated the Communion with the seven members of this mission. Back to Jatai, we took a train for Nova Dantzig. We went, by auto, about 13 miles, to the house of Mr. Mano, where we stayed, I inspected the Chapel of Santo Andre, built by Mr. Mano. It is small and simple, made of hardwood with a capacity for 40 people. After dinner, at the residence of Mr. Mano, the archdeacon read the Vespertime Office and gave the instruction. I pronounced absolution and gave the benediction.

24. At 7:45.,., At the Chapel of Santo Andre assisted by the Ven. Archdeacon, I celebrated the Communion for the five communicants. At 10:30 a.m., I confirmed one candidate, I dedicated the chapel and preached. After lunch, we continued our trip, by auto, for Rolandia, the terminal of the Sao Paulo-Parana railroad. I went to the house of Mr. Henning where I met 30 people gathered, all members of our Church. I held an informal service and spoke. We went, by bus, to Londrina, founded seven years ago and already a city of some proportions. At 8:00 p.m., Mr. Yoiiti Zakoji's, the archdeacon Ito baptized three persons and presented one person for confirmation.

25. At 9:14 a.m., we left for Ourinhos. Thus I finished my first official visit to the State of Parana, where I found five nuclei of church members who are in need of pastoral care. I confirmed 8 persons and I dedicated a small private chapel.

26. At 8:00 p.m., at the house of Mr. Saburo Takahashi, in Bastos, the Ven. Archdeacon baptized a child and presented a girl for confirmation. I preached to a small group.

27. At 9:30 a.m., at Mr. Sugai's, a faithful parishioner, 10 miles from the village of Bastos, after a few baptisms, performed by Rev. Ito, I confirmed 2 candidates. I preached and celebrated the Communion for five members of this mission, assisted by the archdeacon.

28. We left, at 6:00 a.m., by bus, for Marilia, where we arrived at noon. At 8:00 p.m. at the residence of Mr. Nishizawa, 17 people gathered, and we held a devotional service. The Rev. Ono presented a young man for confirmation. I preached.

29. We got up at 6:00 a.m., and went by bus to Colonia Linda. There, at Mr. U. Kuronuma's home we improvised a chapel. The Rev. Ono baptized three adults and four children and presented for confirmation one of the baptized persons, the venerable mother of Mr. Kuronuma. We ate lunch and continued our trip for Guaimbe by an auto kindly provided by Mr. Kuronuma where we were lodged at the parsonage.

30. At 9:00 a.m., at the Church of Ascencao, the Rev. Ono baptized 9 persons and presented 10 for confirmation. I preached. Assisted by the two elders, I celebrated the Communion. at 8:30 p.m., at the house of the pharmacist and parishioner Mr. Sakuda, in Lins I confirmed one person, who was presented by Rev. Ono. I preached and celebrated the Communion for the 10 communicants who were present, assisted by Rev. Ito and Ono.

31. We left, by bus, at 7:00 a.m., for Guaicara. We visited the couple Murata. At his house Rev. Ito baptized a child. I celebrated the Communion and preached. We went, by truck, to Mr. Satow's home, in Bairro Aurora. Assisted by Rev. Ito, I celebrated the Communion for a small group of parishioners and I preached. After lunch, Mr. Satow sent us to the house of Mr. Marco Ito, in Colonia Gonzaga, 19 miles far. At 4:00 p.m., Rev. Ito read the Vespers Service and I preached.

August 1. At 7:30 a.m., at the house of Mr. Marco Ito, I celebrated the communion, assisted by Rev. Ito. Soon after breakfast we went to Borra. At the house of Mr. Hainu, I confirmed 2 candidates, presented by Rev. Ito. I preached and celebrated the Communion, always assisted by Rev. Ito. At lunch the archdeacon made an exhortation and I preached. We went back to Gonzaga, staying overnight again with the Ito family. After supper, I attended the instruction, ministered by Rev. Ito to a small group which was present.

2. We went to Promissao, from there to Birigui. We stayed at the Lamacchia Hotel, where Rev. Takeo had ordered a special and excellent dinner. At 8:00 p.m., at the hall of the tailorshop of Mr. Tijima, I confirmed 2 candidates, presented by Rev. Takeo, I preached and celebrated the Communion, assisted by Rev. Ito and Takeo.

3. At 8:00 a.m., we went, by auto, to Brejo Alegra. At 9:30 a.m., at the Chapel of Sao Lucias, I spoke to 60 pupils of the Sunday school. I confirmed, following that, 2 candidates. I celebrated the Communion, assisted by Revs. Ito and Takeo, and I preached. After lunch, at the home of the Sanos, I attended a meeting of 28 parents of the pupils of the parochial school. I gave a lecture on education and led a discussion. We continued our trip to Nipolandia, where I was lodged by the Shimanuki couple. After tea, I inspected the new building for classes built by the congregation for the Collegio Sao Mateus. At night, we went, by auto to the house of Mr. Maki Torao, in Jangada. I presided at a devotional meeting and spoke as did also the Rev. Ito and Takeo.

4. At 9:00 a.m., at the Church of Sao Mateus, I spoke to 90 pupils of the Sunday school. Immediately after that the Revs. Takeo and Ito baptized some children. Rev. Takeo presented 28 persons for confirmation. I confirmed them, and addressed them a few words, preached and celebrated the Communion. At noon, at the new school building, luncheon was served to 150 persons. I dedicated the building offering appropriate prayers and making a short speech. There were five or six more speakers.

We left, two hours late, for Agua Limpa. At the house of Mr. Sakamoto I confirmed one person, presented by Rev. Ito, I preached and celebrated the Communion. We had supper with the Sakamoto family and afterwards we went, by auto, to Aracatuba.

5. At 9:00 a.m., we embarked for Lussanvira. The Rev. Yuba was waiting for us and the company of the colony kindly sent us by auto to Novo Oriente, the headquarters of the Colonia Fazenda Tiete. At the house of Mr. Kimoto, I baptized three children. Rev. Ito baptized four, and I confirmed one and preached. We stayed overnight at Mr. Wako's.

6. At 7:30 a.m., at the house of the parishioner Kimoto, I confirmed one person, presented by Rev. Ito, and celebrated one person, presented by Rev. Ito, and celebrated the Communion, assisted by the Revs. Ito and Yuba.

We left, at 9:00 a.m., by auto put at our disposal by the Company, for Second Alianca, 25 miles away. At parishioner Mr. Kimbara's, after some were baptized, I confirmed one person. I preached and celebrated the Communion for five members residing in that point.

We continued our trip for Primeira Alianca. When we arrived at the Katahara's, who kindly lodged us, we ate lunch. At night, we went by horse, to the headquarters of the Colony. At the Church of Aliance I led a devotional service, assisted by Revs. Ito and Yuba, and I preached.

7. We went, by horse, to the Chapel of Sao Marcos, four miles away. At 9:00 a.m., I attended Sunday School. There were speeches of greeting in Portuguese, and an attendance of 76 pupils. I spoke. After a few were baptized by Rev. Ito, I confirmed three candidates. I preached and celebrated the Communion, assisted by the two companions of the journey. I dedicated the Chapel with appropriated prayers. When the services ended at 12:30 p.m., we had luncheon with Kobayashis. I confirmed, afterwards, two persons.

At 4:00 p.m., we went, by horse, to the other section of the village, right after we had arrived and had performed one baptism. I confirmed 3 candidates. I celebrated the Communion and preached. After supper I led a meditation and a discussion, which ended with tea and candies at 11:00 p.m.

8. We got up at 4:30 a.m., went by horse for two hours to the Station Guaracai, where we took the train. We arrived in Guararapes at 11:00 a.m. At the house of Mr. Obow, after baptism, I confirmed 2 persons, preached and celebrated the Communion. We continued our journey for Aracatuba. At 8:00 p.m., I led a devotional service, at the home of Mr. Nakagawa, assisted by Revs. Ito and Yuba, and I spoke.

9. In the company of Rev. Ito, I embarked at 8:00 a.m., for Guarantan. There we took a bus to the settlement. They were expecting us on the following day, but soon they notified the parishioners and other persons of neighborhood, so that at 8:00 p.m. the house was full. I preached and celebrated the Communion.

10. At noon we held a memorial service in memory of the father of Mr. Hitokata and of the wife of Mr. Sakuda, two faithful parishioners of that mission. We returned by auto to the station, and embarked for Sao Paulo.

11. We arrived in Sao Paulo.

14. At 9:30, at the Capela de Sao Joao, the Rev. Ito baptized two children and presented 8 candidates for confirmation. I confirmed them, preached and celebrated the Communion.

20. We embarked, at 7:00 a.m., for Registro; from there to Manga Larga, where we were lodged at the parsonage. At the Church of Todos os Santos, a devotional service was held at 8:00 p.m. I addressed a meditation to 60 attendants.

21. At 9:30 a.m., I spoke to the pupils of the Sunday School. After the baptism of seven persons, I confirmed 3 candidates, presented by Rev. Ito. I made a brief elocution, preached and celebrated the Communion.
After lunch, I went, by auto, to Quilombo, in company of Rev. Ito and Iso. At 8:00 p.m., at home of Mr. Yoshikawa, I led a devotional meeting, speaking to the persons who were present for the Litany, which was read afterwards by Rev. Ito.

22. At 9:00 a.m., at the home of Mr. Yoshikawa, assisted by Rev. Ito, I preached and celebrated the Communion; received by all the communicants of that mission. The Old Mr. Yoshikawa, who is 86 years old, was sick in bed. We took the sacred elements to him also.
We continued the journey for Registro and Sete Barras, where a good part of the congregation was waiting for us at the dock. After tea at the home of the Freitas, I confirmed at the Capela de Santo Andre 6 candidates, presented by Rev. Timoteo, and I preached. We returned to Registro, where we stayed overnight.

23. We embarked, at 7:00 a.m., for Juquia, where we spent a night.

24. At 5:20 a.m., we took a train for Santos. I embarked for Rio.

25. I arrived in Rio at 8:00 a.m. I finished thus a
journey of five weeks, in visiting the congregations and
missions of our Church in Sao Paulo. I had to travel by 17
trains and 55 automobiles, buses, ships and other means of
transportation. I traveled 2486 miles. I took part in, or
led, 101 divine offices, I celebrated the Communion 26 times
and confirmed 109 candidates. I visited 40 churches or
missions, 10 of them for the first time (Thomas in Atas e
Outros Documentos do 4lo. Concilio da Ingreja Episcopal
Brasileira (1939:47-52).

As we have seen it was a very busy and extensive schedule.
It was a very hard and tiring itinerary which Ito made two or
three times a year. He would carry a rucksack and take a cane
for his journey. Sometimes he went hungry with nothing to eat,
and so he had to ask a traveler for piece of bread; sometimes
night fell where no house could be found and he had to spend the
night under a tree. One day darkness fell while he was walking
on a path in the midst of a jungle. He was afraid to stay there
over night because of wild animals and yet it was so dark to
continue his journey. He did not know what to do. But after a
little while it began to thunder and lightning. So each time
lightning struck he could see and advance a few yards. Thus,
he arrived at his destination where he held a cottage meeting,
preaching on Jesus as the light of the world, and applying his
experience to his message, reminding his listeners that every
dark time of life there is light if we look up to God (Ito...
1970:143-144). Here was a true missionary who had determined to
preach the gospel "where Christ has not already been named."

GROWTH AND DECLINE

If we look at graphs 3 and 4, we notice that the period of
growth for the Episcopal Church among the Japanese in Brazil
continued up to 1955, after which it began to lose members. Now
if we break down the period of growth by decade, we note that
the decade of the thirties was the period of most rapid growth,
when the Church grew 181.42 percent. The decade of the forties
and the first quinquennium of the sixties are the period of slow
growth, when it grew at 50.48 and 29.29 percent respectively.
Now the yearly growth of these two decades and one half is
respectively 10.8, 4.2 and 5.4 percent. This indicates that the
Episcopal Church grew rapidly in the period 1930-1940, while in
the following 15 years its growth slowed down. Why did the
Church grow more rapidly in the pre-war period than in the
following years? In answer to this question we can mention a
few factors that we consider important.

FIGURE 3

COMMUNICANT MEMBERS OF
THE JAPANESE EPISCOPAL CHURCH

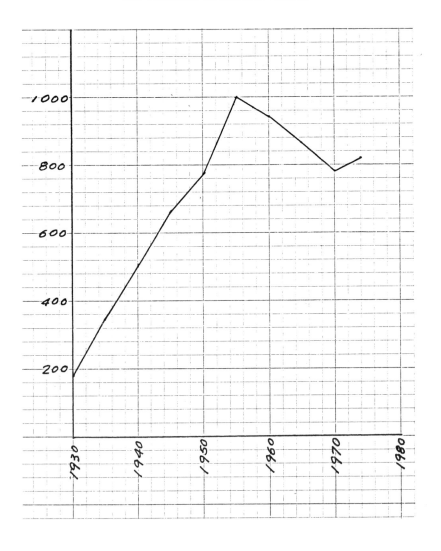

FIGURE 4

COMMUNICANT MEMBERS OF
THE JAPANESE EPISCOPAL CHURCH

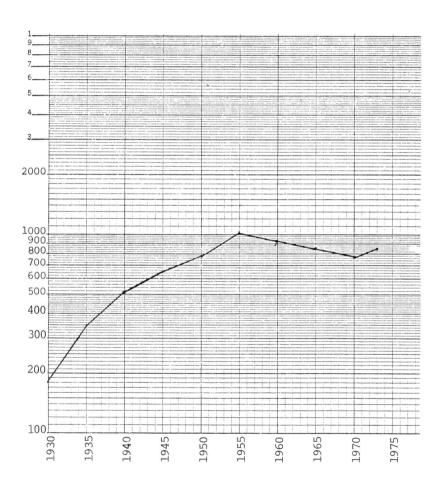

The years before the war were what is known as the pioneer stage of the Japanese immigrants. Migrating to a new country, they were uprooted, insecure, and lonely. They were also free from the social control of family, society, tradition, and religion. They were looking for new associations, for a new orientation in life and were more open to new ideas or beliefs. They did not have Buddhist temples nor Shinto shrines, nor Buddhist or Shinto priests in Brazil. Under these circumstances Ito could work fairly free of competition from other religions, except for the Catholics which had missionary work among the Japanese in the Registro and Sao Paulo areas. His visitation and messages were a source of encouragement and hope for many immigrants newly arrived, as is attested by one of them:

> It was in 1924, when I was living alone a few kms. from Guicara, near Lins. It was in the midst of a forest where I had felled trees to form a pasture of about 2 alqueires (about 12 acres). As I did not have much money I was living in a cabin covered with coconut leaves and since I was the only one living there I wore only underwear, living seminude. In order to protect myself from wild animals, I used to have a wood fire burning all night, and the noise of burning wood was my only friend. It was a life similar to Robinson Crusoe's. "Asamisan ogenki desuka" (Are you well, Mr. Asami?). It was Rev. Ito who had come to visit me in such an inconvenient and far off place. He was wearing a khaki suit and gaiters, and carrying a heavy rucksack. As I did not have a luxurious thing like bathtub, I took him to a stream and asked him to wash himself there. Meanwhile, I went out to borrow a plate and a spoon, for the only tableware I had was what I used myself. I killed a chicken and fixed supper.

> Under the beautiful and twinkling constellations, around the woodfire, sitting on sacks, we two sang hymns, prayed and read the Scriptures. It was a quiet world where you don't hear anything but bird's songs. The cool breeze would refresh our faces. The pose of Rev. Ito looked to me like the apostles of the early Church, so precious it was. His words on God were like water that sank as in sand into my heart.

> Next day, we walked on the desert-like sand, under the hot, bright sun of Noroeste, from settlement to settlement, from home to home, where Rev. Ito would preach the gospel. I carried his heavy rucksack. His talk, while we were walking together, became part of my blood and flesh. After having repeated this type of experience several times, I was baptized and later confirmed at the home of Rev. Ito's brother, in Gonzaga, a district of Promissao (Ito...1970:132).

Another factor of growth is undoubtedly the dedication of a man like Ito. We have seen the time and energy he spent in soul-winning and in church planting. He was a man determined to pay the price for church growth and did not spare any sacrifice to achieve that goal. The Christianization of his people was his top priority and concern.

One more important factor is the aid given by the American Episcopal Missionary Board. The substantial financial aid given by the Mission to building churches and to paying the workers enabled Ito and his five fellow ministers to devote full time to church work. In this point the Episcopal Church had an enormous advantage over the Holiness Church which started from the very beginning on an almost entirely self-supporting program. Ito's mobility throughout his wide area of missionary work without having to worry about his family's living was possible only through the financial help given by the Mission. Add to this the attention paid to the Japanese work by Bishops Kinsolving and Thomas who would spend about one month yearly visiting the Japanese churches and missions. Bishop Kinsolving retired in 1928 and was succeeded by Bishop Thomas. Bishop Thomas's interest in the Japanese work was so great that even during the war he didn't stop visiting Japanese churches, although sometimes he was questioned by government agents who thought he was a German. Right after the war when the Japanese community was under the threat of a fanatical group who did not believe in Japan's defeat and who threatened to kill the leaders of the *colonia* who said Japan had been defeated, the bishop was advised not to travel among the Japanese. But for him his responsibility as a bishop was more important than his life, and he told Ito that they perhaps would become martyrs. Yet he continued his episcopal visitation to the Japanese churches.

We shall now try to explain why the Japanese Episcopal Church slowed down in its growth during the war and afterwards, and why it declined after 1955.

The slowing down during the war is understandable when we know that in that period no public meeting in Japanese was allowed to be held. Since all the ministers were Japanese-speaking, we can understand how difficult it was to have services or Sunday school in Portuguese. And even though some of them actually did preach in Portuguese, it was very difficult for their listeners to understand. No doubt this limited the growth of all the Japanese churches, not only the Episcopal, during that period. The church as a whole continued to grow, though more slowly, during the war, except for the church of Guaimbe which lost members because its pastor was in prison.

The decline of growth after 1955 we may explain by pointing to the factor of migration into the cities. Many Japanese, following the general trend, moved form the country to the city, particularly to Sao Paulo and its vicinities. Most of the Episcopal churches (five out of eight) were located in rural areas like Manga Larga, Bilac, Guaimbe, Alianca, Pereira Barreto. Ito was right when he built churches in the rural areas during the twenties and thirties because at that time the great majority (90 percent) of the Japanese lived in the country. But with migration of rural people to the cities after the war, a more correct strategy would have been to move the churches to the cities where the Japanese were moving. But as this was not done the churches have suffered membership erosion as we can see in graph 5. Two rural churches which were prosperous in the thirties and in the first half of the forties, Manga Larga and Bilac, died out in 1960. The other two rural churches, Guaimbe and Aliance stopped growing in 1955. The only church that has grown consistently from the beginning up to the present is the one situated in the megalopolis of Sao Paulo. This was the church located where the influx of Japanese has been greater and greater since the end of the war.

Another important factor of non-growth and slow growth after the war was the integration policy adopted after the war. During the war, as we have already mentioned, no church was allowed to hold a public meeting in Japanese. So some churches shifted to Portuguese in order to continue their Sunday school or church services. Ito, for instance, held Sunday school and church services in Portuguese. When the war ended and churches were allowed again to use Japanese in their public meetings, Ito would not shift, thinking the right way of the Japanese in Brazil should be toward integration and that the churches should take the initiative (Ito...1970:1970:81). Later this philosophy of integration would have its influence not only on the language but on the appointment of ministers. Thus some Brazilian ministers were appointed to the Japanese churches. It is obvious that a Brazilian minister would have a limitation in reaching Japanese, particularly those who were Japanese speaking. Man has a tendency to associate with those who are like him, and when integration within the church is pushed too strongly before a minority group is totally integrated into the main stream of the larger society, the church will naturally suffer. In the United States we have the example of the Methodist Church which integrated the Japanese churches after the war with unsatisfactory results. Now that cultural pluralism is being advocated, the Church leaders think that that policy was a mistake, but at the same time they think it is too late to reverse it now. Yuba, the successor of Ito, thinks that it is an error to form churches composed only of Nisei, for this will slow down even more the Japanese amalgamation and integration into Brazilian life and culture (this comes from his statement made when he was interviewed by Wesley King, a Free Methodist missionary to Brazil, in

FIGURE 5

COMMUNICANT MEMBERS OF
THE JAPANESE EPISCOPAL CHURCHES

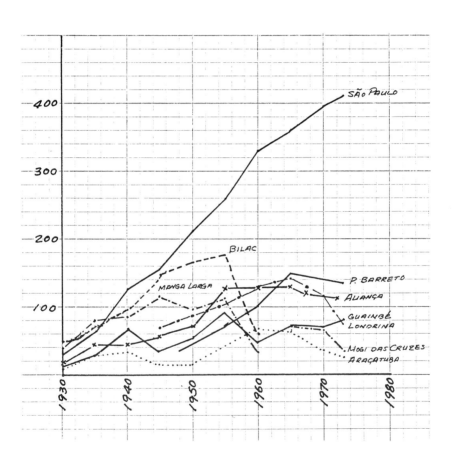

1963). In 1963, eleven out of fourteen churches were totally
integrated, that is, were having their services only in Portuguese. This must have been a very important factor for the slow,
non-growth of the Episcopal Church in the past fifteen years.
The Free Methodist and Holiness churches have not adopted this
policy of integration.

One more important factor that may have affected the growth
of the Episcopal Church is the cutting of financial aid from the
American Mission. As we have mentioned, the American financial
aid contributed to the growth of the Episcopal work among
Japanese in its early years. But it seems that this financial
dependence went on for too long. The Episcopal work among
Japanese began in 1923, and in 1963, forty years later, thirteen
out of fourteen churches were still receiving financial aid from
the United States, accounting for 50 percent of their budgets.
Only one church (Sao Joao church in Sao Paulo) was totally
autonomous (information given by Yuba to W. King in 1963). In
the past few years financial aid has been cut substantially, and
as a result many ministers have been taking secular jobs in
order to support themselves. Thus they are not giving fulltime
to ministry which, doubtless, affects their work. This is the
reverse of what has happened with the Igreja Evangelica Holiness
do Brazil whose ministers began with self-support and are now
all fully supported by the churches.

Another fact that we have to note is the retirement of Ito in
1958, the death of two ministers, Ono and Shimanuki, and the
retirement of two more ministers, Iso and Kaneko. Thus the
Japanese Episcopal Church has lost five of its ministers. New
ministers have appeared, but not all of them are working in the
Japanese churches due to the policy of integration.

We should also mention the fact that the Episcopal Church has
not multiplied churches in the past twenty years. Ito was a
church planter and thirty years after the beginning of his work,
1953, he had established 10 churches and 35 missions. By the
time he retired in 1958, however, the number of churches remained
the same, whereas the number of missions has even diminished. A
fact known to the students of church growth is that in order for
a church movement to grow it must multiply congregations. This
was not done by the Japanese Episcopal Church. Compare the
Episcopal Church with the Holiness and the Free Methodist Churches in Table 16.

Finally we can mention as a factor of the non-growth the
facts that often missions forget to continue establishing new
churches once they have established a certain number. Missions
become more engaged in taking care of the established churches
and forget the task of establishing new ones. The Japanese

Episcopal Church in Brazil did not escape this general rule. Most of its churches had been established by the time the war started, and it seems that in the post-war period, which was an unprecedented opportunity for evangelism, they were more occupied in taking care of themselves.

TABLE 16

NUMBER OF CHURCHES PLANTED AND MEMBERS
BY YEARS AND DENOMINATIONS

Year	Episcopal		Holiness		Free Methodist	
	Churches	Members	Churches	Members	Churches	Members
1930	2	183	1			
1935	5	350	3			
1940	6	515	4		3	
1945	6	661	5		3	
1950	7	775	6		8	173
1955	7	1002	9		8	517
1960	9	947	11	797	9	1081
1965	8	871	12	1018	14	
1970	7	785	15	1233	16	1636

Source: Atas e Outros Documentos de Igreja Episcopal
Brasileira, 1930–1970.
Resumo do Relatorio do Secretario de Estatisca
Prestado ao Concilio, 1950–1970 (Free Methodist).
Annual Report of the Holiness Church of Brazil.

3

The Evangelical Holiness
Church of Brazil

THE BEGINNING

The Holiness Church of Japan has been a phenomenal movement in the history of Japanese Christianity. Its growth in the fifteen years preceding World War II was simply remarkable (Yamamori 1974:119). This Holiness revival had its repercussion in Brazil too. In 1924, Juji Nakada, a founder of the Holiness Church of Japan, wrote an article on the evangelization of the Japanese immigrants in Brazil. And in 1925 Takeo Monobe was sent as the first Holiness missionary to Brazil (Burajiru Holiness Kyokai 1935:28,29; Edwards 1971:81; Yamasaki and Chiozaki 1970:83).

Takeo Monobe was born in Nagano-ken, Japan, on June 23, 1893, as the second son of Jitsuichi Kanei. He was later adopted by the Monobe family and thus changed his family name. From his early age he was very obedient to his parents and kind to his brothers and sisters. After his formal education he went to Tokyo where he attended school for four years. Then he became a trainman and worked very diligently, maintaining a good and friendly relationship with his collegues. In 1915 one of his collegues died suddenly and that led the sensitive young man to think seriously about life and death. He sought an answer to his problem in several places but in no place was he able to find the answer he was seeking. Finally he came to a Holiness Church, and there he heard the gospel, came to the experience of new birth, and found peace in his heart. On August 6 of the same year he was baptized by the Bishop Juji Nakada. In 1917 at a *seikai* (*Holy* assembly) held in Nagano-ken, God spoke to him through Isaiah 6:8: "Whom shall I send, and who will go

for us?" His reply was the same as that of Isaiah: "Here am
I! send me" (Burajiru Holiness Kyokai 1935:1).

Monobe's father was a Buddhist priest of a *Shinshu* sect and
enjoyed a good reputation in the community. He strongly opposed
the conversion of his beloved son to Christianity, and when he
found out that Takeo was going to be a Christian minister, his
disappointment was so great that he disinherited him and secluded
himself at home for one year. Takeo's decision was firm, however, and he endured that trial and persecution. He quit working
for the railroad company and entered the Holiness Seminary on
April 9, 1917. During his two years at the seminary he prayed
earnestly for his family, and God answered his prayer. His
younger brother and sister were converted to Christianity and
his father came to change his attitude toward Takeo. When Takeo
graduated in 1919 and then married an adopted daughter of the
Monobe family, he had his father's approval. And when Takeo was
appointed to be the pastor of the Koike Holiness Church his
father gave him his blessing and encouraged him to do his best
in his ministry. In May of 1922 he was transferred to Shinagawa
Holiness Church (Burajiru Holiness Kyokai 1935:1-2).

In 1925 Takeo dedicated himself to be the first Holiness
missionary to Brazil. He arrived on July 15 of the same year.
He was a man of love and faith and of a peaceful personality,
tireless in service. On the third day after his arrival, he
made his first missionary journey to the interior of the State
of Sao Paulo, including also a part of the State of Minas
Gerais. From July to November of that year he visited the
vicinities of Sao Paulo, Mogiana, Juquia, Douradense, Arara-
quarense, and Noroeste (Burajiu Holiness Kyokai 1935:29). In
December he accepted the invitation to be the pastor of the
Registro Union Church (Interdenominational) and moved there. By
the end of that year there were in the Holiness Church 36
believers (including those who had come from Japan) and 63
seekers (Burajiu Holiness Kyokai 1935:29).

Until September of the year 1926, Monobe was busy teaching at
the Japanese language school and preaching the gospel day and
night, using all his spare time. He proved to be an excellent
teacher and missionary. At school his care for children was
unusual. For example, he would take barber shears and cut the
children's hair. He was very efficient and the children's progress in learning became evident. Parents often said that it
would be difficult for the teacher who would come after him. He
was very efficient in his ministry too. He was able to baptize
eighteen people that year (Barajiu Holiness Kyokai 1925:10-11).

In October of the same year his family arrived from Japan and
he left Registro for Sao Paulo to join his family and to initiate

his ministry in a wider area. In December of that year he began
the Holiness Church on 7 Conde de Sarzedas Street, Sao Paulo.
His objectives were to establish self-supporting churches and to
preach the Biblical gospel. That year, in May, he made a missionary trip to Mogiana (including Minas), Paulista, and Araraquara
zones and baptized three people, bringing to twenty-one the number he had baptized (Burajiru Holiness Kyokai 1935:29).

In February of 1927, the Holiness Church of Brazil was composed of ten members who had come from Japan, forty who had been
converted in Brazil, and 120 seekers. On June 10 of the same
year six more people were baptized in Sao Paulo, and preaching
stressed the keeping of the Lord's day and tithing. He spent
the month of July in Registro and September in Mogiana and Minas
Gerais. On these trips he baptized twenty people (Burajiru
Holiness Kyokai 1935:29).

In the year 1928, Monobe visited the Mogiana and Paulista
zones in January, Douradense in March, again Magiana in June,
Sorocabana and Noroeste in July, Paulista in August. This year
a new missionary couple, Koji Tamura and his wife, came from
Japan on August 16. Tamura was appointed to work in Registro
in December of the same year (*Loc. cit.*).

In 1929 Monobe traveled 22000 kms. (13,750 miles). Besides
Noroeste, Mogiana, Sorocabana, Registro, Santos, he went to
Cambara, State of Parana. The year 1929 was historical because
of the visit of Bishop Juji Nakada to Brazil. He arrived on
May 29 and spent five weeks in Brazil. With him came Juro Yuasa
and his family, who came as the third Holiness missionary to
Brazil. Nakada held special meetings at the Sao Paulo Holiness
Church, Sao Paulo Baptist Church, Unida Church, Mackenzie
College, and in many of the association halls of the Japanese
colony. Every meeting was very well attended. As the result of
his ministry 59 people were baptized and two native Brazilian
young men, Jose Emilio Emerenciano and Paulo F. Almeida, dedi-
cated their lives to Christian ministry and went to Japan to
attend the Holiness Seminary in Tokyo. Nakada visited Lins,
Aracatuba, Lussanvira, Alianca, Presidente Vencesslau, Cambara,
Registro, and Rio. In Rio he met the President, Washington Luis,
from whom he was assured religious freedom to propagate the
Protestant faith in Brazil (Yoneda 1959:407-409; Burajiru
Holiness Kyokai 1935:30).

In the same year eighty people were baptized and two new
churches were planted: one in Lins by Juro Yuaca and one in
Cambara by Eiichiro Tada, a layman who had arrived from Japan
in December and went to Cambara as a Japanese language school
teacher (Burajiru Holiness Kyokai 1935:30).

The year 1930 was one of great trial for the Holiness Church
in Brazil. Monobe, its founder, died on July 25 at thirty-seven
years of age, a victim of cancer of the liver and over-work. He
began to feel pain in his stomach on May 5, yet on May 12 he
went out for his last missionary journey to Presidente Venceslau
and Bastos. In Bastos he was so weak and the pain was so acute
that he had to preach sustained by local believers. On May 26
he returned to Sao Paulo where he went through terrible suffering for two months. Apparently, because of his belief in divine
healing, he did not go to a doctor for treatment (Burajiru
Holiness Kyokai 1935:30).

The death of its leader left the Holiness Church in a very
difficult situation. There were only three ministers left;
Koji Tamura, Juro Yuaca and Hidesaku Tamura, a *fukuinshi* (a
gospel messenger, as a Holiness minister used to be called), who
had come from Japan in December of 1929 and had decided to be a
fulltime minister in January of 1930. But this year Shimekichi
Tanaami, the future leader of the Holiness Church of Brazil,
dedicated his life for fulltime ministry and went to Japan to
attend Seisho Gakuin (seminary). The Monobe family returned to
Japan on the same ship. In September of the same year the
Church received one more minister from Japan, Masazo Saiki, who
was appointed to Bastos where he started the Holiness church
(Burajiru Holiness Kyokai 1935:31,31).

In July of 1931 Nakada appointed Koji Tamura to be the acting
superintendent of the Brazil District (the Holiness work in
Brazil was a district of the Holiness Church of Japan until it
became independent in 1934). On August 29, Jose Emerenciano and
Paulo Almeida came back from Japan, and in September Eiichiro
Tada resigned from the work in Cambara and moved to Sao Paulo
(Burajiru Holiness Kyokai 1935:31).

In January of 1932 Paulo Almeida and Masazo Saiki resigned
due to their lack of certainty on the divine calling. In April
Koji Tamura moved to Sao Paulo and Juro Yuasa moved to Santos.
On December 15, Guararapes Holiness Church was inaugurated. The
number of baptisms reached 42 that year (*Loc. cit.*).

On January 26, 1933, Shimekichi Tanaami, who had gone to
Japan for study, came back with Katsuichi Namba, another Holiness
minister, and they were appointed to Bastos and Lins, respectively. On May 7 of the same year the first temple of the
Holiness Church was dedicated in Bastos (*Ibid.* 32).

INDEPENDENCE

In October of 1933 the Holiness Church of Japan split into two
factions, the Holiness Church (Kiyome Kyokai) led by Bishop

Nakada and the Japan Holiness Church (Nippon Sei Kyokai) headed
by five seminary professors, Akiji Kurumada, Yutaka Yoneda,
Tosaji Obara, Masakichi Ichinomiya, Kenichi Tsuchiya (Yoneda
1959:464-465). This schism led the Holiness Church of Brazil to
decide what stand to take in face of what had happened to the
mother Church. In the District Meeting held on January 3-8,
1934, the problem was thoroughly discussed and the conclusion
was to take a neutral stand. On July 2 of the same year,
Jisaku Ando, *Fukuinshi*, and his wife arrived from Japan with a
first-hand report on the issue. On July 5-7 a special District
Meeting was held and the final conclusion was that, in order to
avoid a split in the Holiness Church of Brazil, the only way was
to become independent. Thus on July 7, 4:18 p.m., all the
present members stood up and declared the independence of the
Holiness Church of Brazil (Igreja Holiness do Brasil). The
Church restructured to meet the new situation. The First
General Conference met in Sao Paulo on January 3-4, 1935. It
approved the constitution of the newly created denomination.
According to this constitution, instead of a bishop, a committee
of three ministers would rule the Church. It was decided to
divide the field into four districts: Central District,
Southern Sao Paulo, West Sao Paulo, Northern Sao Paulo.
Apparently the Holiness Church of Japan did not ordain its
ministers. Since none of them had been ordained, they had to
seek an ordained minister. Thus Koji Tamura was ordained by an
independent minister, Ishido, and then on January 4, 1935,
Tamura, Jose Emerenciano, Namba, Tanaami (Burajiru Holiness
Kyokai 1935:33).

Another noteworthy event was the organization of a Ministers'
training school in 1934. Since there were no funds, the
teachers would be pastors, and the students would work as
laundrymen to support themselves. Juro Yuasa became the President of the Midian Bible Institute and Koji Tamura, Tanaami and
Emerenciano its professors (*Loc. cit.*).

KOJI TAMURA AND JURO YUASA

We must say a few more words about Koji Tamura and Juro
Yuasa, who also were pioneer missionaries from Japan. Koji
Tamura was born in Akita-ken, Japan, in 1903. He was converted
at the age of nineteen under the work of the missionaries of
the Christian Church. Two years later, at the Nagayama
Methodist Church he heard a message on the need of entering
through the narrow gate and came to experience a real conversion. In the same year of 1924 he went to Tokyo and began to
attend the Yodobashi Holiness Church of Tosaji Obara. In the
beginning he did not feel at home at that church, which was
very different from what he had attended before, but he was
impressed by the faith of the pastor, Obara. It was at that

church that he began to feel a divine calling to be a preacher.
He spoke to Obara and under his advice entered the Holiness
seminary, which he attended for three years, graduating in 1927
(Interview, Tamura 1975).

In 1928 he received a divine order to go to Brazil which he
was reluctant to obey. But God assured him that He would provide all his needs, and so he came to Brazil on August 16 of the
same year. After a missionary journey to Alta Paulista, he went
to Registro where he worked for one year for the Registro Union
Christian Church, where Monobe had worked before. Then he went
to Santos where his ministry was really blessed with the conversion of many families. About 20,000 Japanese immigrants were
arriving at the port of Santos yearly, and he would go to meet
each ship that came in in order to speak about Christ to them.
After the death of Monobe in 1930, Tamura moved to Sao Paulo to
take over his responsibilities. There he worked as the acting
District superintendent, pastor, and Bible school professor
until 1937, when he left the Holiness Church. After arriving in
Brazil he had begun to read "Seisho no Kenkyu" (Bible Study), a
monthly periodical edited by Kanzo Uchimura, and this gradually
led him to the conviction that the true way to preach the
gospel is through the way of self-support and independence of
faith and finances. Thus he left the Holiness Church and
started a Non-church (*Mukyokai*) movement in Brazil (Interview,
Tamura 1975). The Mukyokai movement in Brazil is discussed in
the Appendix.

Juro Yuasa was born on January 24, 1895, in Kyoto. His
parents were Christians. His father moved to Kyoto in order to
help in the financial management of Doshisha University, a
vanguard of liberal theology. His older brother, Hatiro, became
the President of that school, and after World War II, the President of the International Christian University (Yoneda 1959:
406-407).

Although born in a Christian family, Juro received no
orientation toward evangelical faith in his childhood. What he
learned was basically Christian ethics and morality. Thus at
elementary school he wrote a composition on prohibitionism. He
was baptized but without knowing that Jesus Christ was his
Savior. The Holy Spirit was at work, however, and he was led
to think that without the blood of Jesus Christ there is no
forgiveness of sin. He wanted to be a righteous man and he knew
also that he could not be righteous without the help of Jesus
Christ. He read and thought much, but he was not able to understand God. Baptism had not helped him in any way. When he was
about seventeen years of age he had a nervous breakdown due to
overstudy. He wanted to retire to the country and rest or to
become a farmer. But because his father wanted him to attend

college, he went back to high school with the intention of studying agronomy in college. He was, at that time, seeking the life
which is taught in the Bible but all in vain. He was desperate
and went to the place where the grave of Jo Nijima is and
attempted suicide by hanging. But as the pain was too much, he
succeeded in untieing the belt and did not die. He went back to
his dormitory and prayed earnestly: "Oh God, or Buddha, if you
exist, reveal yourself to me" (He was not sure yet whether it
was God or Buddha to whom he should pray). He does not remember
how long it took, whether hours or days, but there was a student
of philosophy who was a very fine young man, whom he liked to
hear. He was listening to him and while doing so (he thinks
there was no connection between the two things), he felt that he
received the touch of the living God. It was a real sense of
the glorious presence of the living God. "I prayed as earnestly
as ever in my whole life. I was thankful for God who had
answered my prayer. Prostrated I wept with joy." Afterward
the teacher took him to his room and put him on his bed. While
he was in bed he heard a voice: "I am Christ." As he did not
have enough knowledge of the Bible it was difficult for him to
understand the relationship between Christ and himself. But one
thing was sure: He had no wish to commit suicide. Before, every
time he saw a river or a lake, he was tempted to throw himself
into water to commit suicide. As he was extremely tired, a
doctor recommended a two-weeks rest. He went up to Hieizan
(Hiei mountain), crossed it and went down, saw the water, but
had no temptation to kill himself. But in spite of that marvel-
ous experience he could not recover from his nervous breakdown.
Satan tempted him. He had to return home for rest. At home
when his mother was praying, he danced semi-naked, he would
laugh, just to displease his mother. His illness got worse and
worse, and he became like a living corpse. His mother prayed
for him and gave advice. There was a woman evangelist who had
led the brother of his sister's friend to Christ. His mother
asked the evangelist to come and help her son. She came and told
him to read the Book of Ecclesiastes. He read it and was some-
what impressed by it but his reply to her was that he did not
believe in the Bible. She asked him whether he would mind
being her friend. In his situation no friendship really mattered
to him. So he accepted her friendship from that time on. He had
some feeling that he might be saved through that evangelist. She
was a very godly lady. She had decided to fast for seventy days
in search of God's appearing. She wouldn't stop fasting until
God would appear to her, which He did on the fortieth day. She
fasted and prayed for Yuasa, and his thinking was changed, perhaps due to her prayer. He started to read the Bible seriously.
He came to know that the final destiny of man is either hell or
heaven. Then he thought on which one to choose, Buddha or
Christ. The written life of Buddha is a masterpiece of art,
while the written account of the life of Christ in the Bible is

rather rustic. He thought the truth must be in the artless life
of Christ. So he chose Christ. But Christ had said that his
destiny was the lake of fire, and so did his conscience. He
fell into despair, and he realized that hell is despair. He
suffered much. His mother told him to go to bed and rest. While
he was dozing, he felt God was with him. He was so real to him
that he could no longer doubt his existence. As he was not able
to bear the suffering, he cried, and his mother came and prayed
for him. His father came too. He cried out "Oh Christ, help
me," and suddenly the hell-like suffering passed away. He
realized that Christ, who he had thought of as a person who had
lived two thousand years ago, is living right now in heaven and
that He is the Savior. He had answered him because he had
called Him. That faith was given from heaven. He cried with
his heart filled with gratitude and so continued for about two
hours. He repeated: "Thank you, thank you." The next day his
mother gave him a Bible to read, and as he read it he felt
indeed that the Word of God is sweeter than honey. He testified
to his brothers that he had become a servant of Christ and asked
them to forgive him for the trouble he had caused (Interview,
Yuasa:1975).

He returned to high school in Kyoto, where he was so earnest
that he began to evangelize whomever he met. He had another
nervous breakdown and had to return home for a while. He read
the biography of St. Francis of Assisi and came to know the need
of a total consecration. In 1915, at the retreat of Hakone, he
consecrated his life to Christian ministry. He returned to high
school and after he graduated three years later he entered Tokyo
Seminary (Tokyo Shingakusha) which he attended for three years.
But as there was a liberal professor of Old Testament, a doctor
of theology, who stated that he did not know whether God existed
or not, he felt he should not stay in that school any longer.
So he then went to the Holiness Seminary which he attended for
over two years as an auditor. After that he went back to the
Tokyo Seminary to finish his study and spent three more years
there. This he did because of the advice given by the pastor
who was the father-in-law of his brother, Hachiro. The pastor
thought it was better to have a seminary degree. Professor
Takakura had returned from study overseas and he enjoyed his
lectures on systematic theology, Romans and Galatians. About
one year before his graduation, he began to think about where he
should go to work afterward. He thought he could do nothing
without Christ's help, and only in obedience to his will could
he accomplish something. So he and his wife prayed earnestly,
particularly six months before his graduation. One night, when
he was sleeping, he heard a voice: "Go to Brazil." He woke up
with surprise and read Takeo Monobe's report on the work in
Brazil. In that report Monobe mentioned that his parish was
very extensive and that more workers were badly needed. Still

he was not sure whether God really wanted him to go to Brazil.
He prayed and went to sleep. While he was sleeping, he heard
the same voice saying: "You go to Brazil." This time he could
not doubt it was God's will for him to go to Brazil. Next
morning he told his wife and his mother about the voice. His
mother approved the idea, but his father said he couldn't
believe it and that he wished he would stay in Japan. But Juro's
heart was peaceful, for he was sure that it was the will of God.
"If He has called me, He will provide all my needs," he thought
(Interview, Yuasa 1975).

Yuasa and his family came to Brazil on the same ship as
Bishop Nakada arriving on May 29, 1929. He worked for two
years in Lins, another two years in Santos, and then moved to
Sao Paulo to start the Midian Seminary. He has lived in Sao
Paulo ever since. His wife was a great helper, managing the
finances by working as a midwife and by providing board and room
for students. She cooked for her children and for the students;
she sewed, and taught Japanese to her children and students.
She had time to have family devotions every evening and to tell
Bible stories to children (Interview Yuasa 1975; Suzu Yuasa Lee
in Burajiru Rengo Fujinkai Kaiho 1969, 3:38-39). Two sons, Jun
and Kei, are ministers, and one daughter, Suzu, is a minister's
wife. Jun is the chairman of the executive board of the
Holiness Church of Brazil, and Kei, a doctor of theology, is a
missionary to Peru.

THE GROWTH OF THE CHURCH

Unfortunately we only have complete data for the past sixteen
years between 1957 and 1973, making an accurate analysis of the
growth of the Church difficult. Before 1957 we only have data
for the years 1927, 1928, and 1933. Thus our analysis must be
limited mainly to the period 1957-1973.

The growth of the Evangelical Holiness Church of Brazil in
the last sixteen years, although steady, has been rather slow—
an average of 2.85 percent per year. This annual growth rate is
about the same as the biological growth, which in relation to
the total population does not mean growth. One reason for this
relatively slow growth is, as Table 2 indicates, the fact that
five out of fifteen churches have not grown. Guararapes church
declined at the rate of 5.7 percent per year; Paraguacu church
has not grown at all; the rate of growth for the churches in
Bastos and Tupan has been only 1.1 percent per year. Before
giving the reasons for slow or non-growth, however, let us see
the factors of growth. Table 2 indicates that there are eight
churches that have grown faster than mere biological growth:
Campo Grande, Santo Andre, Londrina, Liberdade, Maringa,
Curitiba, Adamantina, Bosque. The rapid growth of Campo Grande

and Santo Andre can be explained in terms of time and location.
They are new churches (founded in 1971 and 1970 respectively)
located in large and growing cities. Churches usually grow
faster in their early stages. Londrina, Liberdade, Maringa,
Curitiba, Adamantina and Bosque churches are all located in the
large cities (although Adamantina is not as large as others)
where the Japanese population and the population in general
are growing. In these cities Japanese are moving in, and people
become more receptive to the gospel as they come to a new
environment. As is true for the population in general, the
trend of the Japanese is to move from the country to the cities,
and from small cities to large cities. Curitiba is the capital
of Parana, while Londrina is the metropolis of the Northern
Parana.

TABLE 17

ANNUAL AVERAGE GROWTH RATE OF THE HOLINESS CHURCHES
(1958-1973)

Campo Grande* (5 years)	20.0%
Santo Andre* (5 years)	10.0
Londrina*	6.7
Liberdade* (Sao Paulo, 13 years)	6.5
Maringa*	4.4
Curitiba*	4.1
Adamantina	3.4
Bosque (Sao Paulo)*	3.1
Casa Verde (Sao Paulo)*	2.6
Getuba (10 years)	2.7
Vencesslau Bras (7 years)	2.4
Tupan	1.1
Bastos	1.1
Presidente Prudente*	1.0
Paraguacu Paulista (6 years)	0.0
Guararapes	-5.7

*Large City

Source: Computed from the date obtained by the
author through questionnaires.

TABLE 18

PLACES AND YEARS HOLINESS CHURCHES WERE FOUNDED

Place	Year
Bosque	1926
Bastos	1932
Guararapes	1932
Presidente Prudente	1938
Londrina	1942
Case Verde	1950
Curitiba	1952
Adamantina	1953
Maringa	1953
Tupa	1956
Liberdale	1958
Getuba	1964
Venceslau Bras	1968
Paraguacu Paulista	1969
Santo Andre	1970
Campo Grande	1971

Source: Mizuki 1974, Questionnaires

Bosque, Liberdade and Case Verde are sections of the Sao
Paulo city, and particularly the first two have a heavy concentration of Japanese. Thus, those churches growing yearly at the
rate of 3.1 percent and up are located in the cities whose population is over 200,000, except for that in Adamantina, whose
population is less. But we have to remember that Adamantina is
a very important and large city of Alta Paulista. There is one
exception to the rule which we must explain. The city of
President Prudente is a large city of about 200,000 people, and
the Holiness church in that city has declined since 1963. That
church has been strong in membership, finances, and influence
within the denomination, being second only to the Bosque church
which is located in the magalopolis of Sao Paulo. The reason
for its decline has been in great part due to the death of
Zentaro Nomura who was the pillar of the church. He was an
outstanding Christian who had immigrated from Japan with a large
family, really a clan. His family was spiritually, socially,
and financially the backbone of the church. But with his

illness and later death and the later moving of that family, the
church really suffered. Also other influencial families migrated
to the city of Sao Paulo, which resulted in the decline of the
church in spite of the size of the city. Migration of people
to the city of Sao Paulo has seriously affected the growth of
the churches in the interior.

Another important factor in the growth of the Holiness Church
is the fact that it has planted churches after the War. The
number of the churches has grown from five in 1942 to seventeen
in 1971 as Table 18 indicates. This means that the number of
churches has more than tripled in the past twenty-five years.
This is contrary to the Episcopal Church that had added only
three churches in the post-war period. It is a well-known
fact that the multiplication of churches is a key factor of
church growth.

Another important factor is the training of ministers. The
Holiness Church has succeeded in adding younger ministers when
the older ministers reach retirement. The fact that eleven out
of nineteen ministers are Nisei is an indication of how well
the Church has done in the training of its younger leaders.
And even among the Japanese-speaking ministers, two out of seven
are young men who have come to Brazil after the War. This is
very different from the Free Methodist Church which has only
one Nisei minister out of eleven. Considering that 80 percent
of the Japanese population in Brazil are Nisei and Sansei, the
number of Nisei ministers that the Holiness Church has is very
significant.

Now let us explain the slow growth of the Holiness Church of
Brazil. As we have already pointed out, five out of sixteen
churches have not grown. They are located either in rural
areas or in small towns or cities where the erosion of people
is great. As we have already said, the trend of migration is
from the country to the cities and from small cities to large
cities. Churches located in the country or in small cities have
very little chance to grow, and about one-third of the Holiness
churches are located in such places. Bastos, Guararapes, Getuba,
Paraguacu Paulista, Venceslau Bras are small towns and cities
and offer a very little chance for church growth. The non-growth
of these churches weighs negatively on the general scale of
growth.

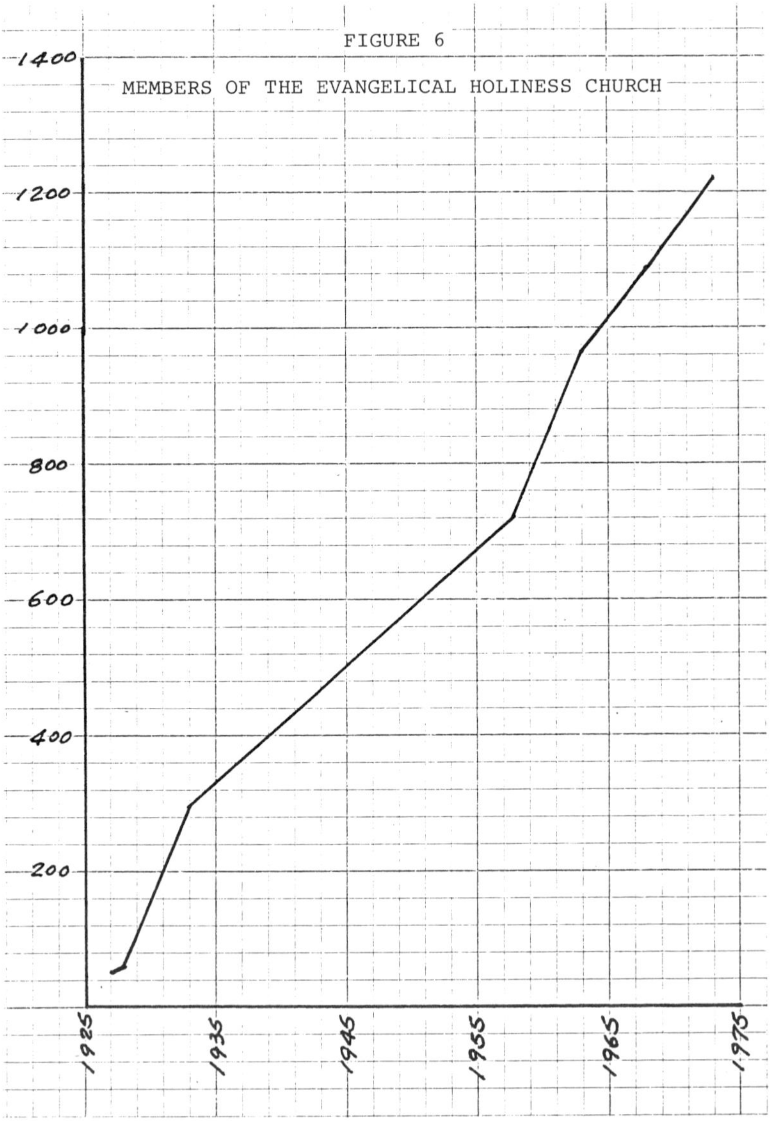

FIGURE 6

MEMBERS OF THE EVANGELICAL HOLINESS CHURCH

FIGURE 7

MEMBERS OF THE
EVANGELICAL HOLINESS CHURCHES

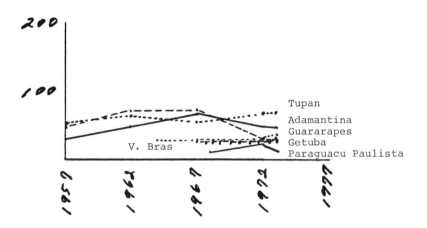

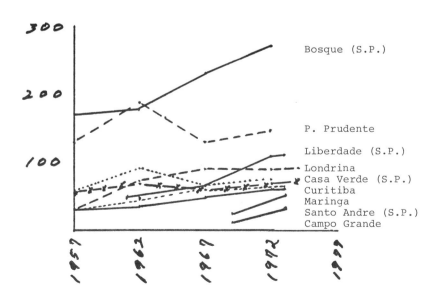

FIGURE 8
LOCATION OF THE
EVANGELICAL HOLINESS CHURCHES

One more important factor of slow growth of the Holiness Church may be financial. The Church has been practically self-supporting from the very beginning. Although until it became independent in 1934 it received aid from the mother Church, it never enjoyed the situation of full support for its ministers, as did the Episcopal and Free Methodist Churches. Holiness ministers had no salary. They had to live by faith depending on what their congregations were able to provide. No doubt they had to face much hardship, and in their struggle for living the effectiveness of their ministry was hindered. For the pastors without children they may not have been so much a problem, but for those having six, seven, and eight children, we can imagine the difficulties they faced.

Finally we can mention the membership leakage. According to pastor Samuel Sakuma, 70 percent of the members who move from his parish to Sao Paulo are lost, and according to pastor Kajimura 40 percent are also lost. These do not seem overstatements when we observe the growth of the churches located in Sao Paulo--Bosque, Liberdade, Casa Verde. These churches, we may say, are not growing as fast as they could considering the convergence of Japanese to that city and the members of the churches in the interior. It seems that they are not succeeding in following up the migrant members from the interior.

4

The Free Methodist
Church of Brazil

Free Methodist work in Brazil started in 1928 when a young
graduate of the Osaka Free Methodist Seminary, Danial Masayoshi
Nishizumi, went to that country. Nishizumi was born in Osaka on
December 22, 1900, as the fourth son of Kohachi Nishizumi. After
he finished his formal education, he worked and attended a
commercial school at night and graduated in 1919.   In 1923 he
became sick and went to Awaji island for recuperation, and there
he came to hear the gospel and became a believer. The following
year he entered Osaka Free Methodist Seminary from which he
graduated in 1928.   It seems an article on the Japanese immigrants in Brazil which he read in a newspaper awakened in him a
desire to go to Brazil. Thus, in the same year he graduated
from Seminary, he sailed for Brazil, arriving on August 6.   First
he went to the Granbery Methodist Seminary in Minas Gerais to
study Portuguese and changed to the Instituto Jose Manual da
Conceicao the following year. In 1931 he married Yoshie Fujita
and went to Juqueri (later Mairiporan) to teach at the Japanese
language school there. He used his spare time to visit and
preach the gospel. He had to teach in order to support himself
(Ono 1947:39).

   There were two laymen of the Kishinosato Free Methodist
Church, Osaka, who followed Nishizumi to Brazil. One was
Yoshikusu Wada who was then sixty-nine years old and another was
Shoh Koh Cho (later Shoh Koh Mita), a young Korean of seventeen
years old. Wada was a businessman and officer at the Kishinosato
church, and he had a real concern for Nishizumi going alone to a

foreign land. Cho came from a poor family of tenant-farmers in
Korea. He was converted in his early teens and went to Japan at
fifteen years of age. In Japan he was mistreated for being a
Korean, but at church he found an entirely different attitude
toward him. People were kind and friendly, and he knew the
difference between Christians and non-Christians. Now when
Nishizumi decided to go to Brazil, Wada and Cho volunteered to
go with the young missionary to help him. Because of the visas
Wada and Cho could not go in the same ship and they thus came to
Brazil one month later, Setpember of 1928 (Paulists Shinbun
1972, May 18; Interview, Cho 1972). While Nishizumi was attending Grambery Seminary and Instituto Jose Manuel da Conceicao in
1929 and 1930, these two laymen worked on the farm in Juqueri
(later Mairiporan, a vicinity of Sao Paulo), raising vegetables
to support Nishizumi. Wada returned to Japan two years later as
Nishizumi finished his study. Wada's son, who died recently,
became a very prosperous businessman in Osaka. Cho married a
Japanese girl and changed his family name to Mita. He is a
retired man now, father of nine children. Although he had very
little education, his selfless service to all, and particularly
to the Korean immigrants which have come to Brazil in the sixties,
has become widely known. He helped them to resettle in Brazil
and became a guarantor in renting their houses to more than
three hundred families. His service came to the knowledge of the
Korean President who invited him and his wife to go to Korea to
receive official recognition for what he had done for his people
(Paulista Shimbun 1972:5,18). He has been the salt of the earth
and a light of the world among Japanese and Koreans and
Brazilians.

While Nishizumi was doing his pioneer work, God called
Hiroyuki Hayashi and his wife, Kaoru. Hayashi was born in
Matsue, Japan, in 1908. Of a non-Christian family, he was con-
verted in his late teens. He attended and graduated from the
Osaka Dentistry School. After that he went to Kobe where he
practiced his profession and at the same time attended a Bible
school. One night he had a dream of skeletons and palm trees.
He interpreted that dream as God's calling him to go to Brazil
as a missionary. So he obeyed the divine calling and sailed for
Brazil with his wife and daughter in 1933. First he went to the
Amazon basin where there were a few Japanese settlements. But
there he, his wife, and his daughter all got malaria which
forced them to move Southward to Sao Paulo the following year.
In Sao Paulo, in 1935, he met Nishizumi and they talked about
working together. As we can see there had been no communication
between the two men prior to this time, neither had they learned
that there was another Japanese Free Methodist missionary in
Brazil. Their meeting was rather providential, for neither of
them, it seems, knew about the presence of the other in Sao
Paulo (Burajiru Jiyu Messodisuto Kyodan 1956:1).

THE FIRST CHURCH

By the year 1936 there were a few converts and seekers plus about ten Free Methodists who had migrated to Brazil. Up to then Nishizumi had no regular meetings. His ministry had been confined to literature, visitation, and personal evangelism. Now he came to realize the need of planting churches. Thus on November 1, 1936, Nishizumi and Hayashi, with other believers and seekers, about twenty in all, met for worship services at 10:00 a.m., at the office of Shinichiro Murakami (dentist) at 40 Conde de Sarzedas. The people who attended the first meeting were: Daniel and Yoshie Nishizumi, Hiroyuki and Kaoru Hayashi, Yoshitaro Fujita and wife, Akio Watanabe and wife, Keizo Hamada, Mamoru Onoda, Chumatsu Yamada, Yoshiga, Suzuki, Masakatsu Fujita, Kiyoko Fujita, Watanabe's daughter, Masahiko Maruyama, Michiko Hasegawa, Katayama, Kanegae (Letter, Onda 1976). That was the inagural worship service of the Sao Paulo Free Methodist Church, and it became the date of the official beginning of the Free Methodist Church in Brazil (Letter, Nishizumi 1937 in Mattaki-Ai April 10, 1937; Burajiru Jiho, October 16, 1936). It is interesting that all the three major denominations—Episcopal, Holiness, Free Methodist—had their beginnings at the office of Doctor Murakami, although in 1936 it had moved from number 7 to 40 of Conde de Sarzedas Street.

From that date on regular services were held on Sundays and Wednesdays. Three men, Nishizumi, Hayashi, and Yoshitaro Fujita (Nishizumi's father-in-law) occupied the pulpit alternately. They stayed in that office for two years and in that period two of the new converts, Kinzo Uchida and Ryoshi Izuka, dedicated their lives to the Christian ministry. These two men, filled with the Holy Spirit, began to evangelize a few families living in Jandira, about twenty miles from Sao Paulo. A young man called Shinichi Yamamoto accepted the gospel and later his whole family and three other families were converted. These families became the foundation of the Jandira (later Itapevi) Free Methodist Church.

From Conde de Sarzedas, the Sao Paulo Free Methodist Church moved to Ouvidor Peleja in May of 1938, and then to Sao Joaquim Street, Onze de Junho Ave., Linda Batista Street, and finally to its own newly built temple on 40 Veriano Pereira (Burajiru Jiyu Methodisuto Kyodan 1956:7). The Sao Paulo Free Methodist Church experienced a phenomenal growth after the War and gave birth to four more Free Methodist churches now existing in Sao Paulo.

CONNECTION TO THE PACIFIC COAST
JAPANESE CONFERENCE

In May of 1938 Nishizumi left Brazil to visit Japan. On his
way to Japan, he stopped in the States where he spent over six
weeks. This trip to the States and to Japan was important for
it had its influence upon the future work of Brazilian Free
Methodism. He arrived in the port of Los Angeles on June 21,
and in six weeks he visited practically all the Japanese Free
Methodist churches in the area, including those in Los Angeles,
Anaheim, Redondo, Stockton, Berkely, and Phoenix, Arizona. He
went to Seattle too, and thus he had the chance to see four
states. On July 1, he met the Free Methodist General Missionary
Secretary, Harry F. Johnson, and talked to him about the
possibility of sending missionaries to Brazil. According to
Johnson there were four South-American countries--Panama, Peru,
Chile, and Brazil--where the Missionary Board was thinking of
starting Free Methodist work. Of course, Nishizumi wanted the
Board to send missionaries to Brazil. His thought was that if
American missionaries came, they could start a work among
Brazilians too. His vision was to extend the Free Methodist
work among Brazilians, and he thought for that he needed help
from the American Missionary Board. To have American missionaries in Brazil was a subject of prayer for Nishizumi as we can
see in his diary (Nishizuni 1947:14-23). This meeting with
Johnson must have had its influence upon the future decision of
the Missionary Board, for, when it sent its first missionaries
to South America, Brazil was one of the two countries where they
came. Another country was Paraguay instead of the three other
countries which the Missionary Board had thought as a possibility.
There was a mission that had an orphanage in Paraguay which it
wanted to turn over to the Free Methodist Mission.

Another thing Nishizumi did while in the United States was to
make the Sao Paulo Free Methodist Church a part of the Pacific
Coast Japanese Conference at the retreat and conference held on
July 26-August 2, 1938, at the Pacific Palisades Camp Ground.
He was ordained an elder by Johnson and Hiroyuki Hayashi was
given a local preacher's license (Ono 1937:26,29). Why
Nishizumi connected the Brazilian Free Methodist Church to the
Pacific Coast Japanese Conference instead of to the Free
Methodist Church of Japan is not clear, for nothing is mentioned
in his diary. What we may conjecture is that since the headquarters of the Free Methodism is in the United States, he may
have thought it was more logical to have the Brazil work linked
to this country. The Missionary Board's plan to send missionaries to Brazil may also have influenced Nishizumi to decide for
the States. Another reason that may have influenced Nishizumi
is the affinity existing between the Pacific Coast Japanese
Conference and the Free Methodist work in Brazil, since both
were working with Japanese immigrants and their descendants.

Nishizumi arrived in Japan on August 20, visiting his fatherland after ten years. During those ten years in Brazil he had
felt very strongly the need for more workers for the vast task
of evangelizing the Japanese. He had felt lonely working without colleagues. Thus he made his Macedonian appeal wherever he
had chance to do so. In the Arima retreat he spoke about the
need of workers to evangelize 300,000 Japanese living in spiritual darkness, in a condition thirty years behind that of Japan.
Sukeichi Ono, who was the Free Methodist youth leader, responded
to Nishizumi's appeal, making his decision to go to Brazil. He
and his family came to Brazil on July 15, 1939 (Ono 1947:99).

There was one more person, Seiichi Shimizu, who responded to
Nishizumi's appeal. Seiichi Shimizu was the pastor of an Inde-
pendent church in Osaka. Nishizumi went to that church and
spoke on Brazil, and Shimizu decided to give up the church that
was his own property and go to Brazil. The Shimizus went to
Brazil on the same ship with Nishizumi, arriving in Brazil on
December 24, 1938 (Ono 1947:95-96; Burajiru Jiyu Mesodisuto
Kyodan 1956:3).

Thus Nishizumi's trip to the States and Japan had the significant results of linking the Free Methodist Church of Brazil with
the American Free Methodist Church and of getting two more
missionary families from Japan.

Let us now turn to the lives of Seiichi Shimizu and Sukeichi
Ono, who, with Nishizumi and Hayashi, were the pioneer missionaries who came from Japan. Seiichi Shimizu was born in Osaka
on October 17, 1908. His family was not Christian but he
attended a kindergarten of missionary orientation. Although
baptized at the age of nineteen, he came to experience conversion only when he was twenty-six years old while reading a book
by Kanzo Uchimura. He was a graduate of business school and was
working for Mitsukoshi, a large business company, where his
grandfather and father had worked. A year after his conversion
he was called to the Christian ministry, and so he gave up a
good job to begin his study at the Free Methodist Seminary in
Osaka. While attending seminary he worked as the pastor of the
church he started. He had received an inheritance from his
father, and with that money he purchased a property and built
his own church. He worked together with his brother-in-law who
was a minister. Four years later he graduated from seminary.
In that same year he heard the report of Nishizumi on the need
of Brazil. He turned the work over to his brother-in-law and
went to Brazil. He worked in Sao Paulo with Nishizumi for about
one year, but because of financial reasons he had to be engaged
in secular work for six years. Starting in 1947 he resumed a
full-time ministry, making a remarkable contribution to the
growth of Sao Paulo church (Interview, Shimizu 1975).

Sukeichi Ono was not a minister when he came to Brazil. In Japan he had worked for the Youth Evangelistic Band, of which he was a leader. After he came to Brazil in 1939 he began to teach at a Japanese language school in Embura, about twenty miles from Sao Paulo. There he remained as a self-supporting minister until 1955, spreading the gospel in the area and founding a church. In 1955 he became a full-time minister and was appointed to the Apucarana Free Methodist Church in the State of Parana.

As we have seen, all four missionaries from Japan came by their own initiative and not as missionaries sent by the mother church, but with their blessing. In this way the Free Methodist Church had a very different beginning from the Evangelical Holiness Church whose pioneer missionaries were sent by a mother church that felt the need of evangelizing the Japanese living overseas.

THE WAR PERIOD (1941-1945)

Between the year that the Sao Paulo Free Methodist Church was organized, 1936, and the year the Pacific War started, 1941, a few people had been won in Sao Paulo, Jandira, Mairiporan, Cambara, and by 1941 there were four ministerial candidates. In 1939 in Cambara, four instance, a seminarian, Kinzo Uchida, on vacation had over twenty converts and several cases of divine healing (Burajiru Jiyu Mesodisuto Kyodan 1956:4). Thus the Free Methodist Church was beginning to expand when the Pacific War started, practically paralizing the work. As we have already seen in 1942, Brazil, following the United States, declared war against Japan. As Japan became an enemy country, any public meeting in Japanese was prohibited. If two or three Japanese were together and speaking their language, they were immediately arrested. Japanese citizens were not allowed to travel, except with a safe-conduct permit issued by the local police department. This safe-conduct was given only if it was assured that the travel was really necessary. Under these circumstances, the only meetings Japanese Christians could hold was at different homes, and even this, very secretly. It was impossible to hold public worship services and Sunday school until the end of the war. These four years of gap certainly frustrated the progress of the work.

The work was not totally stopped, however. There was a Portuguese evening service held on Sundays at Nishizumi's boarding house on Sao Joaquim Street. Nishizumi had a boarding house for students at that place from 1940 to 1946. There was also a young people's meeting held every Sunday morning at Shinichiro Murakami's. Kinzo Uchida and Taisuke Sakuma, both seminarians, obtained safe-conduct permits and went to Cambara and Cravinhos. In 1943 they visited the Takiyas in Cravinhos

and they stayed in that home for two weeks, holding cottage
meetings every night. The head of that family, his wife and
their daughter were already Christians, but their oldest son,
who had resisted before, became a Christian during those days.
As a result of those meetings they decided to have worship services and Sunday school at Takiyas' from January of the following year, bringing them more than forty converts during those
war years. After the war the Japanese community was divided
into two factions, the *kachigumi* (victorists or those who did
not believe in the defeat of Japan) and the *makegumi* (defeatists
or those who believed in the defeat). As Christians believed
that Japan had been defeated the *kachigumi* accused them of being
makegumi and the parents took their children from Sunday school
and many stopped coming to services. As a consequence the
attendance dropped drastically. But the faithful ones remained
in the church. Later these faithful families had to move, some
to Barretos, some to Apucarana, and some to Sao Paulo and
Marilia. The Barretos and Apucarana churches were started by
these Christians who moved from Cravinhos (Burajiru Jiyu
Mesodisuto Kyodan 1956:4,11-13). From the Takiya family came
two ministers and one minister's wife. Gisuke, the oldest son,
is now a pastor in Sao Paulo. Yoshikazu, the youngest, earned
his Ph.D. from Drew University and is now the President of the
Free Methodist Seminary and superintendent of the Brazilian Free
Methodist Conference. Tazuko, the only daughter, is the wife
of Kinzo Uchida, the pastor of the Sao Jose dos Campos Free
Methodist Church.

THE FIRST MISSIONARIES FROM THE U.S.
AND THE DEATH OF NISHIZUMI

The General Missionary Board had been for a good number of
years interested in starting Free Methodist work in South
America. In April of 1940, three men, Harry F. Johnson, the
General Missionary Secretary, B. H. Pearson, the Free Methodist
General Youth Director, and E. E. Shelhammer, a Free Methodist
evangelist, had made an exploratory trip to South America. As
we have seen, the General Missionary Board had four countries
in mind; that is, Panama, Chile, Peru, and Brazil. The Board
did not know in what country it should begin to work. In March
of 1946, Bishop Mark D. Ormston and Byron Lamson, General
Missionary Secretary, visited South America. They spent a few
days in Sao Paulo with Nishizumi and among other things decided
to support Jose Emilio Emerenciano in starting a free Methodist
work among Brazilians and to provide a scholarship for three
seminarians, Kinzo Uchida, Taisuke Sakuma, and John Mizuki.
They also informed the Brazilian Church that the Board would
send two educational missionaries to Brazil.

Thus, in June of 1946, the first missionaries from the United States, Lucile Damon and Helen Voller, arrived. Four missionaries, Harold and Evelyn Ryckman, Ruth Foy, and Esther Harris, went to Paraquay. As we can see, of those four countries where the Missionary Board had planned to start Free Methodist work, only Brazil was chosen. The reason why Paraquay was chosen has already been mentioned. Now the reason why Brazil was chosen we can presume was due to the already existing Free Methodist Church there and to the influence Daniel Nishizumi had upon the Board through his meeting with Johnson in 1938 as well as his subsequent correspondence with the Board. We can also presume that those who visited Brazil were influenced in their decision by the impression made on them by the Free Methodist Christians of Brazil.

That year, when the Church was very happy and encouraged with the arrival of the missionaries from the United States, it had to face the tragedy of the sudden death of its leader, Daniel Nishizumi, who was killed in a car accident. The Church was greatly shaken, but with the loss of the leader, each one, minister as well as layman, became more aware of his own responsibility. They began to work harder in discipling and building churches.

Nishizumi was only forty-six when he died unexpectedly. It was very regrettable that he died when his leadership was most needed and when he was looking forward with such hope for even greater days. But when we look back we realize that he made a substantial and far reaching contribution to the Free Methodist Church in Brazil. He founded the Church in 1936; he brought Shimizu and Ono to Brazil, he influenced the Missionary Board to send missionaries to Brazil; and he determined the type of missionaries who were sent to Brazil. The Board sent educational missionaries because of his request, for Nishizumi had the idea of evangelizing through education--the school approach. Both Lucile Damon and Helen Voller were school teachers. Nishizumi also contributed to the beginning of the Free Methodist Church among Brazilians. His idea was to initiate the Brazilian Church through the aid of the Missionary Board. He was the one who worked for having Jose Emerenciano leave the Presbyterian Mission and join the Free Methodist Church. Thus Jose Emerenciano joined the Free Methodist Church in that same year and began a work in the middle class community of Mirandopolis in Sao Paulo. It was the beginning of the Mirandopolis Free Methodist Church, the largest Brazilian church today.

Lucile Damon (later Lucile Ryckman) was born in Wisconsin in 1912. Both her grandfather and father were Free Methodist ministers. She was converted when she was a teenager in a camp meeting. After she graduated from Greenville College she became

a high school teacher and taught Latin for six years. After
that she went to work at the Free Methodist Headquarters in
Winona Lake, Indiana. She worked there for four years and during
those years she was led to be a missionary. After she came to
Brazil in 1946, she worked for ten years helping in church work.
She helped the Mirandopolis church in its early years, particularly with the youth program. She also spent one year in Campos
do Jordao, being responsible for church work while her colleague,
Helen Voller, was in the States. Then she moved to Vila Galvao
to help start the church. From 1956 to 1966, the year she
returned to the United States to be married to Harold Rychman,
she taught psychology and Christian education at the Free
Methodist Seminary. In 1970 she went back to Brazil and taught
for two more years at the seminary. She has made a significant
contribution in the training of church leaders and in the leadership of the youth. Ever since she came back to the United States,
except those two years she spent in Brazil, she has helped her
husband, who was the Latin America Area Secretary until two years
ago, when he retired. She is working now for the Pacific Coast
Latin Conference and will be retiring in a year (Interview,
Lucile Ryckman 1975).

    Helen Voller was born in Michigan in 1908. After graduating
from Greenville College, she became an elementary school teacher.
For two years prior to her going to Brazil in 1946, she had
worked as a child evangelist. In her early years in Brazil she
helped the Mirandopolis church in the Sunday school where she
developed an excellent program. Her contribution in the field
of religious education and child evangelism was not on the local
level alone. She helped the Sao Paulo Japanese church to start
a vacation Bible School with such a result that it has become a
part of the Sunday school program in more of the churches. In
1949 she got tuberculosis and had to move to Campos do Jordao
for recuperation. By 1950 she had recovered and started a work
among the Japanese living in that area. She planted a church
there and worked for four years. Even today people recall her
with much gratitude. In 1955 she moved back to Sao Paulo to
start a Christian day school, Escola Americana de Mirandopolis,
which became a standard school in the community. Her unusual
devotion to the school led her to overwork which resulted
finally in a nervous breakdown. That illness forced her back to
the United States in 1960 (Interview, Lucile Rychman 1975).
Unfortunately that day school was closed recently for financial
reasons.

STRUCTURING AND RESTRUCTURING

    Up to 1954 the Free Methodist Church of Brazil was a District
of the Pacific Coast Japanese Conference. In 1954 the South-
American Provisional Conference was organized under Edmund

Snyder, Latin America Area Secretary. Harold Rychman was
appointed its Superintendent. This newly-organized conference
would have three divisions (districts): Brazilian, Japanese,
Paraguyan. When they met for the Annual Conference three
languages were used: Portuguese, Japanese, and Spanish.

With the change of status from a mission conference to a
provisional conference, the South-American Conference became
more autonomous with its constitution, though this constitution
was an adaptation of the North-American constitution of the Free
Methodist Church.

In 1964, the South-American Conference was changed from a
provisional to a full conference. This change of status affected
the relationship of the conference to the Mission and the
general Church but did not change its internal structure. In
January of 1966, under the chairmanship of Bishop Paul Ellis,
the South-American Conference was officially dissolved, and
three different conferences emerged: the Nikkei Conference, the
Paulista Conference (later Brazilian), and Paraguayn. Nikkei
and Paulista were organized as full conferences while the
Paraguayan conference became a provisional one. This restructur-
ing of the former three divisions into three conferences was
significant because it was done according to the three different
ethnic groups that used to compose one single conference. The
Nikkei Conference has been a fully self-supporting conference
since 1967, while the Brazilian and Paraguayan Conference still
receive aid from the Mission.

At this point we should mention something about Harold Ryckman,
who was the superintendent of the South-American Conference for
a long time. He was born in Dale, North Dakota, in 1902. When
he was eight years old his family moved to Southern California.
Although accepted at the California Institute of Technology, he
was not able to attend because of sickness during his first year
of college and for financial reasons during the second. In
order to find God's will he entered Los Angeles Pacific College
and in the first year became sure God was calling him into
Christian ministry. After having finished two years at LAPC, he
went to Greenville College in Illinois, graduating in 1927. He
married Evelyn Bartholomew in the same year. He began his
ministry in 1929 working for the Southern California-Arizona
Conference for seventeen years until 1946 when he went to
Paraguay (Interview, Ryckman 1975).

In 1948 he was appointed superintendent of the South-American
Mission and so remained until 1963, when he returned to the U.S.
to be the General Secretary of the Free Methodist World Fellowship and the Latin American Area Secretary. He resigned from
the position of the World Fellowship Secretary but continued as

Latin America Area Secretary until 1973 when he retired (Interview, Ryckman 1975).

Among many contributions he made as the superintendent we can
mention just a few. One was that he organized the Free Methodist
Church of Brazil. Up to 1948, the Free Methodist Church was
poorly organized, but under his leadership it came to assume the
more usual Free Methodist structure. Ryckman made a remarkable
contribution in building the Mirandopolis church, the mission
house and seminary. He built a hall, which served as a place
for Sunday school and worship service, and a mission home which
was dedicated in 1948. He spent a number of years in the construction of the seminary--building the main class rooms, two
dormitories, the dining hall, and three houses for professors.
He also provided good leadership, and the churches really grew
in the period he was the superintendent.

THE GROWTH OF THE CHURCH

Graph 9 indicates that the Free Methodist Church of Brazil
has had three different periods of growth; the period of
accelerating growth (1948-59) in which the Church grew from 136
members to 1091 members, an average annual growth rate of 20.0
percent; the period of slow growth (1959-64) when the membership
grew from 1091 to 1385, an AAGR of 3.6 percent or a little over
the expected biological growth; and the period of slower growth
(1964-74) in which the AAGR is 1.6 percent, much slower than the
expected biological (2.7 percent). This indicates that although
the overall AAGR of the period 1948-1974 has been 10.0 percent
(or 260% per decade), in the past ten years the Church has not
grown enough to catch up with the natural growth of the population. To understand why in the period 1948-1959 the Church
experienced a phenomenal growth and slowed down after that is of
vital importance for the future of the Free Methodist Church of
Brazil. Let us first explain the reasons for growth in the
eleven years between 1948 and 1959, and then the reasons for
slow growth in the following period.

One important factor of rapid growth in the first period was
the aid, financial and in missionary personnel, given by the
Missionary Board. The financial aid enabled the national workers
to give full time to church planting. Shimizu who was engaged
in secular work returned to a full-time ministry in 1947. Three
seminarians, Kinzo Uchida, Taisuke Sakuma, and John Mizuki, who
graduated respectively in 1947, 1948, and 1949, went directly
into full-time ministry of planting new churches. Ono became a
full-time worker in 1955. By saying that the financial aid of
the Missionary Board contributed to the growth of church, we are
not formulating a theory that financial aid is necessary for
church growth. There are many instances--the Pentecostal

churches particularly--in which churches have grown without
financial aid. We are only stating that in this particular
case of the Free Methodist Church the financial aid helped its
growth as it did with the Episcopal Church in its early stage.
Now in the case of the aid in personnel, we may say that
although most of the missionaries were educational missionaries,
they helped existing churches or started new churches since
neither seminary nor a day school was in existence at that time.

Another factor was the revival that started in 1947 and continued for over ten years. In an annual retreat held in Santo
Amaro, a real outpouring of the Holy Spirit was experienced.
Juro Yuasa of the Holiness Church was used by God, and his
message sank deep into the heart of each attendant who began to
weep during the preaching. There was no extravagance but a real
melting of the spirit. The revival lifted up the spiritual condition of the Free Methodist people who enjoyed a wonderful
spiritual unity which contributed for the growth of the Church
in the following years.

The defeat of Japan in World War II created a faith-vacuum in
the minds of Japanese immigrants. Although there was a faction
who would not believe in the defeat of their country, those who
believed it began to look for a new orientation in life and seek
a new faith that could fill that vacuum. Doubtless Christianity
was an answer to that problem. Like Japan of the post-war
period the Japanese of Brazil in that same period offered an
unprecedented opportunity for evangelism. It was a harvest time
and many people became very responsive to the gospel.

The use of the Japanese language in Sunday school was a factor
of church growth too. The Japanese of the post-war period were
still very much interested in teaching Japanese to their children. The Episcopal churches had already shifted to Portuguese,
but the Free Methodist Church, because of a lack of Sunday school
teachers who spoke Portuguese and because of some leaders who
wanted to use Japanese in Sunday schools, did not make that
shift. And this fact became a factor of attraction to the
Japanese parents. Graph 12 shows how the Free Methodist Sunday
schools grew in that period.

The phenomenon of urbanization had to do also with the
growth of the Free Methodist Church. Industrialization of Brazil
had begun and in the post-war period that process was accelerated
and a great move of population to the great urban centers like
Sao Paulo was taking place. Many Japanese were moving from the
country to the cities and from the cities to the megalopolis of
Sao Paulo. The Free Methodist Church, with its spiritual zeal
of revival and a good Sunday school program conducted in Japanese
was waiting for these migrants who were looking for new associations and for a place that would provide moral and spiritual
education for their children.

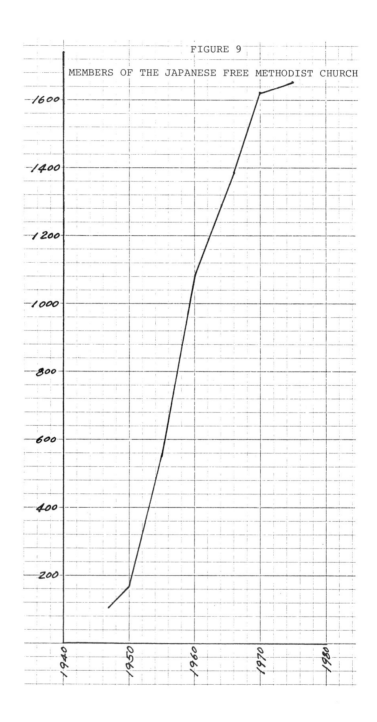

FIGURE 9

MEMBERS OF THE JAPANESE FREE METHODIST CHURCH

FIGURE 10

MEMBERS OF THE JAPANESE FREE METHODIST
CHURCHES IN THE CITY OF SAO PAULO

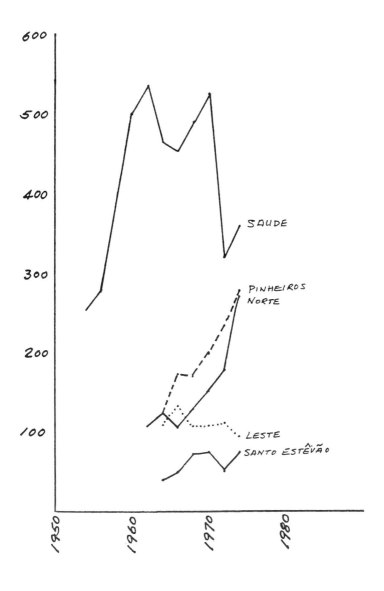

FIGURE 11

MEMBERS OF THE JAPANESE FREE METHODIST CHURCHES
OUTSIDE THE CITY OF SAO PAULO

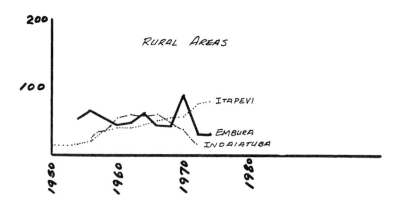

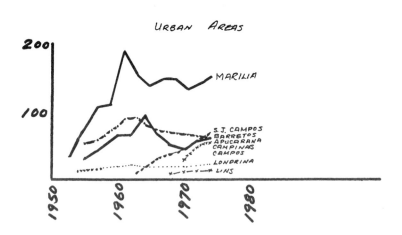

The non-committal stand taken by the Free Methodist Church on the issue of "victory and defeat of Japan" may have contributed to its growth. This issue divided the Japanese society in two factions. The Episcopal and Holiness Churches took the stand on the side of the defeatist and put a good deal of their effort in clarifying the issue (*Ninshiki-undo*). The Free Methodist Church took the stand that its main task was to communicate the gospel which is needed by both *kachigumi* (victorists) and *makegumi* (defeatists). Thus they tried to be friendly to both, assuming that if they became saved, which was essential, they would come to know the truth sooner or later. This stand helped the Free Methodist churches to win people of both factions.

One more important factor of growth is the involvement of laymen in evangelism. The Free Methodist Church has since its beginning had a very active laity. In the early days Hayashi was a layman and so was Ono; Yamamoto who has been in charge of Itapevi church is also a layman, and so are Oshima (Barretos) and Koishi (Lins). Masao Kinoshita, the first Japanese to become a lawyer in Brazil and who was a long-time in charge of the work in Suzano, is a layman too. In the Saude church there is Mamoru Onoda, a dentist, and his brother who is a dental techni-tian, both very active laymen. Koretora Takemura and Shiozaki, who started respectively the Marilia and Apucarana churches, are laymen. Moreover the rural churches were mainly under lay leadership. The church in Indaiatuba had Minamide as its leader, and Tochizawa was in charge of Embura church. Many preaching points were and still are under the responsibility of laymen. In particular Hayashi, himself a layman, is very able in his use of laymen, and churches have always grown under his leadership.

Finally we should mention the fact that the Free Methodist Church of Brazil has planted churches after the war. In 1945 there were only three churches but after that year the number of churches has increased consistently up to 16 in 1970 as Table 19 indicates. Except the church of Indaiatuba, all the churches planted in the post-war period were planted in urban areas. Of the 12 churches planted in the urban areas four were planted in the city of Sao Paulo. Considering the populational move of the post-war period, the Free Methodist Church was wise in estab-lishing churches in the cities and in concentrating mainly in the city of Sao Paulo. The Saude Church that was experiencing a phenomenal growth and had reached over 500 members, gave birth to four new churches--Zona Norte (1962), Pinheiros, Santo Estevao, and Zona Leste, all in 1964. The membership loss in the sixties is due to the members she gave to her children churches--over 100 members to each except Santo Estavao Church as we can see in Graph 10. This concentration in the cities, particularly in the megalopolis of Sao Paulo made the Free

Methodist Church grow faster than the two other Churches of our
study. And outside Sao Paulo, both Campinas and Sao Jose dos
Campos are booming cities where the Japanese population is also
growing. Graph 11 indicates that in these cities also the
churches are growing. Thus we may say that in the choice of
locations the Free Methodist Church is doing right strategically,
for its congregations are located in the places that promise
growth. The churches in Sao Paulo are growing except the one of
the Zona Leeste. The Free Methodist Church has planted churches
in right places which is a very important strategy.

Now we want to see the factors that have been responsible for
the slowing down of growth in the sixties and in the seventies.
One factor that may be mentioned as responsible for the slowing
down of the growth was the nationalization of the Church.

TABLE 19

THE PLANTING OF THE FREE METHODIST CHURCHES
BY NAME AND YEAR

Church	Year
Saude (Sao Paulo)	1936
Itepevi	1939
Embura	1939
Campos do Jordao	1947
Marilia	1949
Barretos	1949
Lins	1950
Apucarana	1950
Indaiatuba	1957
Zona Norte (Sao Paulo)	1962
Sao Jose dos Campos	1963
Pinheiros (Sao Paulo	1964
Santo Estevao (Sao Paulo)	1964
Zona Leste (Sao Paulo)	1964
Londrina	1968
Campinas	1970

Source: Questionnaire 1974

In 1964 the South-American Provisional Conference became a full
conference. As a provisional conference it was under the jurisdiction of the Missionary Board, but by becoming a full conference it became a part of the General Conference which gave much
more autonomy to the national churches. The annual conference,
formerly presided over by the mission superintendent now came to

be presided over by the area Bishop. In 1966 when South-American
Conference was dissolved and three different conferences emerged,
the autonomy of each conference became even more accentuated.
Now each conference would have its own national superintendent
who would work totally independent from Mission. When the conference was under the jurisdiction of Mission the missionary
superintendent had the final word in deciding certain important
issues. But once they realized that they were no longer under
Mission jurisdiction, the dispute for the leadership among
national emerged. The unity that existed before among the
workers was broken and was replaced by rivalry which came to
prejudice the growth of the Church (Interview, Sakuma 1975). By
saying this we are not trying to induct a theory that nationalization per se halts church growth. What we are saying is that,
in this particular case of the Japanese Free Methodist Church of
Brazil, it did due to a new situation that nationalization
created, which resulted in a power struggle of its leaders. In
the process of nationalization the Church had to be restructured
twice--once in 1964 and a second time in 1966. When a Church
goes through a process of restructuration usually its growth is
affected somehow. In the case of the Free Methodist Church what
happened was that the Mission superintendent is appointed by the
Missionary Board and it is more or less a permanent job whereas
a conference superintendent is elected yearly among ministers
who are elders. When the Japanese Church gained its status of
a full conference, it was able to elect its own superintendent.
This change of situation from having a superintendent appointed
by the Mission to a superintendent elected among their own
elders, meant each national elder could see himself as a
potential superintendent. In this kind of situation, a power
struggle may arise if the Church is not mature enough or is
down spiritually.

Another important factor for the slowing down of membership
growth may have been the decline of the Sunday school enrollment,
a great source of membership. Up to 1957 the number of Sunday
school pupils had been three times larger than that of church
members, but in that year the decline began and from 1960 on the
Sunday school enrollment became smaller than church members as we
can see in Graph 12. Why did this happen? One answer may be the
prolonged use of Japanese. Japanese was a factor of attraction
in the post-war period as we have already seen. But as the
assimilation of Japanese progressed, the Japanese language became
more and more difficult for the growing children. Thus what had
been a factor of attraction in the fifties may have become non-
attractive to children and a hindrance to growth. We may also
presume that even parents had become less interested in Japanese
in the sixties as a result of assimilation. We think the finding
of Izumi supports our view (see page 20). We may also say that
the Free Methodist Church did not update its methods of teaching

FIGURE 12

THE JAPANESE FREE METHODIST CHURCH
MEMBERSHIP AND SUNDAY SCHOOL ENROLLMENT

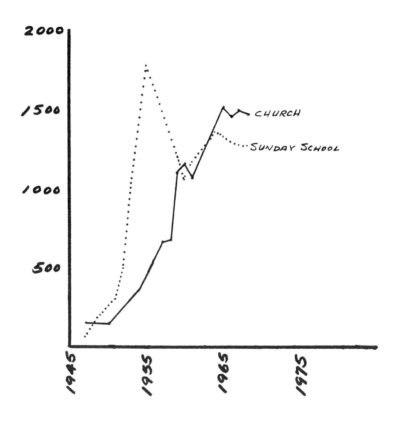

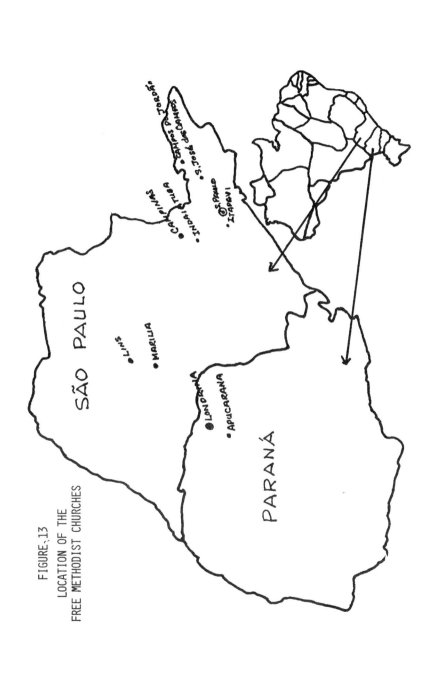

FIGURE 13
LOCATION OF THE
FREE METHODIST CHURCHES

Sunday school children. There were experts in Christian education at the seminary and day school, but the Church, it seems,
did not take full advantage of that.

The failure to train and use *Nisei* leaders is another factor
of slow growth. *Nisei* and *Sansei* constitute 80 percent of the
Japanese population in Brazil, and they can be better reached by
Portuguese speaking Nisei leaders. Yet, in the Free Methodist
Church, there is only one Nisei minister out of eleven ministers.
In the past forty years only three Nisei male ministers have
graduated from seminary: John Mizuki in 1949, Yoshikazu Takiya
in 1959, and Makoto Ono in 1969. John Mizuki was transferred to
the Brazilian division in 1952, as was Yoshikazu Takiya in 1972.
Only Makoto Ono is working for the Nikkei Conference. The lack
of *Nisei* leaders has been a great gap in the Nikkei Conference,
and its outreach ministry has been greatly handicapped. Unless
the Free Methodist Church trains more capable *Nisei* leaders
within five years or so, its growth will be greatly limited.
The training of *Nisei* leaders is the most urgent need of the
Nikkei Conference at present. Regarding this problem, Harold
and Lucile Ryckman, both missionaries to Brazil for over twenty
years, wrote to the author in answer to the question, "Why did
the Nikkei Conference stop growing in the sixties?" Here is
their view:

> The *Issei* were largely born and raised in Japan. They
> went to Brazil before the cultural changes that came to
> Japan during and after the war years. They neither took
> on the new Japanese culture nor the western culture of
> Brazil. The *Nisei* are Brazilians and raised in western
> culture. They are not influenced by the oriental way of
> thinking as their fathers were. I believe the *Isseis*,
> in general, though they had great success in former
> years in winning *Isseis* to Christ, made little attempt
> or progress toward understanding the westernized minds
> of the *Niseis*. The *Niseis* lost confidence in the
> Issei's ability to guide them. They could not as easily
> reach the *Niseis* for Christ as they had their parents
> before them.

> With natural turn of events, the *Nisei* became the field
> for evangelism, but the *Isseis* had not adapted to the
> extent that they could reach them. The *Niseis* became a
> separate culture group which could only be reached by
> other *Niseis* themselves.

> You will notice that the only *Nisei* pastor in the
> Nikkei Conference is Makoto Ono. With the exception of
> Makoto, all our pastors in the Nikkei conference were
> born and raised in Japan.

Largely speaking, the only possibility for growth in the
Nikkei Conference is the conversion of the *Nisei*. The
majority of the pastors are not prepared to reach them
(Ryckman 1974).

Spiritual decline may have been another reason for the slowing down of growth. As we have mentioned, for about ten years
starting from 1947 the spiritual life of the Nikkei Conference
was very high. There was unity among workers and a strong evangelistic zeal existed among both ministers and laymen. In the
sixties, however, that spiritual zeal was vanishing and instead
criticism and rivalry among leaders arose and this doubtless
affected the growth of the Church (Interview, Uchida 1975).

The seminary may be mentioned as another factor that has
indirectly contributed to the slowing down of church growth.
The seminary was founded in 1958. It was amazing how $65,000
were raised by the faculty and students of the Spring Arbor
Junior College (now a four-year college), Spring Arbor, Michigan,
to purchase the land to build seminary facilities and professors'
homes. But when we look back, we may say the foundation of the
seminary retarded the growth of the Church because it diverted
the attention from evangelism. Although most of the early
missionaries were educational missionaries, up to the date of
the foundation of the seminary, they helped the churches, including the Japanese churches. Helen Voller was in charge of Campos
do Jordao church. Don Bowen and Lucile Damon also helped in
youth and Sunday school works. But when the seminary started,
five missionaries and one national became engaged full time in
theological education. Moreover, since Mission began to spend
a good amount of money on the seminary, it did not have as much
to spend on evangelism.

The failure to integrate Sunday school pupils into church
also was a factor hindering growth. This happened due to the
lack of Nisei leaders. Many Sunday school pupils became youth
members, but did not go beyond becoming church members. And
even those who became church members did not grow spiritually to
be fully integrated into church life due to the lack of Nisei
ministers to nurture and guide them to become responsible church
members.

The lack of growth in the seventies is mainly due to the
drastic cut of non-active members (*yurei kai-in*, ghost members)
of the Saude church in 1972 which number over two hundred as we
may see in Figure 10. Here we note the problem of membership
leakage which is a very serious one. Why were there so many
non-active members? To find out why this took place is one of
the crucial points in the study of the growth of the Japanese
churches, for as Boschman, Watson and Yamamori have stressed,

this phenomenon is very common in Japan too (Boschman 1964:31;
Watson 1968:142-94; Yamamori 1974:78-82). One reason for membership leakage in the Saude church is the fact that the nurture of
the Portuguese-speaking members were neglected due to the lack
of Nisei ministers. Another reason more general may have been
the lack of an adequate post-baptismal care given to members.
People who have become members as individuals have left churches
more easily than those who have become members as a family. So
the individualistic approach instead of the family approach is
another possible cause of leakage. With the churches of the
interior the major cause of membership leakage has been migration to the city of Sao Paulo. We shall discuss this subject
further in Chapter VI.

    The economic stability of the Japanese in the seventies may
also be responsible for the slowing down of the growth. As they
become economically more stable and begin to feel more secure,
they become less responsive to the gospel feeling less need for
religion (Interview, Sakuma 1975).

    The syndrome of church development may be mentioned as
another cause of the slow growth of the sixties and seventies.
The churches, once they are established, become busy taking care
of themselves and evangelism with resultant church growth
suffers. It is too easy for churches to become self-centered
and to forget the needs of those who are outside. The Free
Methodist Church has not, it seems, escaped this syndrome. In
the period 1948-1959 when the Church was busy planting and
establishing churches, it grew rapidly, but once the churches
were established growth slowed down.

5

How They
Have Become Christians

In this chapter we are going to deal with the factors related
to conversion such as religion before conversion, age of conversion, ways, happenings, messages, persons used for conversion,
and the commitment of the Japanese Christians of the Free
Methodist and Holiness Churches to their faith.

THEIR RELIGION BEFORE CONVERSION

According to Figure 14 the majority of our *Issei* respondents
came from Buddhism, as expected. Some of them (13 percent) were
already Protestants before their conversion, while 14.4 percent
gave no answer to the question. We note also that very few of
them--only 2.8 percent--were Catholics. One important fact
that we should note here is that 87 percent of the *Issei* respondents came from non-Protestant sources, and this reveals that
the Protestant Churches in Brazil are growing by converting non-
Protestants.

What surprises us in the case of the Nisei is that almost
one-half of our respondents declared that they didn't have a
religion before their conversion. This indicates that there are
many Nisei who are without a religion because they do not become
followers of the religion of their parents nor embrace the
religion of the country they are born in. This may be due to
the fact that they do not receive religious instruction at home
nor are approached to become believers of the religion of the
majority--Catholicism. This means that many Nisei are neglected
as far as religion is concerned and they grow up without any
religious orientation. Also noticeable is the fact that among

FIGURE 14

RELIGION BEFORE CONVERSION BY GENERATION

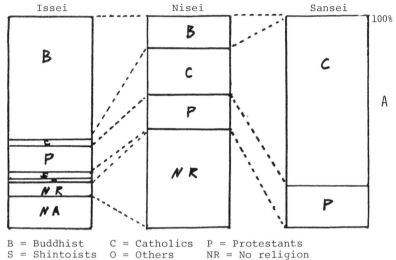

B = Buddhist   C = Catholics   P = Protestants
S = Shintoists O = Others   NR = No religion
NA = No answer

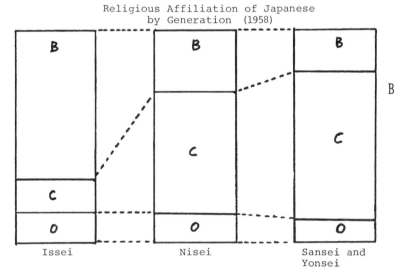

Religious Affiliation of Japanese
by Generation (1958)

Source: A - Mizuki 1975, questionnaire
        B - See Table 9, page 17

Nisei respondents there were more who came from Catholicism than
from Buddhism (21 percent to 15.7 percent), and that the great
majority (84.3 percent) of them came from non-Protestant backgrounds.

In the case of the Sansei we wonder whether any valid conclusion can be drawn because of the size of our sample, which is
only five people. But when we compare it with the general
religious trend of Sansei as it is shown in Figure 14 B, we see
the closeness of our sample to its population, and this makes us
more confident about making some remarks about Sansei. What we
notice about our Sansei respondents is that the great majority
of them (80 percent) came from Catholicism, 20 percent from
Protestantism, while no one came from Buddhism. So 80 percent
of the Sansei respondents came from non-Protestant backgrounds.

Figure 14 reveals that the great majority of the Japanese
Protestants (an average of 83.7 percent) have come from non-
Protestant backgrounds, which means that the Japanese Protestant
Churches in Brazil are growing mainly by conversion and not by
biological growth or by transference. Both Figure 14 A and B
shows that, in order to evangelize *Nisei* and *Sansei*, a missionary or evangelist needs to know Catholic religious thinking and
practices rather than those of Buddhism. In the religious shift
from Buddhism to Catholicism, we see that *Issei* and *Sansei* are
the two opposite poles while *Nisei* stands between them.

Let us see now how the Buddhists have become Christians as
related through their own testimonies:

> Until I was converted to Christianity, I did not think of
> Christ except as one of the three great saints of the
> world and of Christianity as a Western religion for intel-
> lextuals. Up to then my religion was Buddhism of the
> Shinshu Nishi Honganji sect, of which my mother was a
> devout believer. But I did not understand the meaning of
> the sutras at all. I had heard that salvation is by faith
> (*tariki-hongan*) and if I rely upon Buddha I could go to
> *gokurakujodo* (Land of perfect bliss, Paradise), but this
> did not convince me. Before my conversion I was timid
> and so I used to drink a lot to deceive myself. As I had
> to work alone to support a family of eight people, I
> lived as though always persecuted by poverty. Looking
> back now I feel sorry for the trouble I caused my wife.
> I was a carpenter and I barely made our daily living.
> It was around August of 1964 that Rev. H. came to church
> for once-a-year-special-meetings. A church officer and
> local preacher, brother S, came to invite me for those
> meetings. As he came from far away, I went to the Sunday
> evening meeting, compelled by a feeling of obligation

(*ogiri*) towards him. I do not recall the content of the
sermon, but I was more moved by the unusual zeal of the
preacher who spoke with tears rolling down his cheeks.
After having finished his preaching, the preacher and
four more laymen (T,H,S,T), layed their hands upon our
(my wife's and mine) heads, shoulders, backs, and prayed
earnestly. On April 18, Easter morning of 1965, my wife,
my older daughter, and I, plus five more brethren,
received Christian baptism by Rev. N. Ever, since we had
been attending Sunday service, Midweek service, cottage
meeting, even in the rain or wind, unless there was a
major obstacle. Thanks to the guidance of the Holy
Spirit, Hallelujah. (Testimony taken from the questionnaire).

I was born and reared in a Buddhist family. As a
Buddhist I was married to a man whose family was running
a prosperous business. Among the employees there was a
Christian who, in spite of living a life of misfortune,
endured it with joy, and that impressed me. By that time
I received Christian literature from an Adventist church.
I read it and little by little I was led to church. My
husband was led too, and on October 10, 1935, when I was
thirty-seven years old, we both believed in Christ as our
Savior and accepted Him into our heart (testimony from
questionnaire).

AGE OF CONVERSION

The largest number of *Issei* are converted in their thirties,
while those who are converted in their twenties and in their
forties are equal in number. The next most likely ages of conversion are (in order of frequency) those in their teens, their
fifties, their sixties, their seventies, and lastly, children
under ten. Among *Nisei*, conversion usually took place between
ten and twenty-nine (73.6 percent of them), while almost all the
Sansei were converted in their teens. This difference between
Issei on the one hand, and *Nisei* and *Sansei* on the other hand, is
not difficult to understand when we consider the ways in which
they became Christians. For *Nisei* and *Sansei* the primary method
of conversion has been the Sunday school. They have been brought
to Sunday school in their childhood and youth, and have been converted there. So it is understandable that their conversion took
place while they were attending Sunday school or youth meetings--
that is, in their teens or twenties. Most *Nisei* are presently
in their thirties and forties, while the *Sansei* are mostly under
twenty. We expect that these groups would come to know the
gospel at a younger age than Issei who were already adults when
they came to Brazil. Figure 15 indicates also that one need
not worry much about age limitations when evangelizing the *Issei*.

FIGURE 15

AGE OF CONVERSION BY GENERATION

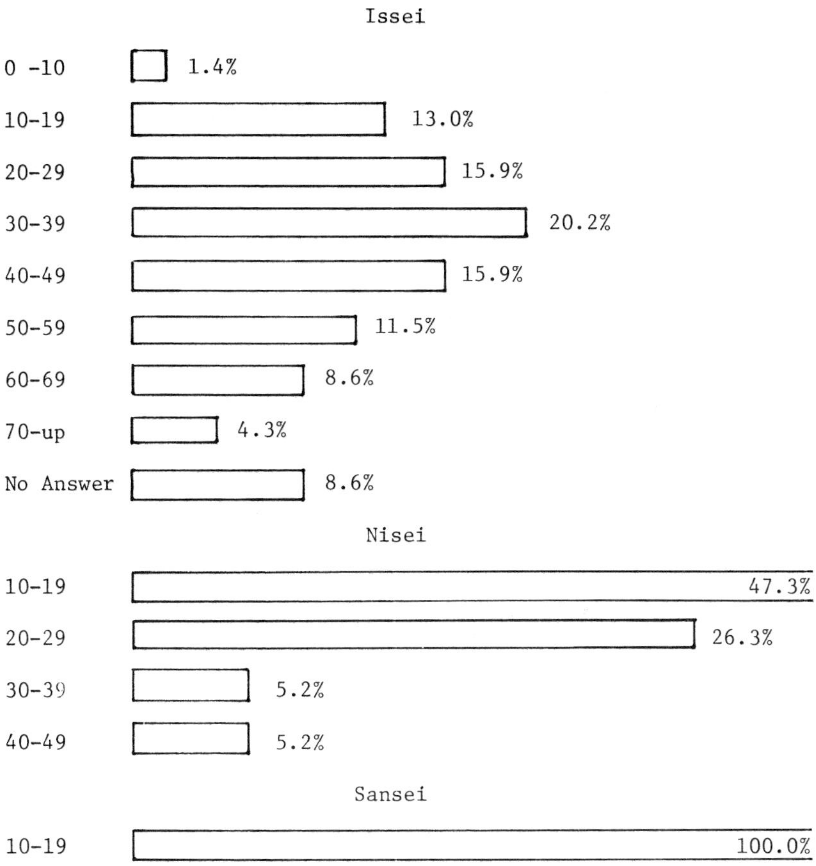

Issei

Age	Percentage
0 -10	1.4%
10-19	13.0%
20-29	15.9%
30-39	20.2%
40-49	15.9%
50-59	11.5%
60-69	8.6%
70-up	4.3%
No Answer	8.6%

Nisei

Age	Percentage
10-19	47.3%
20-29	26.3%
30-39	5.2%
40-49	5.2%

Sansei

Age	Percentage
10-19	100.0%

Source: Mizuki 1975, questionnaire

WAYS OF CONVERSION

    Figure 16 shows that many different ways are used for the
conversion of the *Issei*, while Sunday school and its related
activities are almost exclusive ways used for the conversion of
Nisei and *Sansei*. While the *Nisei* and the *Sansei* are being won
through Christian education ministry, the *Issei* are being
discipled through direct evangelism.

FIGURE 16

WAYS USED IN CONVERSION BY GENERATIONS

Issei

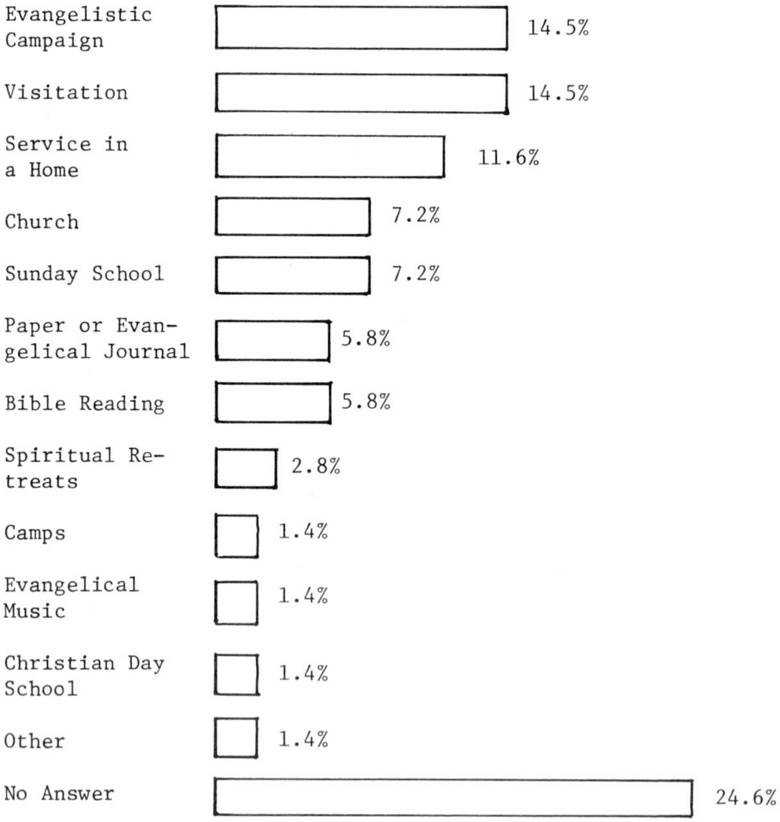

Way	Percentage
Evangelistic Campaign	14.5%
Visitation	14.5%
Service in a Home	11.6%
Church	7.2%
Sunday School	7.2%
Paper or Evangelical Journal	5.8%
Bible Reading	5.8%
Spiritual Retreats	2.8%
Camps	1.4%
Evangelical Music	1.4%
Christian Day School	1.4%
Other	1.4%
No Answer	24.6%

This is understandable because there are not any *Issei* at
Sunday school age. Figure 16 also reveals that *Nisei* and *Sansei*
are not being reached by other methods of direct evangelism.
For instance, the evangelistic campaign which is being used to
convert the *Issei* is not used for reaching the *Nisei* and *Sansei*.
This may be due to the fact that most of the evangelistic
campsigns are conducted in Japanese and do not serve to reach
the *Nisei* and *Sansei*.

FIGURE 16 (Continued)

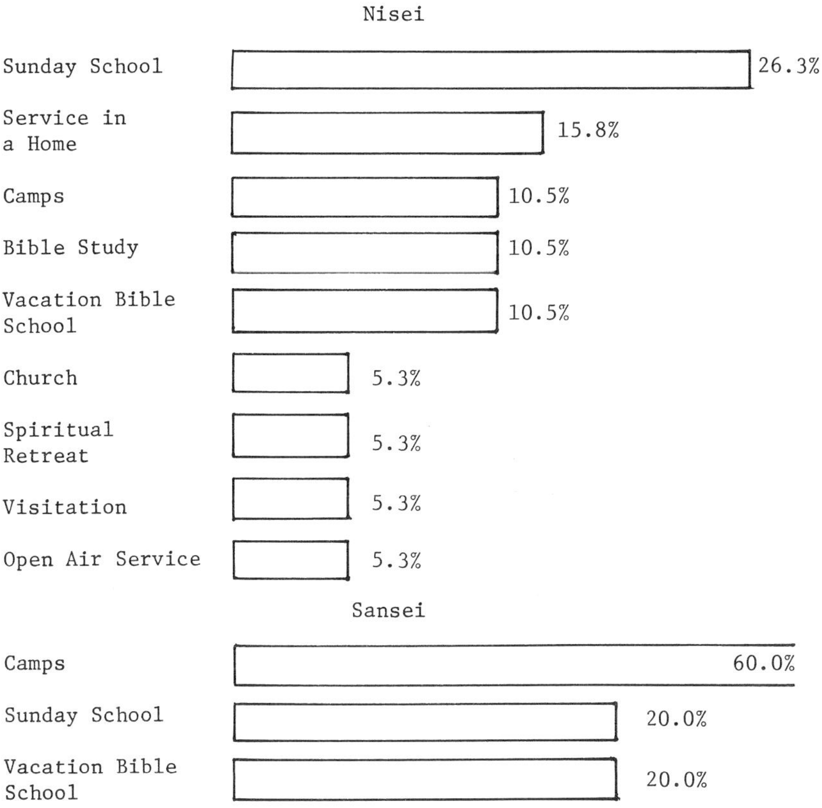

Nisei

Sunday School	26.3%
Service in a Home	15.8%
Camps	10.5%
Bible Study	10.5%
Vacation Bible School	10.5%
Church	5.3%
Spiritual Retreat	5.3%
Visitation	5.3%
Open Air Service	5.3%

Sansei

Camps	60.0%
Sunday School	20.0%
Vacation Bible School	20.0%

Source: Mizuki 1975, questionnaire

PEOPLE USED IN CONVERSION

The pastor plays a decisive role in the conversion of the
Issei, whereas the Sunday school teacher is the key person for
the conversion of the *Sansei* and also in a lesser degree of the
Nisei. The *Nisei* and *Sansei* are converted through the instru-
mentality of the pastor too. Figure 17 also reveals that except
Sunday school teachers, the ministry of soul winning is not being
carried on by other church officers.

FIGURE 17

PEOPLE USED IN CONVERSION BY GENERATION

Issei

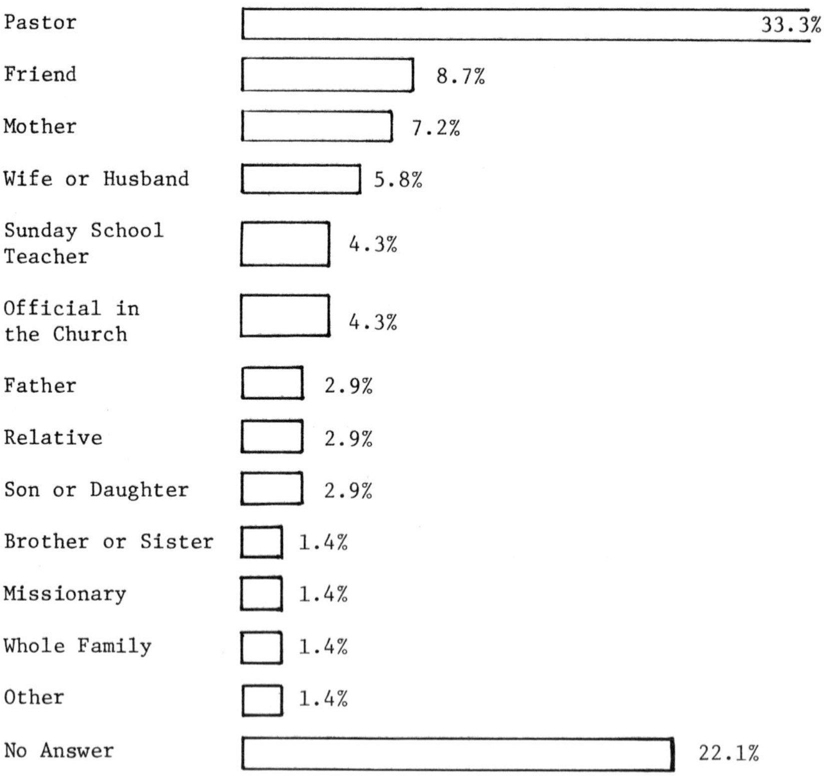

Pastor	33.3%
Friend	8.7%
Mother	7.2%
Wife or Husband	5.8%
Sunday School Teacher	4.3%
Official in the Church	4.3%
Father	2.9%
Relative	2.9%
Son or Daughter	2.9%
Brother or Sister	1.4%
Missionary	1.4%
Whole Family	1.4%
Other	1.4%
No Answer	22.1%

Only 4.3 percent of the *Issei* respondents said that they were
converted through an official in the church. We notice also the
important role that a family member plays in conversion. If we
add the people who have become Christians through their mother
or father, husband or wife, brother or sister, or another relative, they reach 24.5 percent of the total converts in the case
of the Issei and 15.6 percent in the case of the Nisei. Next to
family members come friends as instruments of conversion.

FIGURE 17 (Continued)

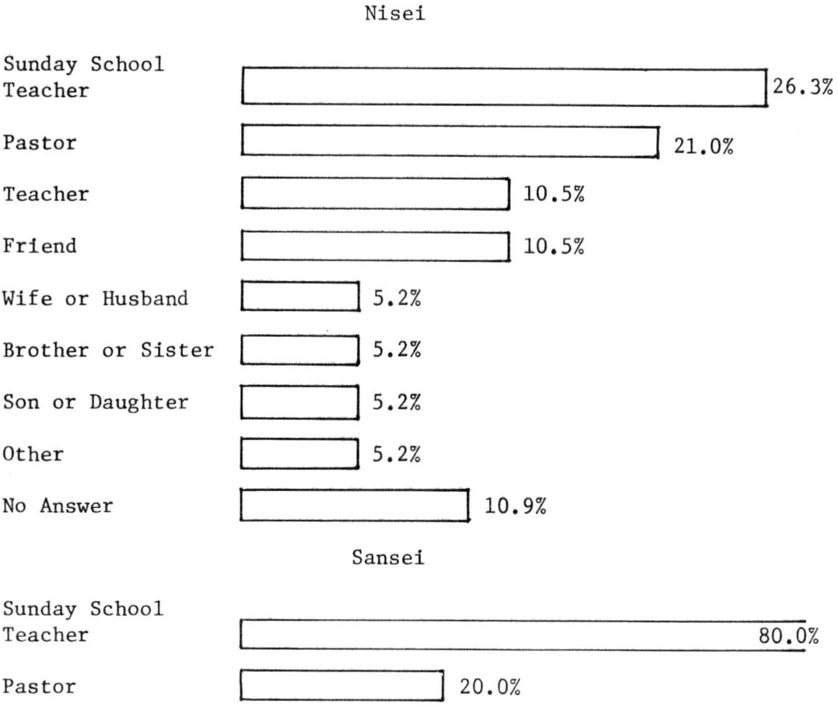

Nisei

Sunday School Teacher	26.3%
Pastor	21.0%
Teacher	10.5%
Friend	10.5%
Wife or Husband	5.2%
Brother or Sister	5.2%
Son or Daughter	5.2%
Other	5.2%
No Answer	10.9%

Sansei

Sunday School Teacher	80.0%
Pastor	20.0%

Source: Mizuki 1975, questionnaire

CIRCUMSTANCES LEADING TO CONVERSION

The circumstances that have led the Japanese to conversion
vary, but in general terms we can say that for *Issei* various
crises and hardships--death in the family, sickness and other
difficulties--have been the major reason for becoming Christians
(38.8 percent).

FIGURE 18

CIRCUMSTANCES USED IN CONVERSION BY GENERATION

Issei

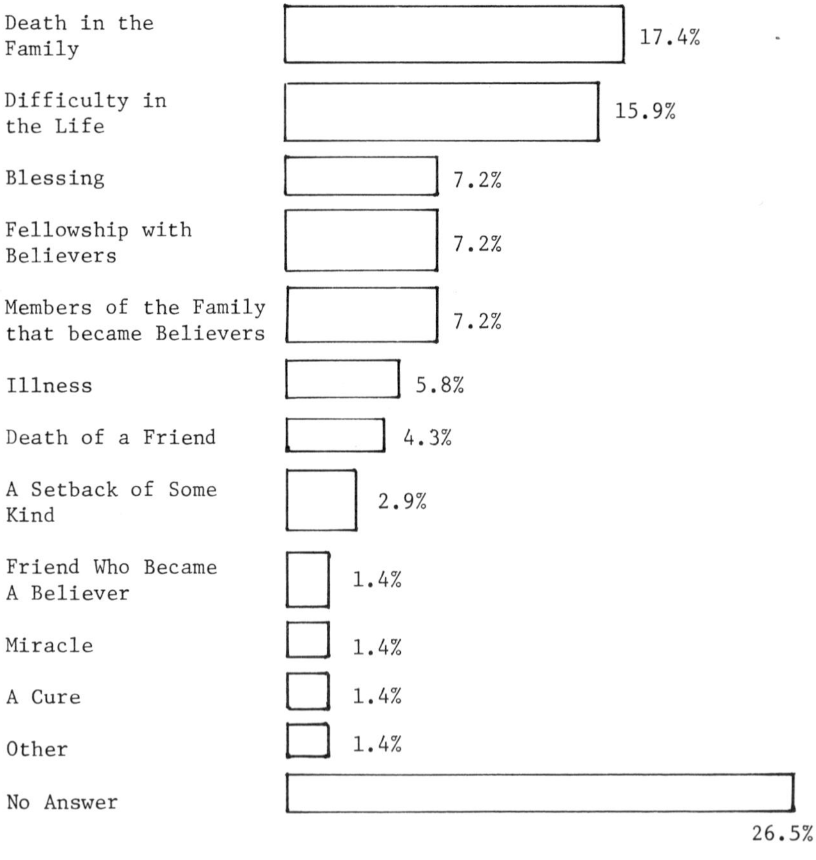

Death in the Family	17.4%
Difficulty in the Life	15.9%
Blessing	7.2%
Fellowship with Believers	7.2%
Members of the Family that became Believers	7.2%
Illness	5.8%
Death of a Friend	4.3%
A Setback of Some Kind	2.9%
Friend Who Became A Believer	1.4%
Miracle	1.4%
A Cure	1.4%
Other	1.4%
No Answer	26.5%

For *Nisei* (13.5 percent) and *Sansei* (60 percent) the main cause has been their friendship with believers. Let us see how God has used certain crises, difficulties, and good examples of believers, friendship with Christians, etc. to lead people to conversion.

FIGURE 18 (Continued)

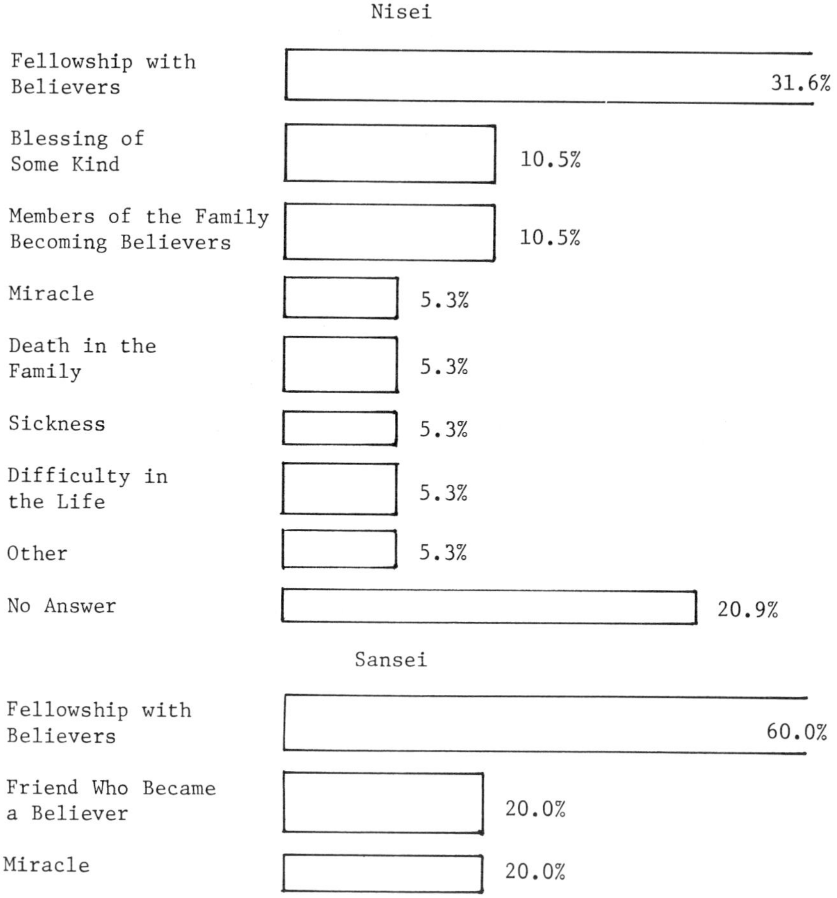

Nisei

Fellowship with Believers	31.6%
Blessing of Some Kind	10.5%
Members of the Family Becoming Believers	10.5%
Miracle	5.3%
Death in the Family	5.3%
Sickness	5.3%
Difficulty in the Life	5.3%
Other	5.3%
No Answer	20.9%

Sansei

Fellowship with Believers	60.0%
Friend Who Became a Believer	20.0%
Miracle	20.0%

Source: Mizuki 1975, questionnaire

Cases of Death in the Family.

I lost my mother when I was six years old, and because of
this I grew up with only the love of my father and brothers.
But one day, my father passed away too.

Then I felt something I had never experienced before--
loneliness. I was then eighteen years old. With so many
problems and missing my father, I wanted to die. My young
brother was very fearful.

One day, one of our sisters wrote to my brother telling
him to go to church. He did, and he continued to attend
church every Sunday. He stopped complaining and I thought
that was good. One Sunday, a friend of mine came to invite
me to go to the Holiness church and so I did. I liked it
very much for I had an unforgettable welcome. I continued
to attend that church and one day a man asked to have a
meeting in our home. We accepted that request and at one
of these meetings I came to discover Christ. He showed me
the life, another life, in which I have the joy of living,
thanks to God (Testimony from questionnaire).

It was the death of our son that led us to become members
of the Free Methodist church. Before that, my wife went
to Mrs. O's home, and she met Rev. H's wife who spoke
about the Free Methodist Church and my wife was very much
impressed. When our son became sick she remembered the
talk with that pastor's wife. Our son had worked hard for
our family but he had no religion and we became very much
concerned about his destiny. We wanted him to have a
religion before he departed, so we requested Pastor H
through Mrs. O to visit our son. Thus he came to see our
son every two or three days and when he could not come,
his wife did. Before his death he began to understand the
message of the pastor and his wife, and one day he requested
to be baptized. We were very happy for his understanding
and earnestness. As the doctor had told us that he had
cancer in the stomach and that it was advanced, we were
expecting his passing any time. He left to be with the
Lord on February 20, 7:20 a.m., 1975 (Testimony from
questionnaire).

Let us now hear from his wife about the same experience.
The reason I decided to believe in Christ came on the death
of our second son. He was forty-nine years old. When the
doctor told me that his disease was cancer of the stomach
and that it was advanced, for the first time in my life I
thought about what would happen to his soul after his death
and I cried all night. That night I remembered Rev. H. I
had met him and his wife several times at the funeral and

memorial services of my relatives. I had heard him and had
respect for him. So I thought I should ask him to help my son.
When I was thinking this, my relative, Mrs. O came to see us
and I asked her about Pastor H. The pastor came many times and
prayed for my son and thanks to that, my son was happy and
passed away peacefully. I am thankful for the kindness of the
pastor and other believers. Now I have Jesus as my spiritual
and moral support and am praying thankfully (Testimony from
questionnaire).

I came to Brazil on November 1, 1935, and on August 29,
1937, my husband died in the interior leaving five children
for me to take care of. The teacher of the Japanese
language school was a Christian from Sao Paulo. One day
two pastors came from Sao Paulo and they held an evangelistic service at school. I attended the meeting and heard
the story of God for the first time in my life. The
preacher said: "Whoever has made the decision, raise your
hand." I was the first one to respond to that appeal and
he prayed for me. It was in April of 1938 (Testimony from
questionnaire).

When I was twenty years of age, in September, my beloved
older brother died as a victim of pioneer work. In 1935,
the third year of the colonization of the city of Asai, in
the midst of the jungle, I became sick due to deep grief.
I read the account of the incident in the life of Luther,
the Reformer, who was depressed one day and was encouraged
by his wife who cited Romans 8:31: "If God is for us, who
is against us." The account said that Luther was encouraged
with that word, stood up, and continued his fight. I read
also a poem by a professor of Aoyama Gakuin which says that
above the cloud there is sunshine. With these words, I
also stood up from the midst of my grief, I got a Bible
and began to seek the God of Christianity (Testimony from
questionnaire).

I grew up in a Christian home. I knew about God, the Lord
Jesus, and the Bible, but did not think of becoming a
believers. When my father, who was a Christian, died, I
became aware of the seriousness of death and, at the same
time, I was impressed with the wonderfulness of his death
which was full of victory. On that day I became a believer.
I was exactly forty-two years old (Testimony from questionnaire).

Cases of Sickness.

My wife had a serious illness that neither the doctor nor
the accupuncturist, the massagist, the charmer, nor anyone
else was able to heal. But when she believed in Christ,

repented of sin, and was saved, her disease was also healed
completely. I used to see her going to church joyfully.
One day she opened up and shared her joy, and said that she
was indeed thankful and asked whether I wouldn't like to
believe in the same wonderful God, and urged me to go to
church with her. In the beginning I went more because of
her insistence. It was hard, though, for I liked to drink
and smoke. I kept my cigarettes in my pocket while in
church and smoked on the way to and from. The pastor used
to speak on the cross from Luke 23, about the prodigal son
and about sin. Each time he spoke I was touched, but I was
not able to jump in and believe. In a worship service, however, I was led to the conviction of sin from Ephesians
5:18 which says: "And do not get drunk with wine, for that
is debauchery; but be filled with the Spirit." I felt bad
about the many troubles I had caused people because of my
drinking and smoking habit and I really repented. I went
home with the determination to quit drinking and smoking
from that moment on, and to give away to my neighbor all
the liquor and cigarettes I had. So I spoke to my wife
about my determination. To my embarrassment her reply was
that to give someone what was bad for me was an evil even
worse, and she advised me to throw away the liquor and burn
up the cigarettes. What I was unable to do with my power
I could do easily by the power of God. I am thankful that
I did not give those cigarettes and liquor to my neighbor,
for the salvation that I received, and for the protection
God has granted me up to this age of seventy-eight years.
"Believe in the Lord, and you will be saved, you and your
household." According to this, God's promise, all my
children have been saved and they are in the church.
Hallelujah! (Testimony from questionnaire).

I was born in a Christian home but never came to truly
believe. I married a *Seicho-no-Ie* believer. When I was
twenty-four years old my first son was born. When he was
three years old he caught the measles, which resulted in
meningitis. After giving him treatment, the doctor gave
up. Then we took him to a specialist in Sao Paulo. After
one month of treatment this doctor gave up too. When we
brought him home he was pitiful indeed, I had no one to
go to except God. When I was in deep grief, my father and
pastor came to see me. They urged me to have faith and so
I was converted and saved. On December 25, 1960, I was
baptized. My husband opposed this strongly, but after I
was saved I regained the hope to live, my son was healed,
and I was able to keep my faith, although struggles continued. Now I am thankful that all my six children were
led to Sunday school and through it, to God, and they have
kept their faith up to now. This is of course thanks to
the work of God (Testimony from questionnaire).

Praise the Lord! Three years ago my body condition
unexpectedly became bad. I went to Dr. S for a check-up
and he told me I had diabetes. According to the doctor
there was no medicine at that time that could cure it
completely. When he said it was like cancer, I thought,
why have I to suffer from this kind of disease? I felt
queer and when I thought I was going to die because of
the disease, suddenly I began to feel the fear of death,
and I could not sleep at night. I was having nervous
prostration, and those days of agony continued for some
time. Then I thought of asking God, Jesus Christ, whom
my wife believed in, to take away my fear and agony. It
was the first time in my life that I was earnestly asking
for something. God gave that trial to break my hard-
heartedness and to give me a happy life. Now I thank my
Lord Jesus for that. On December 25, 1974, under the
ministry of Rev. N, I confessed all my sins and was baptized. Since then I have been living a Christian life.
My diabetes, which was progressing, became better after
I was saved. I quit smoking and drinking and have
controlled my diet. I feel much better now and for this
I feel truly thankful (Testimony from questionnaire).

A Case of an Accident.

Praise the Lord! Although I did not know God, I was
living a happy and busy life. But when I was living a
happy life, a big occurrence took place. I was then
forty years old and had four children, the youngest one
being seven. The occurrence was a big accident that my
husband suffered. It happened when he was transporting
rice to South Parana. The truck fell into a 330 foot
deep cliff and he was seriously injured. The doctor said
he needed seven months of treatment and rest. When I
heard that my heart was greatly shaken. That moment, for
the first time in my life, I looked up at heaven and
prayed: "Oh God, help me!" Lo, and behold! God healed
that injury and seven months later he was able to work
again as before. I truly believe that God exists. My
parents were Christians and each time they came to my
home they told me to become a Christian, but I had not
accepted Christ yet. When my mother died I wept and
asked her to forgive me. My father was tender to me and
said: "Let us believe together in Christ and follow
Him." Soon after that I was baptized and lived as a
Christian with my father for five years, when he too was
called back home at eighty years of age. He called Jesus
twice and went to heaven. I watched his death and my
heart had peace. I thanked God. Amen. (Testimony from
questionnaire).

Delusion, Loneliness, and Hardship Common to Immigrant Life.

When I was eighteen years old I came to Brazil, in spite
of my father's objection. After having led a wandering
life for two years, my dream was gone and I regretted having
come to Brazil. Moreover, I injured my left eye in an
accident and lost my sight. I thought I was a failure and
became very much discouraged.

About the same time Bishop Juji Nakada came from Japan and
spoke at the yough hall in Lins. I was not much impressed
by his message, but from that time on I began to attend
the meetings because I was seeking the way. They were
held at Rev. Y's home (church). He had come with the bishop
from Japan to Lins and started new work there.

In Rev. Y's family I came to see something I had not seen
in my family when I was brought up. At the same time I
came to know that I was wrong and a sinner. Before I had
thought that I was somebody and always right, whereas
environment, friends, and acquaintances were wrong and so
to be blamed. As I was exhorted to repent and to believe
in the cross of Jesus Christ, I did so with simplicity.
From that time on I was born as another person. (Testimony
from questionnaire).

Contrary to my ideal, life was full of contradictions and
this led me to distress and despair. Exactly at that time,
two seminarians came to hold special meetings and I was
invited to attend those meetings. I came to realize that
the only way to overcome sufferings and contradictions of
this life was to go back to God. I confessed my sins that
I remember before God, I believed in Jesus Christ and
accepted Him as my Savior. I entrusted everything to God
and stood up, and ever since my life has been changed to
a life of hope and joy, and I am living daily with thank-
fulness. (Testimony from questionnaire).

Family Problems.

In my case, my wife had received Christian baptism when
we married. I was still young at that time and so did
not think seriously about life. After that, however, as
it is common to every immigrant who is far away from his
birthplace with economic difficulties, the family divided
between Brazil and Japan. Disharmony among brothers due
to a wrong mentality inherited from my parents, made my
family become lonely. Before long my wife's parents died,
and I regretted very much that I was not able to send her
to see them again and that I had caused her much trouble
because of my personality. In spite of this, my wife never

complained, although we have lived together for nearly
forty years. This is perhaps due to the great parental
love she received as a baby and to the fact that she had
lived out of the home for seven years before she married
me. She is brave in enduring hardship and she has been a
great help to me. Later we moved to Sao Paulo, near a
church, and for some reason a home meeting came to be held
in our house, continuing for five years. The sincerity of
the pastor and believers had touched me. God, the Creator,
has become the most important being in my life... (Testimony from questionnaire).

I felt like all the doors surrounding me were closed. I
was sick and tired of the injustice committed in our family
--"supremacy" of the brothers in the firm our parents owned
in Presidente Prudente. They used all means to get my
parents' confidence which meant repudiation for me. I was
the oldest brother but that did not mean much, although I
worked hard for the shop's sake. I really came to realize
that this is a world of injustice and I came to the point
that I could not stand it any longer. To avoid the situation, however, meant defeat to me. When I looked for my
friends, the late Mrs. H advised me to seek the pastor of
the church, Rev. K. His words were like medicine for my
suffering and I felt like one of those doors was opening.
I began to read the Bible, I was consoled and received the
love of God, the only thing capable of healing all the
pains I was feeling at that time. I accepted the Lord
whom I have trusted up to now and will trust until the
end. Amen. (Testimony from questionnaire).

Friendship With Believers and Their Good Example.

My conversion took place in Japan when a friend of mine
became a Christian and quit drinking and smoking completely.
He began to go to church every Sunday to attend worship
services and became an entirely different person from the
usual people. His life was righteous and his character
was pure. I was really impressed by what happened to his
life. Then I came to know how happy is the life of one
who believes in God. I thought "This is the way."
(Testimony from questionnaire).

I knew nothing about Christianity, for I lived in a
Buddhist family and among only Buddhists since my child-
hood. I did not know about the Bible, much less about
Christ. But one day I came to know a Christian girl and
I noticed she was different than other girls. Through her
I came to accept Christ as my only Savior, and up to now I
live happily. (Testimony from questionnaire).

MESSAGE USED IN CONVERSION

According to Figure 19, in the case of both *Issei* and *Nisei*
the messages of the vicarious death of Christ and love of God
has been used more frequently in the conversion of our respondents. But, a wide range of the variety of messages and the
relatively low percentage of each message used in conversion,

FIGURE 19

MESSAGE USED IN CONVERSION BY GENERATION

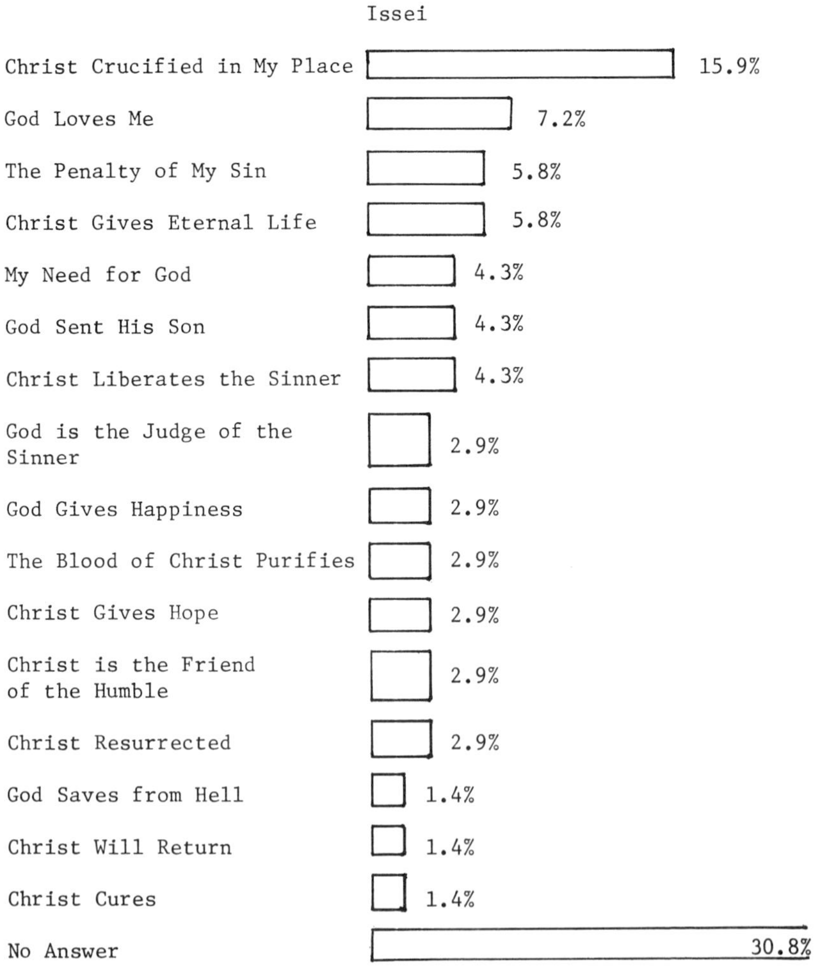

Issei

Message	Percentage
Christ Crucified in My Place	15.9%
God Loves Me	7.2%
The Penalty of My Sin	5.8%
Christ Gives Eternal Life	5.8%
My Need for God	4.3%
God Sent His Son	4.3%
Christ Liberates the Sinner	4.3%
God is the Judge of the Sinner	2.9%
God Gives Happiness	2.9%
The Blood of Christ Purifies	2.9%
Christ Gives Hope	2.9%
Christ is the Friend of the Humble	2.9%
Christ Resurrected	2.9%
God Saves from Hell	1.4%
Christ Will Return	1.4%
Christ Cures	1.4%
No Answer	30.8%

indicate that God uses different types of messages to convert
different people according to each individual need rather than
using one type of message to convert all. Yet we still have to
remember that over 50 percent of the *Nisei* were converted
through the message of the cross and the love of God. So, it
is a good thing for a preacher of the gospel to bear this in
mind.

FIGURE 19 (Continued)

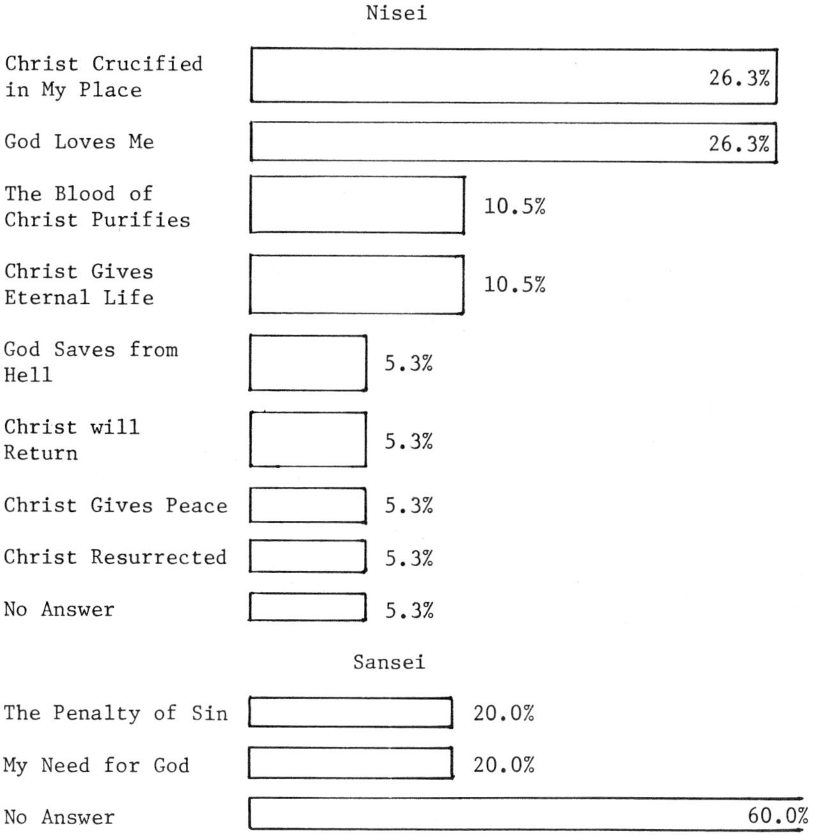

Nisei

Category	Percent
Christ Crucified in My Place	26.3%
God Loves Me	26.3%
The Blood of Christ Purifies	10.5%
Christ Gives Eternal Life	10.5%
God Saves from Hell	5.3%
Christ will Return	5.3%
Christ Gives Peace	5.3%
Christ Resurrected	5.3%
No Answer	5.3%

Sansei

Category	Percent
The Penalty of Sin	20.0%
My Need for God	20.0%
No Answer	60.0%

Source: Mizuki 1975, questionnaire

WHAT HAS HELPED CHRISTIAN GROWTH

While for *Issei* and *Nisei*, worship services have been a major help for Christian growth; for *Sansei*, Sunday school has been the most important help.

FIGURE 20

MEANS USED TO HELP CHRISTIAN GROWTH BY GENERATION

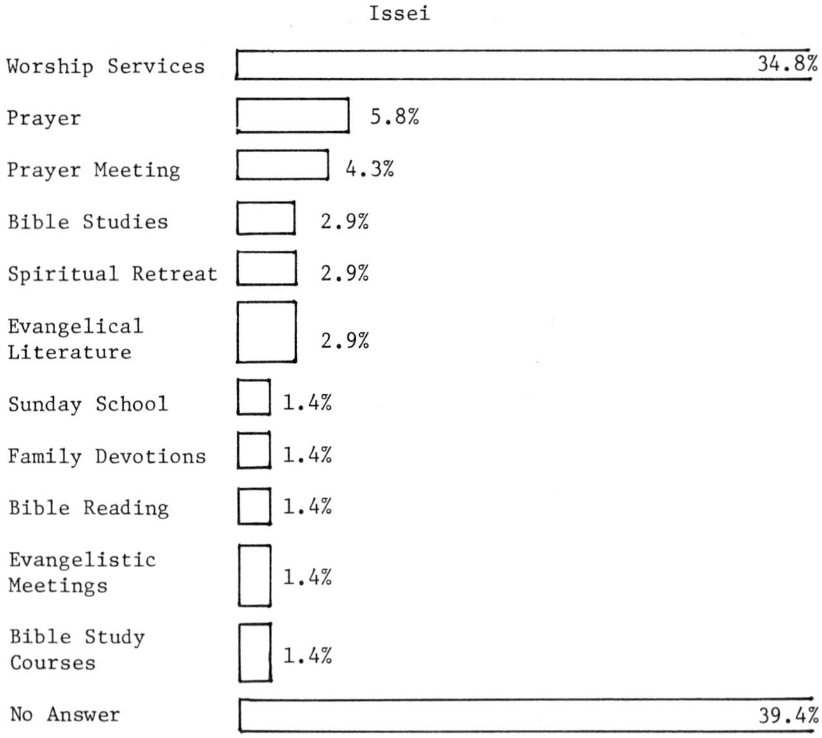

Issei

Worship Services	34.8%
Prayer	5.8%
Prayer Meeting	4.3%
Bible Studies	2.9%
Spiritual Retreat	2.9%
Evangelical Literature	2.9%
Sunday School	1.4%
Family Devotions	1.4%
Bible Reading	1.4%
Evangelistic Meetings	1.4%
Bible Study Courses	1.4%
No Answer	39.4%

Prayer meetings and youth meetings are also helping the *Sansei* to grow spiritually, while the *Nisei* are being helped by Bible reading and studies, and *Issei* are growing through prayer and prayer meetings.

FIGURE 20 (Continued)

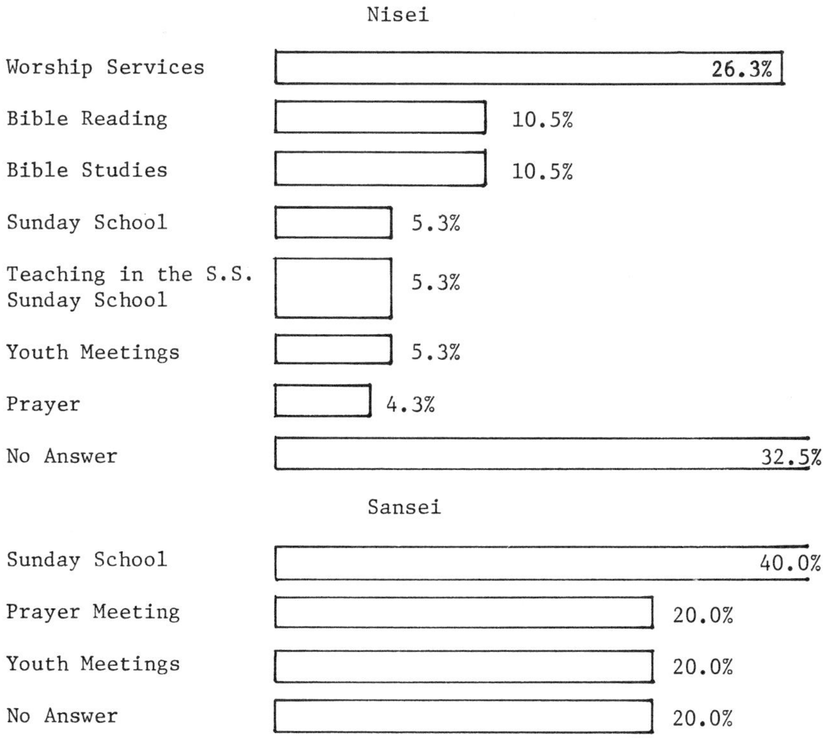

Nisei

Worship Services	26.3%
Bible Reading	10.5%
Bible Studies	10.5%
Sunday School	5.3%
Teaching in the S.S. Sunday School	5.3%
Youth Meetings	5.3%
Prayer	4.3%
No Answer	32.5%

Sansei

Sunday School	40.0%
Prayer Meeting	20.0%
Youth Meetings	20.0%
No Answer	20.0%

Source: Mizuki 1975, questionnaire

COMMITMENT TO CHRISTIAN LIFE

In this section we are going to see the degree of their commitment to church through their church attendance, giving, and involvement in bringing people to church. When we study the level of dedication of the Japanese Christians from the standpoint of their church attendance, tithing, and involvement in bringing new people to church, we may say that their commitment is pretty high.

Figure 21 indicates that 56.9 percent of our respondents attend church one or more times a week, and 22.5 of them attend more than two times a week. This means that 79.4 percent of them attend church one or more times a week.

In giving to the church, 47.3 percent of our respondents declared that they are tithers. This indicates that their commitments to support their church is pretty high, although in this area there is much room for improvement. Since churches are struggling financially, an increase in the number of tithers would help to provide better support to their ministers and to expand their outreach ministry. We have to recognize, however, that this loyalty of Christians has made the Holiness and Free Methodist Churches self-supporting.

The same Figure indicates that the Japanese Christians are interested in bringing new people to church, a factor important to growth. Of our respondents, 79.5 percent answered that they invite others to their churches. Therefore, a great majority are active in making new converts. From this standpoint, too, we may say that churches in Brazil are evangelistically oriented.

This relatively high commitment of the Japanese Christians in Brazil may be due to the fact that a great majority of them are first generation Christians and therefore have their first love. According to the response obtained by our questionnaire, 83.8 percent of them come from non-Protestant religions, and being first generation Christians, they have an enthusiasm to work for the conversion of others.

FIGURE 21

CHURCH ATTENDANCE BY GENERATION

ISSEI
NISEI
SANSEI
Less than once a week
Once or two times a week
More than twice a week
No answer

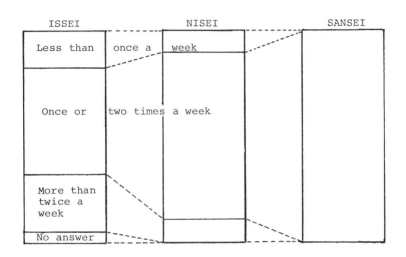

FIGURE 22

NUMBER OF TITHERS BY GENERATION

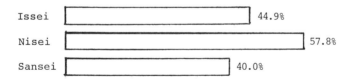

Issei
44.9%
Nisei
57.8%
Sansei
40.0%

FIGURE 23

CHRISTIANS WHO INVITE OTHERS
TO CHURCH BY GENERATION

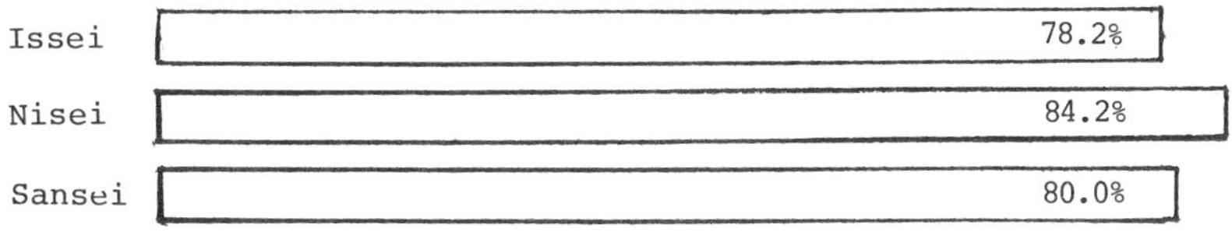

Issei
78.2%
Nisei
84.2%
Sansei
80.0%

6

The Growth as Compared to Counterparts in the United States

Protestant missions among Japanese in the United States began on October 16, 1877 in the basement of the Chinese Mission Hall located on 916 Washington Street in San Francisco, where thirty-five people met to organize a gospel circle. From this small beginning this Christian movement today numbers approximately 20,000 believers and 160 churches. The Japanese Christian churches here celebrated the centennial of Japanese Protestant missions in North America in 1977 (Horikoshi 1975; Shiraishi 1964:7).

THE EPISCOPAL CHURCH

Unlike most of the Japanese-American denominations, which were started by a missionary organization, the Episocpal churches were started by the diocese that encompassed areas of large Japanese settlements (Yamasaki 1976). At present there are four Japanese churches: Christ Church, San Francisco; St. Mary's Church, Los Angeles; St. Peter's Church, Seattle; and Good Samaritan, Honolulu. The Holy Trinity Church in Honolulu was dissolved in 1970. There is one church in Minneapolis, the Japanese Christian Union Church of Minnesota, which is a union church, but has been under Episcopal pastors almost from its beginning in 1947. Although this church is listed in *The Episcopal Annual*, its membership is not given, perhaps because not all are Episcopalian.

Christ Church, San Francisco, was started in June of 1895 by Father Shoichi Tai, who was sent from Japan. He got a building at 421 Powell Street, which was used as church and as parsonage. He returned to Japan after one year. Eleven pastors and lay

leaders ministered to this church between 1896 and 1929 when the
first Nisei pastor, Fr. Joseph K. Tsukamoto, came to minister to
it for the following twenty-nine years (Otani 1976).

St. Mary's Church, Los Angeles, was founded on July 1, 1907.
After the earthquake of San Francisco in 1906, many Japanese
moved to Los Angeles. At that time Miss Mary Patterson came
from San Francisco to work among the Japanese along with
Shinjiro Mayekawa, a lay worker. In 1913, Fr. Misao Yamazaki,
a graduate of the Berkeley Divinity School, assumed the pastorate
and under his leadership the church experienced remarkable progress. He created a kindergarten, a Japanese language school,
and other organizations. For the year 1931, the church reported
151 baptized, 68 communicants, 20 Sunday school teachers, and
318 pupils. In 1932 the present sanctuary and other facilities
were built. During the war the Yamazaki family and the members
of the church went to the relocation camp in Jerome, Arkansas.
Yamazaki's son, John, and John's wife went to a relocation camp
in Gila River, Arizona. John Yamazaki became a priest in 1942.
In 1945 (September), M. Yamazaki returned to Los Angeles and
began the rebuilding of the congregation. At the same time his
son, John Yamazaki, initiated a service in English. The English
speaking congregation is becoming integrated and today about 20
percent of its constituency is non-Japanese. After the war the
name of the church was changed from the "Japanese Episcopal
Church" to "Saint Mary's Episcopal Church." In 1956 the church
became self-supporting. That same year Misao Yamazaki retired,
but he has continued to work as the pastor of the Japanese
speaking congregation (Otani 1976).

Saint Peter's Church, Seattle, was started in June of 1908
with the help of the Trinity Church and its pastor, Herbert H.
Gowen. Two rooms were rented on 216 S. 9th St. to begin that
Japanese mission. Paul S. Uchida served as a lay leader while
Gowen taught Bible class. Under the sponsorship of the Trinity
Church, a night English class was also started. In 1909 Uchida
left and Gennosuke Shoji became the lay leader. He served for
six years as an unpaid minister and afterward received $25 per
month. In 1920 Shoji was ordained to the priesthood. On
September 7, 1932, a new sanctuary was dedicated at 1610 King
Street, and the church began to experience organic growth with
organization of new departments. In 1938 Fr. Daisuke Kitagawa
came to serve as an assistant to Fr. Shoji. In 1940 Shoji
retired because of illness, and Kitagawa became his successor.
In 1942 the Japanese living in Seattle evacuated to the relocation camp in Hunt, Idaho. Daisuke Kitagawa and his brother,
Joseph, accompanied the evacuees and they were appointed to be
administrative priests of the relocation camp, while Shoji and
Kenneth Chujo, also a priest, assisted them. In 1945 the
Japanese were allowed to return to the Pacific Coast and the

first post-war service at Saint Peter's Church was held on
August 19, 1945. According to the church report of that year
there were 10 families, 66 baptized, 34 communicants, and 17
Sunday school pupils. In 1949, Fr. Andrew N. Otani came from
Hawaii to take the pastorate which had become vacant after
Kitagawa had left to assume the pastorate in Minneapolis. Otani
stayed until 1954 when he left for Minneapolis to be Fr.
Kitagawa's successor. From 1955 to 1963 the church had Fr.
Lincoln Paul Eng as its pastor. Fr. Timothy Nakayama, a Nisei
from Canada, has been the pastor from 1966 to the present
(Otani 1976).

   Holy Trinity Church, Honolulu, was founded in April of 1908.
The first pastor was Fr. Philip Y. Fukao who was ordained a
deacon in 1911 and was ordained a priest in 1914. He initiated
a night English language school in 1909, which became a day
language school the following year. This school was created to
help newly arrived young people from Japan. In 1942, Fr.
Lawrence Ozaki succeeded Fukao and under his leadership the
church experienced remarkable growth. His sudden death on
September 29, 1958, was a disaster to the church. From that
year on the pastor was changed frequently, the membership
declined, and the church was finally dissolved by congregational
request on October 30, 1970 (Otani 1970).

   Good Samaritan Church, Honolulu, was founded in 1911. The
first pastor was Benjamin S. Ikezawa who came from Ozaka, Japan.
He was arrested when the Pacific War started and taken to the
relocation camp in Santa Fe, New Mexico. The church was under
the administration of Andrew F. Otani from 1942 to 1944, and in
those years a kindergarten was founded with good results. A
Bible study class for Nisei servicemen was also started and
about 50 of them attended the meeting that was held on Wednesdays.
James S. Nakamura served as the pastor from 1944 to 1955, and
George F. Hayashi, from 1961 to 1970. With no pastor since 1970,
the church has been in a state of stagnation (Otani 1976).*

                    THE HOLINESS CHURCH

   The Oriental Missionary Society Holiness Conference had its
beginning in 1920 when a Japanese church was established. A
group of students who had been attending the Friends Church in
Whittier began meeting at the O.M.S. Trinity Church of Hollywood
for prayer on Sunday evenings. Ugo Nakada, son of Bishop Juji
Nakada, a founder of the O.M.S. Japan Holiness Church, was

---

* Good Samaritan has just completed a building fund drive for
  $40,000 for a new church building. They have a Hakujin pastor
  there now.

ministering to that group of students. To that group belonged
Natsu Yano, Aya Okuda, Paul Okamoto, Toshio Hirano, Hanako
Yoneyama, Teruki Sakuma, and George Yashiro.

In 1921 Juji Nakada came to the United States to hold evangelistic meetings, traveling extensively. His son, Ugo, joined
him several times and assisted him. In J. Nakada's schedule
there was a visit to Asbury College where two Holiness ministers
were studying. One of them was Sadaichi Kuzuhara whom J. Nakada
appointed to take care of the new work in Los Angeles. Thus
Kazuhara interrupted his study to come to Los Angeles in order
to help found the first Holiness church in the United States.
It was loosely tied to the O.M.S. Trinity Church and so O.M.S.
became part of the name of the Holiness Conference (Suehiro 1972:
129-30). Starting in the early twenties a number of churches
have been founded by the O.M.S. Holiness Conference.

TABLE 20

HOLINESS CHURCHES IN THE U.S.

Church	Year Founded
Los Angeles	1922
Modesto	1928
Honolulu	1928
San Lorenzo	1929
San Diego	1930
San Fernando	1934
Baldwin Park	1934
Centerville	1934
Seattle	1939
Cambell (Later the Santa Clara)	1953
Chicago	1954
West Los Angeles	1955

Source: Kishi 1975; Suehiro 1972:131-36.

In 1942 all churches, except the Honolulu Holiness Church,
were closed due to the relocation of the Japanese from the West
Coast. The first Holiness Church to be reopened was at Los
Angeles by George Yashiro in 1945. In the following year,
churches in San Diego, San Fernando, San Lorenzo and Seattle
were reopened (Kishi 1975). At present there are eight Holiness
churches, each one with two divisions, English and Japanese.
There are sixteen pastors and 1714 communicant members (Kishi
1975).

THE FREE METHODIST CHURCH

The Free Methodist Church among the Japanese in the United States was started by American home missionaries, a majority of whom were women—some of the missionaries were Free Methodists, and some joined the Free Methodist Church later. The churches in northern and southern California were started without being dependent upon each other and it was not until 1913 that financial support of the General Missionary Board was instituted when it was voted to grant financial assistance to a Free Methodist missionary working among Japanese at what was then called the Port of Los Angeles (Yamada 1966:22-23).

All the Japanese churches were part of the Caucasian conference up to 1932, when they were organized as a separate missionary conference under the name "Pacific Coast Japanese Free Methodist Conference." As a missionary conference it came under the jurisdiction of the General Missionary Board (Yamada 1966:32). In 1963, the conference became a regular, full conference and thus a part of the General Conference of the Free Methodist Church of North America. Since then it has become self-supporting and now is contributing $18,000 a year to the general treasury of the denomination. It is also supporting a missionary family in Paraguay, and is contributing to other interdenominational missionary agencies working in Japan and in Brazil.

The PCJFMC has nine churches with nine English-speaking and five Japanese-speaking pastors. The locations, year of founding, and the names of the founders are given below.

TABLE 21

JAPANESE FREE METHODIST CHURCHES IN THE U.S.

Church	Year Founded	Founder
Phoenix	1912	D. H. and M. Thornton
Berkeley-Richmond	1916	Lillian Pool (later Burnett)
Los Angeles	1916	Sam Mizukami and Maude Thornton
Anaheim	1916	Chose Miyabe and Yoshimasa Shigekawa
Glendale	1921	Julian Soper and A. W. Van Loon
Venice-Santa Monica	1925	Lillian Burnett
Gallup	1935	Juro Kashitani and Berly Manyon
Redwood City	1951	Frank Omi
Fowler	1954	Yoshimasa Shigekawa
South Bay	1964	Kay Sakaguchi

Source: Yamada 1966:28-32,39,40.

GROWTH COMPARED

We turn now to a comparison of the growth of the three denominations in the United States and Brazil. Looking at Figure 22 we
note that they are very much alike in spite of the fact that they
are situated in two entirely different countries. Ranging
between 800 and 1700 in membership, there is no remarkably large
church. We note also the likeness between the Episcopal Church,
the Free Methodist Church, and the Holiness Church in Brazil, and
these same three groups in the United States.

In the case of the size of the Episcopal Church, in both
countries we see very little difference and the growth pattern of
each is almost identical; a growth period followed by a period of
decline. We have already explained what happened to the Episcopal
Church in Brazil. With respect to the Episcopal Church in the
United States we want to only mention what happened to cause the
decline in membership after fifteen years of a steady and accelerating growth. As Figure 23 shows, there were two fast growing
Episcopal churches in the United States--St. Mary's Church in Los
Angeles and the Holy Trinity Church in Honolulu. As we have
already mentioned, Holy Trinity Church grew rapidly under the
leadership of Fr. Ozaki who took its pastorate in 1942. He
worked in that church until 1958 when he suddenly died. Figure
23 indicates that the decline in membership began in 1960 and
apparently the church went through many crises up to 1970 when
it was dissolved by congregational request. As Trinity Church
was the largest Episcopal church, its decline and final extinc-
tion greatly affected the growth of the Episcopal Japanese
churches in the United States.

When we compare the average annual growth rate of the two
Episcopal Churches we see that the Episcopal Church in the United
States has grown faster than its counterpart in Brazil--6.1
percent against 4.3 percent. In fifteen years it has reached
about the same membership that its Brazilian counterpart took
twenty-five years to reach. The growth of the Episcopal Church
in the United States was accelerated by the fast growth of the
Holy Trinity and Saint's Mary churches, both located in places
of heavy Japanese population, Honolulu and Los Angeles,
respectively.

FIGURE 24

MEMBERS OF THE EPISCOPAL, THE FREE METHODIST,
AND THE HOLINESS CHURCHES IN THE U.S. AND BRAZIL

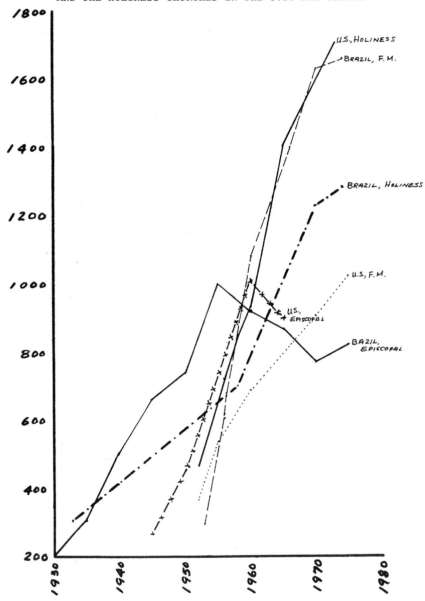

FIGURE 25

MEMBERS OF THE JAPANESE EPISCOPAL
CHURCHES IN THE UNITED STATES

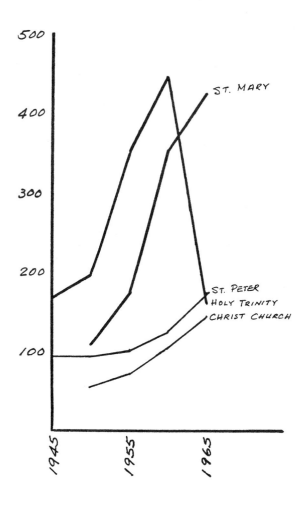

If we compare the Holiness Church and the Free Methodist
Church in the two countries, we have a 6.1 percent per year
growth for the Holiness Church in this country against 3.2 percent for its Brazilian counterpart, and a 5.0 percent per year
growth for the Free Methodist in the United States against 8.4
percent for its counterpart in Brazil. The Holiness Church has
grown faster in the United States, while the Free Methodist
church has grown faster in Brazil. Since we have already spoken
about the growth of these Churches in Brazil, a few words on
their growth in this country will suffice. Both the Holiness
and Free Methodist Churches have grown fairly quickly in the
period we have been studying—1952 to 1972, mainly because of
the incorporation of the *Nisei* (second generation) in the
forties and fifties, and of the *Sansei* (third generation) in the
sixties and seventies. The second generation reached their
adulthood in the forties and early fifties. Many of them were
children of Issei Christians and others came from non-Christian
parents. The main means of reaching them was Sunday school and
activities related to it. The third generation is being won
mainly by the same method. In both denominations, churches have
grown faster in urban areas, especially in the sections of a
heavy concentration of Japanese population. An exception to
this is the Honolulu church which has not grown. With regard
to the growth of the Holiness churches we should mention the
Los Angeles Holiness Church whose membership comprises one-third
of the entire conference. This is one of the few churches within
the homogeneous unit of our study which has exceeded 500 in
membership. Without delving into the why and how of its growth,
we want to mention one factor that may have contributed—its
location. This church is located in an area where there was a
very heavy Japanese concentration until a decade ago. In the
past ten years Japanese have been moving out, and this may be
the reason for its decline after 1970.

When we compare the average annual growth rates we note that
there is much more similarity between churches in the United
States than in Brazil. In this country the growth rates are
6.1 percent (E), 5.9 percent (H), and 5.0 percent (FM), which
are pretty close to one another, whereas in Brazil the rates are
8.4 percent (FM), 4.3 percent (E), and 3.2 percent (H). This
means that denominational difference is greater in Brazil than
in the United States.

We may conclude this chapter saying that from Figure 22 there
is no evidence that the country variable has had an important
bearing on the growth of the churches of our study. More evident
is the ethnicity in Japanese Churches which makes them alike
even though located in two different countries. More noticeable
also are denominational differences between the Episcopal Church
on the one hand and the Holiness and Free Methodist Churches on

FIGURE 26

MEMBERS OF THE JAPANESE HOLINESS
CHURCHES IN THE UNITED STATES

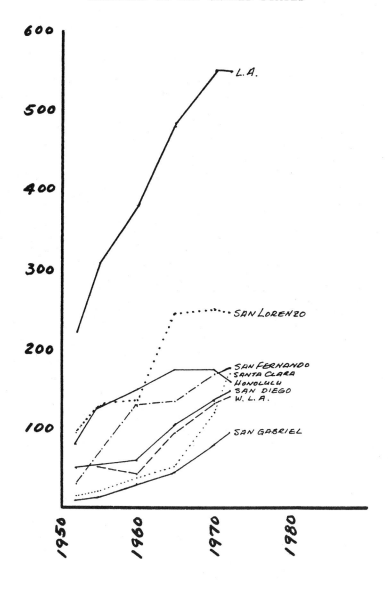

the other. We have cited some factors that may have hindered the
Episcopal Church in both countries, but also contributing to this
may be the absence in this denomination of an autonomous structure to deal with the evangelization of this particular homogeneous unit.

One question that may arise regarding the subject of this
chapter is why Protestant Churches have not grown faster in the
United States than in Brazil. This being a "Protestant country"
shouldn't immigrants and their descendants be more receptive to
the Protestant faith here than in Brazil, a Catholic country?
This is a very reasonable question, but we must consider other
variables that play a role in church growth. Japanese Protestants in the United States have faced some obstacles that their
counterparts to the South have not experienced. One of them is
the presence of very strong Buddhist churches. In this country,
from the early years of Japanese immigration, Buddhist churches
have been established in the Japanese community. They have
adopted the Christian method of religious education (Sunday
schools and songs of praise to Buddha instead of to God) and
Christian titles, such as reverend and bishop for their priests.
Usually they are tied to the Japanese community centers and
exert much influence upon its cultural life relating it to the
Japanese tradition and language. This is attested by the
presence of splendid Buddhist temples wherever a Japanese
community exists, in Hawaii or on the Mainland. There is no
doubt that these Buddhist churches have been a big obstacle to
the evangelization of the Japanese in the United States.

The Japanese government did not allow Buddhist priests to
emmigrate to Brazil, due to the fear that it would sow the seed
of anti-Japanese feeling. Japan had had enough of that sort of
experience in North America, and the thought may have been that
establishing Buddhist churches in Brazil would create problems.
Without Buddhist priests and churches, Protestant missionaries
could work more freely in Brazil. Only after World War II did
some Buddhist priests come to Brazil and Buddhist temples were
built.

Thus, while in Brazil we cannot consider the presence of
Buddhism as the major obstacle to the evangelication of Japanese,
a different obstacle in Brazil may have been the fact that
Protestantism is not a religion of the majority. A proof of
this is that in 1958, 43.5 percent of the Japanese seven years
and up declared Catholicism as their religion (Suzuki 1969:123)
and, in 1974, according to the Jesuit priest, Father Takeuchi,
60 percent of them declared that they had been baptized in the
Catholic Church (Takeuchi 1974).

FIGURE 27

MEMBERS OF THE JAPANESE FREE METHODIST
CHURCHES IN THE UNITED STATES

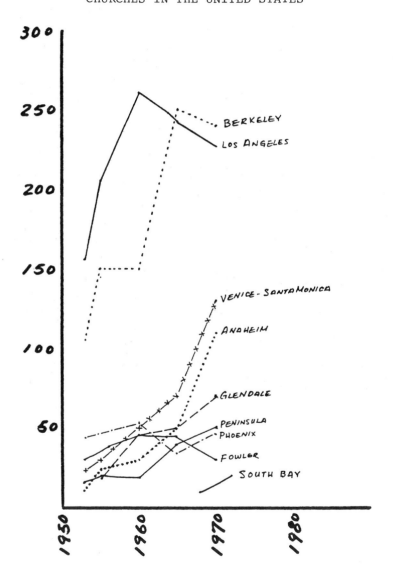

FIGURE 28

THE GROWTH OF THE THREE CHURCHES IN BRAZIL

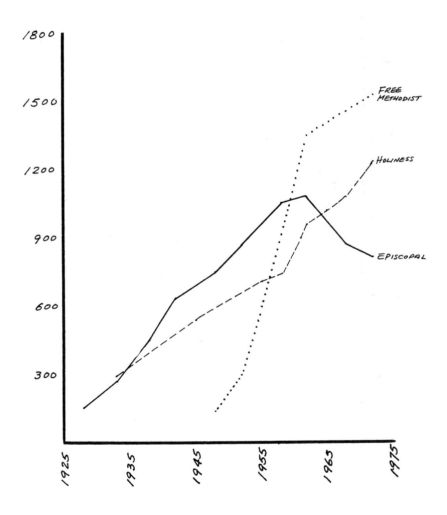

There are other factors that may also be considered as advantageous or disadvantageous for the evangelization of the Japanese living in North and South America, but we will leave this for the study of someone else.

7

Suggested Strategy
for the Future

When we take church membership into consideration, we can say
that Protestant missions have not been successful in winning
Japanese, either in Japan or overseas. The harvest has been
rather meager. After one hundred and seventeen years of Protestant missions, the number of church members is only 0.7 percent
of the total population of Japan; in the United States, after
one hundred years of missionary work, the percentage is about
3.0 percent; and in Brazil, after half a century of discipling,
church membership does not exceed 0.6 percent of the total
Japanese population. This makes any church statesman or
missionary strategist think seriously about the reasons for
this poor result. Aware of the difficulty of this problem, we
have tried to find some reasons for growth and non-growth of the
Japanese Churches in Brazil. Now, using our findings and
insights gained from other sources, we want to suggest a strategy
for the future evangelization of the Japanese in Brazil. In any
strategy it is essential to define the goal we want to reach and
then to find effective means to reach that goal. And this is
what we want to do in this chapter.

THE GOAL

The goal of evangelization is to make disciples of all
nations (*panta ta ethne*). As disciples of Christ we are under
His divine command to go, to preach, and to make disciples. The
Great Commission is given to the Church as "an irreplaceable
task" and she cannot leave it unfulfilled without being unfaith-
ful to the risen Lord. Mission is deeply rooted in the very
nature of God, who is love. Because He is love, even when man

refused to cooperate with Him in reaching His purpose of creation, He sent His only begotten Son to redeem rebellious man.
He is a God who sends. First He sent His prophets, then His Son,
the Holy Spirit, the Apostles, and the Church. As Christ was
sent by the Father so He sends the Church: "As the Father has
sent me, even so I send you" (John 20:21). And Jesus who sends
His Church also commands: "Go therefore and make disciples of
all nations, baptizing them in the name of the Father and of the
Son and of the Holy Spirit, teaching them to observe all that I
have commanded you; and lo, I am with you always, to the close
of the age" (Matt. 28:19-20).

The reason why God gave His only begotten Son was "that
whosoever believes in Him should not perish but have eternal
life" (John 3:16). God wishes no one to perish (Matt. 18:14;
II Peter 3:9). He wants all men to come to repentance and to be
saved (I Tim. 2:4). Christ died, rose again, and ascended unto
heaven, but His redemptive work must be carried out by the Church
to the end of earth and until His second return. The Church is
given this glorious task of partaking in God's work of redemption.
Far from being finished, mission must continue to the end of
human history (Mk. 13:10; Matt. 24:14). Since God's will is to
save all men, He commands His Church to go and to make disciples
through the proclamation of the gospel. According to the Great
Commission as we find it in Matthew 24:19-20, the goal of
evangelization is to make disciples. To go and to preach are
rather means to an end--to make disciples. It is very important
to make this clear, for some people think of evangelism in terms
of presence only or as proclamation only. They think that all
we have to do is to go live a godly life or to go and proclaim
the gospel leaving the result up to God. It is true that the
acts of conversion and regeneration depend solely on the Holy
Spirit, but if our concern is the salvation of the lost, we will
not rest until we see them found and saved. This is what Jesus
teaches us in His parable of the lost sheep (Matt. 18:10-14;
Lk. 15:3-7). The purpose of Christ's coming to this world was
to seek and to save the lost (Lk. 19:10). As children of God
and as disciples and followers of Jesus Christ we should share
the will of the Father and of the Son.

As early as the seventeenth century, the Dutch theologian
Voetius stated the task of mission as threefold: "1) to convert
the heathen, 2) to establish churches, and 3) to glorify and
proclaim divine grace" (Beyerhaus 1971:17-18). To convert the
heathen and to incorporate them into the fellowship of the body
of Christ is the essential task of mission. To make disciples
and to establish churches is therefore the right goal in a
missionary strategy. In our case, to convert the Japanese in
Brazil and to establish churches among them must be the goal.

WHAT IS NECESSARY TO REACH THE JAPANESE OF BRAZIL?

First of all we must find where they are. One advantage we have is their geographical distribution. Figure 27 shows that 75 percent of the Japanese of Brazil live in the State of Sao Paulo, and 18.7 percent in the neighboring State of Parana. This means that nearly 94 percent of them live in an area equivalent in size to the State of California. We may say that this is a heavy concentration of Japanese when it is compared to the distribution of Japanese in the United States. In this country, according to the 1970 census, 36.75 percent of the Japanese live in Hawaii, 36.08 percent in California, and the rest, 27.17 percent, in other states across the country. This scattering of Japanese in a huge country like this makes their evangelization difficult. In Brazil, there are more Japanese in an area the size of California than in the whole United States. This concentration of Japanese in a much narrower area should facilitate the task of reaching them.

Finding the Receptive Area

To find receptive areas is important in any missionary strategy. Our findings have shown that churches located in the city of Sao Paulo have enjoyed a faster growth than those located in the cities of the interior, or in rural areas. And within the city of Sao Paulo, the churches located in the *bairros* of heavier Japanese concentration--for example, Bosque, Saude, and Pinheiros--have grown faster than those located in the less populated *bairros*. This is true also in the United States where the churches in the cities of large Japanese concentration like Honolulu and Los Angeles have grown faster and bigger. Following the general trend, Japanese have migrated from the interior to the city of Sao Paulo and to its surrounding areas such as Campinas, Sorocaba, Atibaia, Braganca, Mogi das Cruzes, and Sao Jose dos Campos. There were 180,000 Japanese in the city of Sao Paulo in 1974 (Consulado Geral do Japao 1974:7). We do not have the exact figure of the Japanese living in the vicinities of that city, but based on the information we do have, we may safely say that there are around 50,000. Since Sao Paulo is where the largest number of Japanese are moving, we may assume that it is the most responsive area. Being a megalopolis where people are threatened with becoming nobodies, the new-comers look for a new association, a fellowship and a sense of belonging. The church can meet this need. Many more churches can be planted in Sao Paulo and all have a good possibility of growth. Besides Sao Paulo, the surrounding cities where Japanese are moving in are also promising. Moreover, other metropolitan centers such as Rio de Janeiro, Curitiba, and Brasilia, where practically no Japanese churches exist, offer a good opportunity for church planting and growth. With the

FIGURE 29

DISTRIBUTION OF THE JAPANESE
POPULATION IN BRAZIL

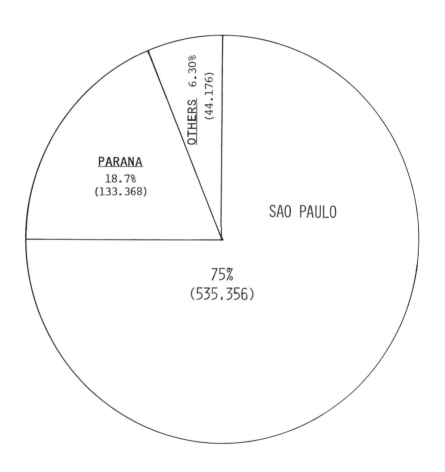

OTHERS 6.30%
(44.176)

PARANA
18.7%
(133.368)

SAO PAULO

75%
(535.356)

FIGURE 30

JAPANESE POPULATION IN THE U.S.
ACCORDING TO THE 1970 CENSUS

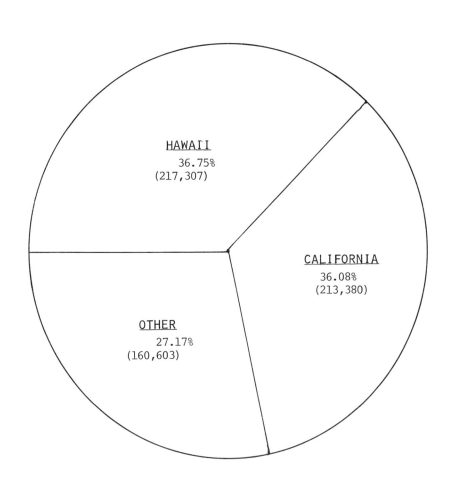

HAWAII
36.75%
(217,307)

CALIFORNIA
36.08%
(213,380)

OTHER
27.17%
(160,603)

ongoing process of industrialization and urbanization, we should
expect that more and more Japanese will be moving from rural
areas to the cities, from small cities to larger cities, and
from these cities to the megalopolis of Sao Paulo. One-half of
the Japanese who still live in rural areas will continue to move
to the cities in the coming years. We should expect that this
mobility and social change will facilitate the receptivity of
the Japanese in the years to come. Willems attributes the
phenomenal growth of the Pentecostal Churches in Brazil and
Chile to the great social change that is taking place in these
countries (Willems 1967:255-56). Japanese too are in the midst
of this social and cultural change and may be won if the
churches use right methods and approaches. The churches must be
sensitive to the phenomenon of migration and urbanization which
is going on in an intensive way and take advantage of this
unique opportunity.

Training Leaders

    At present there are over sixty churches with seventy pastors
and missionaries who are working with Japanese in Brazil. If we
are to reach the population that in ten years will be one
million, the most urgent task is the training of new leaders.
Of course we have to pray to the Lord of harvest to send more
workers, but at the same time we must train those whom God is
calling. In training leaders we have to bear in mind the fact
that 80 percent of the Japanese in Brazil are Nisei and Sansei,
and that the Portuguese speaking segment will increase while the
Japanese speaking segment will decrease as the Issei decrease.
Unless some change takes place in the economical situation of
Japan and in the Brazilian immigration law, we cannot expect
that many immigrants will come into Brazil in the near future.
This means that if we are to reach the Japanese in Brazil we
have to train many more Portuguese speaking leaders. At present
only thirteen out of seventy pastors and missionaries are Nisei.
This ratio is just reverse of what it should be since the total
population of Nisei and Sansei constitute 80 percent, and Issei
only 20 percent. Actually we need more Japanese-speaking
leaders, but also many more Portuguese-speaking leaders. Unless
Brazilian Japanese churches increase the number of Portuguese-
speaking leaders and their Portuguese-speaking constituency,
within ten or fifteen years they will become dying churches as
is the case of Japanese-speaking congregations in the United
States. In this country the influx of new immigrants in the
past twenty years has become a revitalizing factor to the
Japanese-speaking congregations, but in Brazil where the Japanese
immigration has fallen drastically since 1968, it is unlikely
that a similar experience will take place. Thus the training of
Nisei and Sansei leaders is the most urgent need that admits no
delay.

In the training of leaders it is necessary to think of a
multi-level leadership instead of one type of leader. McGavran
speaks of the five classes of leaders. He calls Class One
leaders those who are engaged in the maintenance ministry of the
church. They are deacons, elders, Sunday school teachers,
ushers, and choir members. The Class Two leaders are those who
volunteer for outreach ministry, going out two by two to win
people of the community. The Class Three leaders are unpaid or
half-paid lay ministers who are in charge of small congregations.
The Class Four leaders are paid, professional leaders of large
and well established congregations. The Class Five leaders are
denominational or district leaders (McGavran and Arn 1974:89-97).

For the evangelization of the Japanese in Brazil the first
four classes of leaders are particularly important. Class One
leaders must be trained to improve the quality of the church
maintenance ministry. They are, with the pastor, responsible
for the nurture and perfection growth of the church members.
They contribute by leading each member of the body of Christ to
Christian maturity. In Brazil the Class One leaders usually
have not received an adequate training to discharge their
functions. Class Two leaders are indispensable for the membership growth of the existing congregations. It is strange that
in Brazil and even in the United States due attention has not
been given to such an important subject. Class One and Class
Four leaders are all people think about when they talk of
leadership training. No church can really grow in membership
without this class of leaders. If the Japanese churches in
Brazil expect to grow, a serious consideration must be given to
the training of the Class Two leaders. Class Three leaders are
indispensable for the multiplication and maintenance of small
congregations. To win the Japanese in Brazil we must not think
only in terms of churches with their edifices and paid pastors.
By this method evangelization becomes so expensive and unafford-
able that the Churches will never accomplish the goal of
discipling the Japanese. Only through adequately trained unpaid
lay leaders can the Christianization of Japanese in Brazil
become conceiveable. When the Churches succeed in training
hundreds of lay leaders they may say that their goal is not an
impossible dream. This method is being used with great success
by the Pentecostal Churches, and there is no reason that it will
not work with Japanese. Class Four leaders are also necessary.
They are needed in the well established churches which can
support full-time pastors. Particularly in the cities where
there are more sophisticated people, well trained ministers can
work more effectively. They look up to and listen to a minister
who has *cultura* (a high education).

One question that remains regarding leadership training is
how to do it. There were three theological institutions where

Japanese ministerial candidates have received their training:
the Episcopal seminary, formerly in Poqto Alegre, moved to Sao
Paulo in the early sixties and was closed recently for reasons
unknown to the writer; the OMS seminary in Londrina; and the
Free Methodist seminary in Sao Paulo. There are, of course,
ministers who have received their training in other institutions. For the growth of the Japanese Chruches in particular,
the other Brazilian Churches in general, a revamping of
theological education is necessary. Instead of taking European
and American institutions as a model, they should adapt their
program to the local needs. In a country like Brazil at least
three levels of training programs are needed: one for the
pastors of urban middle-class churches; another for the
ministers who work among urban masses; and finally for the
pastors who work in rural areas. In cases of the Japanese the
situation is a little different, for most of them belong to the
Brazilian middle class, old or new. Still, we can think of two
types of ministers needed: those who work in the cities, and
those who work in rural areas. Seminaries should also provide
a program for the training of Class One, Two, and Three leaders.
For the students who cannot attend seminary because of distance,
age, or the family situation, a Theological Education by
Extension program is the answer. It is widely used in Brazil
with excellent results and can be used in the training of
leaders of the Japanese churches. It offers the great advantage
of training leaders without dislocating them from their social
and cultural milieu which is essential for ministering to their
own. Many ministerial candidates who come from the interior
and receive their training in a city like Sao Paulo have
difficulty in ministering to their own people due to the social
and cultural dislocation they go through.

Another important factor in the training of soul-winners and
church planters is the creation and maintenance of an "atmosphere of perennial evangelism" as says Clark Scanlon:

> To grow to their full stature as soul-winners, students
> must be taking courses and reading books and at the same
> time be at work in searching for the lost. During vaca-
> tion months students can help in or even lead evangelistic
> campaigns.

> Then too, through the year, students should be kept in an
> atmosphere of a perennial evangelism. In El Salvador the
> students of a Bible school carried out the Great Commission
> so well that the number of churches in the immediate area
> grew from 78 in 1954 to 210 in 1960. By the Spirit's help,
> perennial evangelism can produce the same type of results
> in other countries (Scanlon 1962:60).

The participation of the faculty in evangelism is also important for church growth. The problem is that sometimes seminary
graduates with no experience in the pastorate or in church
planting evangelism become seminary or Bible institute teachers.
They are unable to teach evangelism for they have no experience.
Regarding this type of seminary instructor Greenway says:

> A professor who knows nothing about evangelism, church
> planting, and the application of God's Word to society at
> large from personal experience is nothing more than an
> academic mole forever buried in the world of books and
> institutions. He will be a failure in any kind of educa-
> tional system, and he will produce a sizeable number of
> students just like himself (Greenway 1973:195).

The training of leaders for church growth experience in the
pastorate and in evangelism is essential. The future adminis-
trators of the theological institutions in Brazil must bear this
fact in mind when they select new members of their faculty if
they want their institutions to make a positive contribution to
the growth of the churches.

Besides theological institutions, local churches can provide
lay training programs with the help of an expert in each field.
This way the Class One, Two, and Three leaders can receive their
training in the local churches. Each denomination should take
this program very seriously and encourage each local church to
carry out this type of work.

Multiplying Churches

Neil Braun suggests that multiplying churches is the most
important way to evangelize Japan. By this he means starting
new congregations. He presents facts from many countries to
support his theory which is that in order to grow, a church must
"multiply" churches. He shows by statistics how denominations
that have multiplied churches have grown and how those which
failed to multiply churches have not grown. We want to use
some of his data in order to illustrate this important point.

TABLE 22

ALL PROTESTANTS IN JAPAN, BAPTISTS IN BRAZIL,
AND ROMAN CATHOLICS IN JAPAN

Year	Churches	Communicant Members
PROTESTANTS IN JAPAN		
1882	93	4,987
1888	249	25,514
1913	877	89,347
BAPTISTS IN BRAZIL		
1882	2	50
1890	5	500
1900	30	2,000
1910	110	9,200
1920	210	19,200
1930	440	34,000
1940	740	59,000
1950	1,000	100,000
ROMAN CATHOLICS IN JAPAN		
1950	497	141,286
1952	445	174,527
1954	650	218,457
1956	725	246,232
1958	811	261,454
1960	1,028	301,901
1962	1,044	323,599
1964	888	305,832
1966	993	333,265

Source: Braun 1971:21,23,26

Braun also shows how in Japan the United Church and the Episcopal Church did not increase the number of their churches in the period between 1949-63 and consequently did not experience any church growth. On the contrary, the Lutherans and Baptists, which multiplied their churches, experienced a remarkable growth in the same period (*Ibid*. 24-25). He also shows how the Baptists and Methodists in America grew in the period between 1750 and 1950 by multiplying churches. His argument is that if Japan is to be won for Christ, the secret resides in multiplying churches in every village of Japan.

   We think his theory is applicable to the case of the evangelization of the Japanese in Brazil too.* At the rate Churches are
growing in Brazil we will never achieve the goal of Christianiz-
ing the Japanese living there. The rate of growth between the
Japanese total population and Japanese Christians (Protestants)
was 1.8 percent in 1958, and now, after nearly twenty years, it
has not changed. Unless we adopt another method, the evangelization of the Japanese in Brazil is an impossible task. But by
the method suggested by Braun, we think the task does not seem
beyond our reach. In 1800 the church members in the United
States were less than 10 percent of the total population. But
in 1910 they had grown to 43 percent, and in 1960, to 60 percent.
And this is a great encouragement to the churches which are
struggling in the countries where they are less than 10 percent
of the total population. We know that the situation in other
countries is different from that of the United States, but we
still believe that the theory is valid and works in different
situations. If the Japanese Protestant Churches can attain and
maintain an annual growth rate three times faster than the total
population, which is not more than many other churches are doing,
fifty years from now their community will be over 30 percent of
the total Japanese population. Supposing that the Japanese
population of Brazil will grow at a rate of 3 percent per year
for the coming fifty years and that the Japanese Protestant
community will grow three times faster in the same period, let
us see what may happen:

TABLE 23

THE RATIO OF THE JAPANESE POPULATION AND ITS PROTESTANT
COMMUNITY IN THE COMING FIFTY YEARS
(Hypothetical Figures)

Year	Total Japanese Population	Japanese Protestant Community	Percentage
1976	800,000	15,000	1.8%
1986	1,075,133	35,000	3.3
1996	1,444,889	84,067	5.8
2006	1,941,810	199,015	10.2
2016	2,609,630	471,141	18.1
2026	3,507,125	1,115,363	31.8

Note: The rate of the Brazilian population growth is 2.7 percent
       per year and since the fertility of the Japanese of Brazil
       is higher than that of the general population of that country,
       we are estimating its growth rate to 3 percent per year.

* To see the relationship between multiplying churches and
   membership growth in the case of the Japanese Churches in
   Brazil see p. 55.

One pertinent question to be asked at this point is how many
churches should be planted to Christianize the Japanese in
Brazil? In the United States there is one church for every
thousand people. Braun says that in order to evangelize Japan
it is necessary to plant a church in every community. In Brazil
we need to plant one church wherever there are one thousand
people, two churches wherever there are two thousand people, and
so on, if we want every Japanese to hear the gospel and be saved.
This means the planting of nearly 800 new churches and increasing
their number each year proportionally as the general population
increases. Isn't that an impossible dream? Yes, it is an
impossible dream if we think of establishing churches in terms
of traditional edifices and salaried pastors. But we know that
this is not the only method of church planting. It is not the
New Testament method either.

An expensive edifice and a large pastor's salary are the two
most onerous burdens for a church. If we can eliminate the
edifice burden, church planting and maintenance will become less
difficult and more feasible. In the New Testament we frequently
notice Paul talking about house churches (1 Cor. 16:19; Col. 4:15;
Phil. 2). These churches met in the houses of Aquila, Nympha and
Philemon. With this type of small church that meets in the
believers' homes we can multiply to hundreds and thousands without creating an onerous burden to their members. Furthermore,
following this method we can plant and multiply churches in
Brazil wherever a few families of Japanese live.

The second problem in church planting is the support of the
pastor. Here again we should ask whether a paid pastor is
necessary for every church. Recent researches have shown that
it was not until several centuries after the Apostolic churches
were founded that the clergy began to receive full support
(Braun 1971:35-39). It was through unpaid lay evangelists and
pastors that the Methodist and Baptist Churches spread and grew
in the American frontiers in the nineteenth century (Braun 1971:
51-57). The same we may say about the Pentecostal Churches in
Latin America where they are experiencing a phenomenal growth by
the work of their unpaid and half-paid lay ministers. The
Japanese Churches in Brazil have to learn from the New Testament
and from the Pentecostal Churches in developing an unpaid and
half-paid lay ministry. These are the Class Three leaders we
have talked about.

With this we are not saying that edifices and paid professional
clergy are unnecessary. They are needed and important. A paid
professional clergyman has an important role to play in the
church. Our contention is, however, that if we only count on
the paid clergy for the evangelization of the Japanese in Brazil
and think of multiplying churches in terms of building only, we

will never fulfill the great Commission of our Lord. If the
winning of one million Japanese is our goal, we cannot continue
in the present pace of evangelism. A much faster way of discipling must be engineered. We believe that in the multiplying of
the New Testament-type house churches and by using unpaid
ministers, we will find the solution of the problem of the
evangelization of the Japanese in Brazil.

Involving the Laity

Christianity began as a lay movement. Jesus Christ was not a
professional clergyman nor were his twelve disciples. The
priesthood of all believers was one of the three basic principles
of the Reformers. Yet this principle never came to be fully
applied in the Protestant Churches. Recently we have had two
great advocates of the theology of laity, Kraemer and Congar.
Kraemer said that the laity in the modern churches is "frozen
credits and dead capital" (1958:176). Braun's contention is
that if Japan is to be Christianized, the Japanese laity must
be mobilized to carry out the Great Commission. We must say the
same regarding the Christianization of the Japanese in Brazil.
If we leave it up to the clergy alone, this task will never be
fulfilled. Only through the mobilization of the laity can we
realize the discipling of the Japanese. According to the Latin
American mission the three fastest growing movements in their
field were the communists, Jehovah Witnesses, and Pentecostals.
They are very different in doctrine and purpose, but one thing
they all have in common is the mobilization and involvement of
their laity in making converts (Ford 1966:47). Kenneth J. Dale
has done excellent research on the Rissho Koseikai, a Nichiren
sect, that has close to five million members. It has a pattern
of amazing growth for a religious sect that began in 1938.
Dale mentions that all the leaders of the Rissho Koseikai are laymen
or laywomen who are appointed, not on the basis of their educational qualifications, but on the basis of their ability to lead
and teach. Dale says that lay leadership constitutes one of
the keys to the secret of the Rissho Koseikai's success and the
success of other new religions in Japan. Unlike theologically
trained leaders who may be absorbed in theological abstractions,
lay leaders stay close to the everyday life of the people (Dale
1975:156-57).

One important question concerning lay involvement is how to
train them. Braun presents the case of the lay workers' training
by the Presbyterian Church of Korea and the Christian and
Missionary Alliance in the Philippines. In Korea a lay training
class was started in 1890 by Nevius. The first class started in
the house of a missionary with seven men in attendance. In 1891
a rule was adopted requiring every missionary to "work out a
course of Scripture instructions for each sub-station according

to the general plan approved by the mission (Braun 1971:141).
This program developed successfully and in 1909 in the area of
the Presbyterian Mission 50,000 people attended about 800
classes that were being held. Each of 3,000 congregations conducted a Bible class once or twice a year. These classes lasted
from five to ten days. Elders, pastors, and other teachers
taught the Bible in the morning, visitation evangelism was
carried out in the afternoon, and in the evening old-fashioned,
Moody-type revival services were held.

At another level of training were annual Bible institutes, six
weeks for men and ten weeks for women. The annual sessions were
a part of a course designed for completion in five years. In
1936, 4,509 persons attended these institutes. They paid their
own expenses.

Above all these were the seminaries for the training of the
clergy.

Further, a strong Bible correspondence course program was
carried out. In 1938, 10,000 students were enrolled in this
program.

The teachers of these courses were missionaries in the
beginning, but later the national pastors and laymen and laywomen participated in this ministry. The subjects taught were
the Bible, evangelism, and effective church work (Braun 1971:
141-42).

In the Philippines a "Lay Preacher Training" institute was
carried out by the Christian and Missionary Alliance. A one-
week session was conducted every three months. Between sessions
students engaged in home study and practical Christian work in
their spare time. The subjects taught were: Old Testament
books, sermonology, Sunday school, music, evangelism and basic
doctrines, and hygiene. The institutes moved from one place to
another so that people from nearby churches could attend. In
1963 the Christian and Missionary Alliance Board in New York
reported that of over 500 churches, half had been founded and
were currently led by trained laymen (Braun 1971:145).

We firmly believe that lay training programs similar to
those conducted in Korea and the Philippines are possible in
Brazil. First, we think that each local church has to have its
own lay training course. The pastor must be the first teacher.
Then he can train a few capable laymen to be teachers with him.
He can use Sunday school time for that purpose or have one night
a week for training of the laity. The Jehovah Witnesses in
Glendale, California, have their leaders' training session on
Tuesday evenings from 7:00 to 9:00 p.m. That is a good time
for the Japanese churches in Brazil, too.

Lay training programs can and should be carried out on denominational and interdenominational levels. In this way pastors and laymen of a certain area can cooperate, and the problem of a lack of teachers can be minimized.

Seminaries and Bible institutes should be involved in the training of lay leaders. In Sao Paulo, the Free Methodist seminary is ideally located for this type of program. Its accessibility to the Japanese community through the subway and bus-lines makes its site ideal. Thus the seminary professors can be directly involved in the ministry of finding the lost.

Braun says that in Korea the lay training institutes had five to ten day sessions annually or even every three months (1971:141). Like in Japan, in Brazil it is almost impossible to conduct lay training courses with schedules similar to those in Korea and the Philippines. People are extremely busy and they cannot afford setting aside ten or fifteen days a year for training. In Brazil a better schedule would be for most of the schools to function at night. One course could be offered every ten weeks with two-hour classes one night a week. This way about four subjects could be taught in one year. The Bible, Christian doctrine, history of Christian movements, personal evangelism, and homiletics are the more essential subjects for lay workers. The teaching materials of TEE can be used with a good result. For teaching personal evangelism *Kokoro to Kororo no Dendo* by Masumi Toyotome, Campus Crusade's *Four Spiritual Laws* (Japanese, Portuguese), and James Kennedy's *Evangelism Explosion* may be used with adaptation to the Japanese situation in Brazil.

In teaching these subjects, the teachers must be careful to teach them in a simple, clear, and easily understandable way. Dale points out that one of the causes of the Rissho Koseikai's success is the way its teachers teach the difficult doctrines of the Lotus Sutra. They are trained to present the message in a way very easy for the common people to understand. The message is related to the daily life of the people. Japanese Christian preachers and teachers have much to learn from the lay leaders of the Rissho Koseikai.

Homogeneous Unit

To pay attention to the homogeneous unit is very important in understanding church growth or non-growth. According to McGavran, each homogeneous unit Church has its own pattern of growth, its own rate of growth, its own limitations, and its own *elan vital*, and churches grow very differently in homogeneous units (1974:2-4).

From the standpoint of the evangelization of the Japanese in
Brazil it is important to maintain and to multiply Japanese
ethnic churches. The reason is that unless we have ethnic
churches working with this particular group, its evangelization
cannot be accomplished. The fact is that in Brazil there are
many fast growing Brazilian churches but they have practically
no Japanese in attendance. The reverse is also true. There are
some Brazilians who attend Japanese churches because of a Nisei
or Sansei friend or because they have a special liking for the
Japanese people, culture, or language. But these cases are
rather accidental and quite unusual. And this is true in the
United States, too. In the San Fernando Valley, where the
author lives, there are two large Caucasian churches: The First
Baptist Church of Van Nuys and the Grace Community Church. The
former has over ten thousand members and the latter over two
thousand members. Both are very well attended. During one
summer vacation, the author went to visit these churches. To
his surprise he saw only a handful of Japanese in both churches,
and this was in the San Fernando Valley where there are over
1,500 Japanese households. This increased his conviction that
if we are to evangelize the Japanese, ethnic churches are
indispensable. People like to get together with those who are
like them. In a church where there is primary contact, people
like to be where they feel at home.

Of course we should ask, for how long such churches should
remain ethnic? In answer to this question Peter Wagner says
that it depends on how fast an ethnic group is being acculturated.
If the acculturative process is going on at an accelerated pace,
integration should be rapid. But if the process is slow,
integration should also be slow (1971:183). Regarding this same
question, McGavran thinks that when an ethnic church stops
growing faster than mere biological growth, it is time to
integrate. That is, if it is no longer making converts from its
own ethnic group, there is no more reason to remain as a
separate church. To remain as such means stagnation. It should
integrate in order to continue growing. Viewed from this point,
we may say that the Japanese Churches of our study, both in
Brazil and in this country, have a good reason to continue, at
least for the time being, as separate ethnic churches, for they
are growing faster than mere biological growth. Moreover, we
have seen the case of the Episcopal Church in Brazil whose
growth, as we see it, has been affected by the policy of integration.

One thing we have to consider here is that there are homogeneous units within homogeneous units. In the case of the
Japanese in Brazil, for instance, there are *Nisei* and *Sansei*
who linguistically and culturally are different from the Issei.
The reason why there are relatively few Nisei and Sansei

Christians is that the majority of the Christian workers have
been *Issei* up to the present. *Issei* have great limitations in
winning *Nisei* and *Sansei*, and vice-versa. We have to make a
distinction also between the Japanese living in the cities and
in the rural areas. The former are more cultured, more independent, less under social control, and freer to choose their
religion. There are also the post-war immigrants who are
different from the pre-war ones.

Avoiding Membership Leakage

The problem of membership leakage has been a very serious
one for the Christian churches all over Japan. Paul W. Boschman
in his research paper, *Church Growth in Miyazaki Prefecture*,
shows how in the period 1952-1963 the Mennonite Church, the
Southern Baptist Church, and the Bible Baptists gained and lost
their members.

TABLE 24

THE STATE OF THE CHURCHES IN 1963

Church	New Members	Active	Inact.	Rev.	Died	Non-Rev.
Mennonite	321	130(40%)	28(9%)	36(11%)	8(35%)	119(37%)
S.Baptist	253	104(42%)	15(6%)	55(21%)	8(3%)	71(28%)
B.Baptist	62	39(63%)	2(3%)	2(3%)	3(5%)	17(27%)

Source: Boschman 1964:26

The above data shows that if we include migration, death,
reversion, and inactive members, membership loss amounts to 60
percent for the Mennonites, 58 percent for the Southern Baptists,
and 37 percent for the Baptists. This means that over one-half
of the members received in that period by conversion or transfer
were lost. The lower percentage of loss by the Bible Baptists
was due, Boschman says, to the longer period of membership
instruction and the strict covenant at the time of incorporation.
He mentions three causes for this membership loss: the occupations, the ages, and the social structure. The Mennonite Church
constituency included salaried people (29 percent), housewives
(19 percent), and students (12 percent). The salaried people
were unstable because they changed jobs, and were transferred to
other cities. Students graduate from high school or college and
take up their vocations in new areas. The housewives are
unstable members because usually they are the only Christians in
the family and do not have an opportunity to express their faith
due to their subordinate position in Japanese society (Boschman
1964:30).

The second cause of the loss of members is attributed to the age of the people when they are received into the church. Persons baptized between the age of 10-29 constituted 65 percent, 57 percent, and 66 percent of the entire membership of the Mennonites, Southern Baptists and the Bible Baptists respectively. When they were baptized, about the same percentages (61, 53, and 64) were single and below the age of 30. This means that about two-thirds of the people were single and under thirty when they were baptized. With few exceptions they come from non-Christian families where they are the only Christians. In a society where the household and not the individual is the basic unit, the precariousness of these Christians is understandable (Boschman 1964:29).

The third cause for membership loss is due to the individual-istic approach used by the churches in reaching people. Boschman says that much attention must be given to the social structure of Japan. In rural Japan, the individual cannot make a decision by himself. He is under the control of the household he belongs to. But the household (*iye*), in its turn, is under the control of the *Buraku* (village). Because of mutual dependence at the time of planting and harvest, the Japanese farmer cannot act against the interests of the *buraku*. Thus, the interest of the individual is subordinate to that of the household, and this in its turn is subordinate to the *buraku*. When one individual (or a household) acts against the interest of the *buraku*, he is ostracized (*mura-hachibu*). In order to introduce Christianity into rural Japan it is therefore necessary to use a group approach, that is, to try to win one entire hosuehold and also the entire *buraku*. It is necessary to lead the people to make their decision as a group. The cause of much membership loss has been the ignorance of missionaries and pastors of the social structure of Japan. They have used an individualistic approach which in rural Japan has not worked. Instead of trying to con-vert individuals, they should have worked with the households and *buraku*. This way the converts would have been brought into the church fellowship without social dislocation. The possi-bility of their remaining in the church would have been much greater due to the group support they could enjoy.

Leslie Watson made a study on why Christians in Japan leave churches. His findings are based on the data furnished by 24 pastors who responded to the questionnaire he sent. The respon-dents represented six denominations: Non-Church group (2), Spirit of Jesus Church (3), Assembly of God (4), Baptist (10), Mennonite (2), and Lutheran (3). According to his findings people leave churches because of: 1) the lack of fellowship (2.5%), change of denomination (17%), reversion (12.4%), moving (12.4%), too busy (14.2%), marriage (13.2%), dissatisfaction (16.7%), and others (11.6%) (Watson 1968:172-194).

In Brazil, no similar research has been done as yet. But the problem of membership leakage is serious there too. The churches in the interior lose many members because they migrate to Sao Paulo or to other metropolitan areas like Curitiba, where large universities are located and job opportunities are better. When young people reach the age to attend college they move to the large cities, particularly Sao Paulo. And when they graduate the tendency is for them to stay in Sao Paulo which always offers greater employment opportunities. Usually the younger brothers or sisters follow the older ones. When all the children are graduated and settled in Sao Paulo, the parents also move to that city because they want to stay close to them. In this way, an exodus of members from the interior churches occurs. Often those young people who leave for Sao Paulo are leaders of the local youth group. They are the more capable and ambitious young people. When they leave, the local youth program is affected. Almost every pastor the author interviewed complained about this.

Some of those who migrate to Sao Paulo join a church of their denomination or some other denomination, but many of them are lost to Christian churches. An exact figure of those who are lost was not available to us, but according to the pastor of the Presidente Prudente Holiness Church, Kinji Kajimura, the loss is around 40 percent, while according to Samuel Sakuma, pastor of the Maringa Holiness Church, up to 70 percent are lost.

One reason why these young people are lost may be the lack of any Japanese church near to where they have moved. Another reason—probably the major one—is the different atmosphere in the churches of Sao Paulo and those of the interior. The family-like atmosphere of the small churches in the interior is not usually found in the churches in Sao Paulo, where people are less personal, and may seem less friendly to the people from the interior. To those used to the intimacy of the small rural church, this kind of change is quite shocking. Thus they go to church two or three times and then quit. This may be the end of their connection with the Christian church.

How can this problem be solved? One suggestion that we may make is that a follow-up ministry for this type of young migrant be started in Sao Paulo. The minister in charge should have a place where the students who move from the interior could meet regularly for worship, prayer, Bible study and fellowship. When they get used to the life style of Sao Paulo, they may be encouraged to join an existing church if they so desire. A ministry of this type may be supported by an interdenominational fund. It would be worthwhile for it would help bring a solution to the serious problem of membership leakage. Another solution would be to develop several family-like congregations in each local church.

Another problem related to membership loss are the inactive members (*yurei kain*, ghost members). In 1972 Saude Free Methodist Church eliminated 200 inactive members. Why do so many members become inactive? The reasons may be several but one responsible factor is, we think, the lack of post-baptismal care. Usually the church shows enthusiasm toward a person up to the time of his baptism and reception into church. After that the person is usually forgotten. The new members do not usually receive enough care in order to grow spiritually and to get involved in the church ministry. At this point, the example of the Seventh Day Adventist Church in Peru is worth imitating. It grew larger and faster than other denominations due to its very effective post-baptismal training program (McGavran 1970: 141). It would thus seem that an efficient program to indoctrinate the converts and to involve them in the church work, particularly in a soul-winning, outreach ministry, is very badly needed in Brazil.

This problem of the lack of post-baptismal care has been aggravated in Brazil due to the language handicap of the Issei ministers who have not been able to provide an adequate ministry in nurturing their Portuguese speaking Nisei lambs. The Great Commission includes the ministry of teaching: "...teaching them to observe all that I have commanded you" (Mt. 28:20). The same Lord also said to Peter: "Feed my lambs" (Jn. 21:15). We cannot expect the new believers to grow without feeding them satisfactorily.

Although we do not have any data related to the loss by marriage to people of other religions, it is safe to assume that some members are lost because of their marriage to Buddhists or Catholics. For the conservation of members and for their own happiness, Protestant churches must continue to encourage them to marry Protestant Christians.

As is true in Japan, the individualistic approach has its bearing in the membership leakage in the Japanese Churches in Brazil and also in the United States. Our observation supports the theory that a converted family is much more stable in its membership than a converted individual. People who have become Christians as a family have mostly remained in the church, whereas many of those who are won as individuals have left the churches. While a person is in the effervescence of his conversion he remains firm in his faith. As time goes by and his original fervor passes, his church attendance may decline, until finally he does not attend. If his family is Christian, he may receive encouragement to go back to church. He would also have the social support to keep up his faith. But when he is the only Christian in the family, he finds no support at home to remain loyal to the faith he has embraced. The result is the loss of his faith and a return to his former life.

This teaches us that in the case of Brazil too, we should try to win the household instead of isolated individuals. Since, the Japanese community is not divided in *mura* and *buraku*, as in Japan, and since the social pressure upon the household is not as strong as in Japan, the household enjoys more freedom to decide about religious matters. The winning of the family and extended family would be a good approach to the Japanese in Brazil. This is the method used in the New Testament where we see the household of Cornelius, of Ludia, and the jailkeeper of Phillipi being won to Christ.

Sunday School

We have noted that in the case of the Free Methodist Church of Brazil the Sunday school has been a good source for church growth. That Church grew as the Sunday school enrollment grew and leveled off as the number of Sunday school pupils declined. If the Japanese Churches expect to grow they should make efforts to recruit more Sunday school pupils as well as to start new Sunday schools.

A Para-Church Association

If we are to plant a church wherever we find a few hundred Japanese, we need to organize a para-church association (sodality). It would be a voluntary organization, not disassociated totally from the existing ecclesiastical bodies, but loosely tied to them, yet with a good deal of autonomy. The sole objective of this association would be the planting of new churches all over Brazil, wherever there are between five hundred and one thousand Japanese. Its task, however, would not be confined to Brazil, but would extend to other countries in Latin America as follows:

TABLE 25

JAPANESE POPULATION IN LATIN AMERICA
(1971)

Peru	56,513
Argentina	23,185
Bolivia	11,758
Paraguay	7,080
Mexico	9,139
TOTAL	107,675

Source: Rafu Shimpo, August 31, 1971

Since there is a linguistic and cultural similarity among Latin
American countries, missionaries from Brazil would be able to
work effectively among the Japanese living in the aforementioned
countries.

The missionary work of the Catholic Church in the sixteenth
and seventeenth centuries in the New World, Asia, and Africa, is
well known. The success of the Catholic missions was due to the
existence of the Catholic religious orders whose main aim was to
convert the heathens. Luther, in trying to reform the Church,
eliminated the religious orders which were, among other things,
missionary agencies. The result was that for nearly three
hundred years Protestants did practically nothing in discipling
the heathens. Only at the end of the eighteenth century when
William Carey started a missionary society, did Protestant
missions to the non-western world begin in a significant and
substantial way. In the past 175 years, Protestant missions
have done a remarkable work in establishing churches in every
land all over the world. But Protestant missions have failed,
as Ralph Winter has pointed out, in the establishment of other
missions. He mentions two assumptions that may have contributed
to the blindness of missionaries to perceive the need to
establish "younger" missions. The first assumption involved
liberal theology and the other evangelical theology.

First, liberal theology assumed that missionary societies
could only come from abroad. In their eagerness to nationalize
churches, the missionaries contributed to change Missionary
Councils and Christian Councils into Councils of Churches. They
voluntarily withdrew from the Councils of Churches and by so
doign the rule was established under which everything would be
excluded from these Councils except Churches. Thus not only
foreign missionary societies, but also nascent indigenous
missions, were excluded with fatal consequences to the latter.

Secondly, evangelical theology, leading to non-establishment
of younger missions, assumed that the young churches would
automatically be as fervently missionary-minded as their
founders. Evangelical missionaries assumed that missions as
separate entities were necessary only when churches went
"liberal" and lost their missionary zeal. This met with the
same consequence as with the Ecumenist missionaries--the lack of
planting younger missions.

Moreover, the wealthy missionary-sending countries, particularly the United States and their missionaries, accustomed to a
comfortable life resulting in diminished passion for the lost,
hardly are in the spiritual condition to establish missions in
the third world which require much sacrifice and self-denial.
The nationals cannot afford economically to "go and do likewise"

in the pattern of missions as they have experienced them (Winter
1972:141-145).

Traditionally mission strategists have thought of church/
mission/church relations. Winter thinks that a more correct way
of thinking is church/mission/church/mission relations which he
shows in the diagrams on the following page.

According to the diagrams, the U.S. Church sent missionaries
to a field through its mission board. These missionaries
planted new churches in the mission field. Once these churches
were established, the mission and the young National Church
should have created the younger or national-based mission
which could have sent missionaries from the National Church to
a new field as in Diagram B. At this stage the relationship
between the mission and the younger church would logically
cease and a new relation directly between the mother church and
younger churches would arise as well as a relation between the
U.S. mission and the younger mission. The younger mission will
then plant churches in a new field, and when these churches are
established, still another new mission would be created there.
This process could go on indefinitely (Winter 1972:133-36).
Wagner refers to this four-fold ongoing cycle as "360° missions"
(1974:103-5). If this method is followed, missions will become
a never ending work, for until the coming of the Lord there will
always be a place to evangelize. The lack of understanding this
may be one reason for the tardiness of the younger churches to
initiate their own missions.

In the case of the Japanese Churches in Brazil, we may say
that it is not too early to create a missionary society. The
Japanese Churches in this country founded a missionary society
(JEMS) after seventy-five years of Christian missions among
them. In Brazil it is a little over fifty years since the first
missionary came. Brazil, being a poor country and its Churches
having limited resources, cannot and should not think of
creating a missionary society after the U.S. model, which is
beyond the reach of the third world churches. American missions
are the result of 175 years of missionary enterprise and they
are highly institutionalized. A missionary society in Brazil
can start as missions started in Europe, when German candidates
went under the Danish auspices supported by British funds
(Winter 1972:145). As the Japanese Christians in Brazil are
very devout, they may pay their tithes to their churches, and
anything beyond tithes could be given to the missionary society.
If they could support a team of two or three men specializing in
church planting, as did the apostle Paul with his team, in five
or ten years many house churches could be planted among the
Japanese in Brazil. And as the number of contributors grows,
more church-planters could be supported and some of them could be
sent to Peru, Bolivia, Paraguay, Argentina, and even to Mexico.

FIGURE 31

PLANTING OF NEW CHURCHES
AND NEW MISSIONS

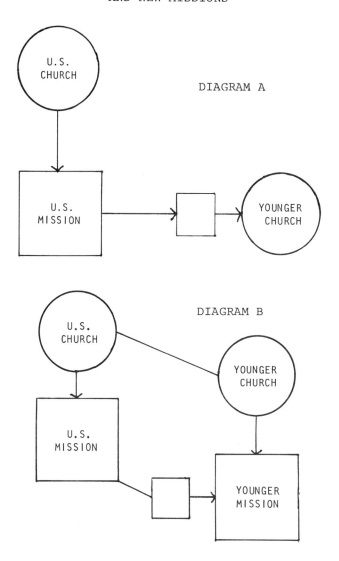

To fulfill this great task, the Japanese Churches in Brazil should welcome the cooperation of foreign missionary associations too. In the Amazon Basin, there are 250 missionaries working among 136,000* tribespeople, but there is no American or European missionary working among nearly 800,000 Japanese. Are the Japanese souls less worthy than the souls of the Indians? No, in the sight of God we believe they are equally precious. Why then has no missionary board thought of evangelizing the Japanese in Brazil? One reason is probably the impression missionary executives have that since the Christian Churches are already established in Brazil, the work of evangelization is being carried out adequately by those existing Churches. Nothing is farther from the truth. After over fifty years of missionary work, the total number of Protestant Christians is not more than 15,000, which means less than two percent. Ninety-eight percent of the sheep are still without Christ. The cooperation of foreign missionary agencies is necessary, for the task is too great and too urgent to be carried out by the existing Christians only. The greatest error some missionary agencies have made is to come to a country, planting ten or fifteen churches and then returning home, thinking that the Church is already established there. Our attention must always be upon those who are outside the Church and not so much as those who are inside the fold.

Another error that many missionaries have made is to stay too long in the established churches. This has sometimes created problems of relationships between the missionaries and the nationals. In caring for the established churches they have some-times forgotten the task of moving on to new frontiers and plant-ing new churches. As Peter Wagner has rightly pointed out, this "church development syndrome" has been a difficulty in many countries (1971:169-171). If missionaries keep themselves busy with their main task of planting new churches, no national Christian would say, "Missionary, Go Home." The work of reaching the unreached is very great. In the case of Japanese in Brazil, mission has barely begun. Much is still to be done.

---

* *Christian Science Monitor* July 8, 1977, gives that figure as 118,000.

Conclusion

By way of summary, we can now draw some final conclusions from
the study of the three denominations which are working among the
Japanese settled in Brazil.

Our research teaches us that time and place are important for
church growth. In the pre-war period the churches grew in the
rural frontier areas where the great majority (90 percent) of
the Japanese lived and where the receptive people were. But
after the War, the receptive people were found in the cities,
particularly Sao Paulo. Once flourishing rural churches declined,
and churches that existed or were planted in Sao Paulo in this
period grew.

This leads us to understand the importance of urbanization for
church growth (people are more receptive in the cities) as a
result of urbanization. In Sao Paulo, where people are continu-
ally moving in, they have been receptive throughout the post-war
period up to the present. A missionary strategist must be
sensitive to the populational shifts and be ready to find where
the receptive people are and to move churches following the
migrational trends.

Financial aid from mission boards is important for church
growth. It should not be too short, nor too long. There is a
right time for it to stop and for the younger Churches to become
self-supporting. Sometimes a severe financial difficulty may
affect church growth.

The hasty integration of an ethnic Church may harm its growth.
As long as it is gaining new converts from its own ethnic group
it is advisable for it to remain separate. Integration should
not be pushed so long as the church is growing within its ethnic
group. For the evangelization of a homogeneous unit the homo-
geneous-unit church is indispensable.

Retirement or death of outstanding church planters or church
builders may drastically affect the growth of a church. A man
with high commitment, determination, and hard work is a key
factor in church growth. There are pastors under whose leadership churches have always grown, whereas there are pastors whose
churches have not grown even in favorable locations.

Multiplication of churches is essential for church growth.
Denominations that have planted churches are growing while
denominations that do not multiply churches are doomed to
stagnation or decline.

In this period of industrialization and urbanization, it is
difficult to build a strong and stable congregation in rural
areas. Small churches or house-church type churches are more
advisable.

Revival is an important factor for church growth. It creates
unity in the church, stimulates zeal and passion for the lost,
and gives the power to witness and evangelize. The power of the
Holy Spirit is a perennial need for evangelism and church growth.
The Christian Church started with the outpouring of the Holy
Spirit, and history atests that revivals have definitely contributed to the growth of the Christian Churches. Edwin Orr
shows through his *The Flaming Tongue* how the 20th century
revivals have contributed to grow churches. The growth of the
Pentecostal Churches in Latin America is attributed to the stress
laid upon the third person of the Holy Trinity (Wagner 1973:30).
Orr says that we can not bring a revival--which only God can--
but we can and must pray for a revival. This we should do that
God may send a revival among the Japanese Churches in Brazil.

In the time of social change caused by war, revolution, and
migration, people are more receptive to the gospel. The post-war
period was the time of harvest for the Japanese people, including
those living in Brazil. That great opportunity was not used by
the Churches as it should have been.

The stand taken by the Church in a critical time in history
may harm or help church growth, depending on the developments
and consequence of the events.

The involvement of the laity in the soul-winning ministry is vital to church growth. The churches that have used their laymen in this way have experienced a faster growth. Mobilization of laity is the key to the evangelization of the Japanese in Brazil.

Internal dispute and lack of unity among church leaders may greatly affect church growth.

The Sunday school is still a great source for new members. An improvement in the Sunday school program and increasing its enrolment will contribute to church growth.

The training of Portuguese-speaking Nisei and Sansei leaders is crucial to the growth of the Japanese Churches in Brazil. Unless they train many more Nisei ministers and lay leaders in the immediate future, their growth will be sealed off. This is probably the most urgent need at the present.

As to the religious affiliation prior to their conversion, our finding is that while the Issei come from Buddhims, Nisei and Sansei come from Catholicism or had no religion before. This shows that those who are going to work with *Nisei* or *Sansei* need to know more about Catholicism than Buddhism.

The age of conversion for *Nisei* and *Sansei* is in the teens and twenties while for the *Issei*, although the majority of them have been converted between twenty and fifty years of age, every age has had its share of converts.

As to the ways used in conversion, the *Issei* have been won through the activities related to church, while *Nisei* and *Sansei* have been won through Sunday school and activities related to it.

The pastor has been used most in the conversion of the *Issei*, whereas the Sunday school teacher has been the person most used in the conversion of *Nisei* and *Sansei*.

A crisis in life is a likely time for conversion. Many people have been led to Christ due to a serious illness, a death in the family, or an accident. The church must be ready to know when there is a crisis and move to meet the needs.

Fellowship with believers has also been a good motive to become a Christian, particularly for *Nisei* and *Sansei*.

The message of the cross and of the love of God has been used most in conversion.

Worship services have been the most helpful means for spiritual grwoth for both *Issei* and *Nisei*, while for the *Sansei*, Sunday school has been most helpful.

The Japanese Christians of the Free Methodist and Holiness Churches in Brazil are very faithful in tithing, church attendance, and in witnessing and inviting non-Christians to church. This should be encouraged.

The comparison of the three Churches in Brazil with their counterparts in the United States shows that the variation from one country to another has little bearing on the pattern and rate of growth, except for the fact that in the U.S. the rates of growth are more uniform, while in Brazil they vary more widely. The growth of the three Churches is very much alike in spite of the difference of country. It seems that ethnicity has more bearing than nationality.

A well-delineated strategy is necessary for the evangelization of the Japanese in Brazil. Such a strategy should comprise a well-defined goal and correct methods to reach that goal. A correct goal should be in accordance with the Great Commission and should include discipling, incorporation, and nurture. To achieve the goal of discipling 800,000 Japanese residing in Brazil, we have suggested means such as finding the receptive area, trining the leaders (lay and clergy), multiplying churches by using the Pauline method, mobilizing the laity, paying attention to homogeneous units, solving the problem of membership leakage by a good post-baptismal care, establishing an effective follow-up ministry for the migrants who come from the interior to the city of Sao Paulo, improving and developing more Sunday schools, and creating a church planting agency, that is, a missionary society whose aim would be the planting of new churches in Brazil and in other Latin American countries where Japanese settlements exist.

Appendices

A.

Other Japanese Churches in Brazil

THE ALIANCA CHRISTIAN CHURCH

The Alianca Christian Church was founded on April 3, 1928, by the Japanese Christian settlers of the Primeira Fazenda Alianca, Lussanvira, State of Sao Paulo. It is about 400 miles northwest of Sao Paulo city. In 1929 it called its first pastor, Giichi Ishido, who served as a self-supporting minister. In 1932 its church building was dedicated, and in 1935 its constitution was written and approved by the church society meeting.

During World War II the church was closed and only the Sunday school was continued, but outside the church building. After the war ended, the meetings were resumed--two Sundays a month in the beginning and every Sunday later. About this time the pastor, Ishido, became ill and resigned. Later he recovered and resumed the pastorate which continued until he was called to be with the Lord on April 14, 1963.

In 1964, a new pastor, Nakamura, came from Japan to minister to that church. He served for two years, baptized about 35 converts, and consolidated the church. Since Nakamura left in 1967, the work has been carried out by laymen who take turns in leading the church services and activities. At the present Hisayoshi Kanizawa is the lay leader of the church. There is a women's society that meets once a month. The church has 50 members at present. The evangelization of *Nisei* and *Sansei* is being done through the Sunday school, but the present leaders have a certain language handicap with them. It seems that there

is no way out except for calling a young minister to reach the
younger generation (Kamizawa 1975).

THE ASSEMBLIES OF GOD

The Japanese Division of the Igreja Evangelica Assembleia de
Deus was initiated by Koretora Takemura in 1964, when he and
seven other members left the Free Methodist Church. He did not
agree with certain theological doctrines of the Free Methodists
including that of entire sanctification and others related to
salvation. Also, an incident that took place in the annual
conference of 1964 caused him to feel unwanted in the Free
Methodist Church. He had been elected to be the delegate of the
Saude Free Methodist Church to that conference, but as there
were more delegates than were allowed by church law, the presid-
ing Bishop did not let him take his seat for the conference
sessions. He resented that, and as he had some doctrinal dis-
agreement with the denomination, he used that incident as an
occasion to leave it. Seven other members followed him to start
the Japanese Assemblies of God church. In 1973 the church
officially became a part of the denomination. Since then he has
been participating in the monthly meeting of the pastors of that
denomination. In these meetings he has met pastors who have
invited him to speak in their churches. Thus he initiated his
visitation to the churches in the interior of the state of Sao
Paulo, Mato Grosso, and Brasilia, and through these churches he
is evangelizing the Japanese. The Japanese won by his ministry
are being baptized and incorporated in these local churches. At
the present there are about 25 cities that he visits from four to
five times a year. He visits the cities which are farther away
on weekends. Among these cities are Batatais, Paulo de Faria,
Cuiba (capital of Mato Grosso), Aracatuba, Cardoso, Votuporanga,
Brasilia, Monte Alto, Morro Agudo, Orindiuva, Itumbiara (Minas),
and Orlandia. In each of the 25 churches he visits there are
from 5 to 10 Japanese. In Paulo de Faria a whole family was
converted recently and there are over 20 Japanese.

There are only two Japanese congregations: one on 701 Galvao
Bueno Street, Sao Paulo, where he is the pastor; and another in
Penha, Sao Paulo, whose pastor is Jorge Nakajima. In his church
there are 36 members, but he does not know how many there are in
another church.

Koretora Takemura thinks that the gospel of Jesus Christ must
be taken to every creature before the coming of the Lord. The
time is so urgent that he believes there is no time to be founding churches, building temples, and organizing congregations.
The work of evangelizing Japanese is difficult because they are
scattered all over Brazil, as are the Assemblies of God. A more

practical way might be to take the gospel to the Japanese through existing Assemblies of God churches (Takemura 1976).

Figuring from Takemura's information we can estimate that there are approximately 230 Japanese who belong to the Assemblies. of God. Since he says that there are between 5 and 10 Japanese Christians in each of the 25 churches he visits periodically, we can multiply that figure by seven which is 175. If we add to this figure the 35 members of the church he pastors plus the members of another church that we can estimate at about 20, we come to a total of 231 Japanese Christians in the Brazilian Assemblies of God.

THE CHRISTIAN AND MISSIONARY ALLIANCE

There are three churches that belong to the CMA: one in Brasilia, which was started in 1960 by Mutsuko Ninomiya; one in Rudge Ramos, S.P., which was started in 1966 by Hiroto Oye; and one in the city of Sao Paulo, which was inaugurated in 1972. Their membership is 12, 40 and 30 respectively, which makes a total of 82 members. Unfortunately we do not have more histori- cal data on the Japanese work of the Christian and Missionary Alliance.

HOSANA EVANGELICAL MISSION

The Hosana Evangelical Mission was started by Ken Kunihiro and his younger brother, Hideo. Ken Kunihiro is a graduate of the Texas Agriculture and Mechanical University in College Station, Texas. After he got his M.A. in sociology from the University of Texas, he went to Prairie Bible Institute in Three Hills, Alberta, Canada.

In 1955, he went to Belem, Para, as a missionary under the Unevangelized Fields Mission, working among the Japanese settlers of Belem, Tomeacu, and Macapa. In 1960 he came back to the United States on furlough.

In the same year he returned to Brazil as an independent missionary, going to Campinas, State of Sao Paulo, where he began his missionary work among Japanese of that area. In 1963, he and his brother founded the Missao Evangelica Hosana. Ken worked in Campinas for fourteen years and in 1974 he moved to Bauru to plant a new church there. In one and a half years he visited every one of the 800 Japanese families which reside in Bauru (Kunihiro 1975).

Hideo studied at Saint Mary University, where he majored in chemistry and biology. Then he did graduate work in atomic science and when he was about to finish his course work for the

Ph.D. program, he was called to the Christian ministry. He gave
up everything and went to Brazil as a missionary in 1958. He is
now in charge of the church in Campinas (H. Kunihiro 1975).

The Hosana Evangelical Mission has four churches which are
located in Campinas, Bauru, Asai (Parana), and Sao Paulo. It
has been self-supporting from its beginning. Beside the
Kunihiro brothers, there are two pastors, Hayashi and Kuroki.
The members of these churches are:

Church	Members
Campinas	70
Bauru	15
Sao Paulo	20
Urai	7
TOTAL	112

The methods of evangelism used by the Hosana Evangelical
Mission are Sunday schools, youth meetings, adult meetings and
visitation. There are 250 pupils enrolled in the four Sunday
schools. According to Hideo Kunihiro, the major problem in the
evangelization of the Japanese is materialism--their attachment
to money. He feels that twenty-four hours a day they are concerned about "self-elevation, self-assertion, and self-
preservatíon" (H. Kunihiro 1975). To the question of whether
the Japanese are receptive, resistant, or indifferent, his
reply was that it depends on what you mean by these words. If
by *receptive* you mean being invited to come in, the Japanese
people are very receptive. But if by *receptive* you mean conversion to Christianity by committing oneself to Christ, they
are resistant (H. Kunihiro 1975). According to Ken Kunihiro,
the responsiveness of the Japanese varies according to where
they reside. In Canada they are more responsive than in the
United States and Brazil. The major obstacles to the evangelization of the Japanese in Brazil are materialism, education, and
other religions (H. Kunihito 1975).

THE LUTHERAN CHURCH

The first Lutheran missionary who came to Brazil to work
among the Japanese was Toshiko Arai. She was born in Suwa,
Prefecture of Nagano. Her family was Buddhist, as were most
Japanese families. She was converted to Christianity when she
was twenty-five years old. When young she became engrossed in
literature but it did not bring her happiness. On the contrary,
she became so disillusioned that one night she left home to
attempt suicide. She came to the brink of a lake but somehow
did not have courage to jump into the water. Thus she decided

to return home, and took the last bus that night. On the bus
she met a missionary who presented Christ to her.

"Where are we going?" asked the missionary, but she was not
able to answer that question. Then the missionary showed her
John 8:12, and read it to her several times. "I am the light of
the world; he who follows me will not walk in darkness, but will
have the light of life." This word sank deeply into her heart.
The missioanry invited her to attend church and there she found
an atmosphere that she had not been able to find among her
literary friends. The lady who led her to Christ was a Lutheran
missionary from Finland.

The family opposed her going to church, and so she went to
work for an American missionary family and from there she
attended church. Later she was encouraged to attend a Bible
institute, which she did. After she graduated, she worked for
five years for a Lutheran church in Tokyo and then for five more
years for the Lutheran church in Shizuoka. A young member of
that church emigrated to Brazil, as did a classmate, Kyoko Suda.
Suda wrote to her from Brazil saying that she was without a
church and asked whether there was anyone who would go to Brazil
to minister to them. She asked for prayer.

Arai prayed for her friend in Brazil, and one day God said to
her: "Why don't you go?" She replied that she was not qualified
for that task. "You did not choose me, but I chose you and
appointed you that you should go and bear fruit and that your
fruit should abide;" (John 15:16) was God's word that came to
her and that made her decide to go to Brazil.

She arrived in Brazil in 1962 and went to Cianorte, Parana.
She traveled extensively to preach the gospel, visiting cities
such as Umuarama, Paranavai, Roanda, Porto Rico, Londrina, and
Marilia. For six years she visited these cities periodically.
Lately she has concentrated her work in three cities: Umuarama,
Cruzeiro d'Oeste, and Cianorte. Many people who were converted
have moved to larger cities after they have been able to amass a
little capital in order to start a new business. Here their
children can get a higher education. As a result, at present
Arai has only 11 members in Cianorte, 8 in Umuarama, and 4 in
Cruzeiro d'Oeste. Arai is supported by a local Lutheran church
in Japan, although initially she was supported by the American
Lutheran Church.

The Lutheran church of Sao Paulo was started in 1964 by
Tsukuru Fujii, who returned to Japan after six years. Hisahi
Shiobara succeeded Fujii. According to the report of 1974 there
were 34 members in the Sao Paulo Lutheran Church.

Among a group of Floriculturists who migrated to Itati, Rio
Grande do Sul, were three families who were Christians. The
local (non-Japanese) Lutheran pastor began to work with them and
one day invited Shiobara to go there and hold services with all
the Japanese families residing there. At that time 21 of them
received Christian baptism. There are about 25 Lutheran
members in Itati now.

According to Toshiko Arai, the work with Issei will take ten
more years. The problem right now is that there are no Nisei
workers or believers. There is one ministerial candidate in the
Sao Paulo church who studied two years in Japan and is the
evangelist of that church, but since he was born in Japan he has
real limitations in reaching Nisei.

The needs now are for Japanese Christian literature which can
be read by the Japanese in Brazil and for more workers. There
is a Norwegian missionary couple who are attending the language
school in Campinas and who want to work among Japanese but it
is not sure whether the Mission will permit them to work only
with Japanese.

For methods of evangelization, Arai has used the vacation
Bible school and a kindergarten, but the problem she has faced
is the lack of workers. She would like to conduct a radio
program, but it is against the law in Brazil to broadcast in a
foreign language.

According to the information given by Arai, there are 82
members of the Japanese Lutheran Church (Arai 1975).

THE METHODIST CHURCH

The first Japanese Methodist missionary to Brazil, Sumiko
Miyamoto, was born in the Prefecture of Yamanashi, Japan, on
May 22, 1920, where her father is an active layman in the local
church. From the time she was small, she wanted to know the
world created by God and the people of different lands. The
fragrance of Christ (*Kirisuto no kaori*) was an idea she always
loved, and she was convinced that when this fragrance fills the
earth, the world will be different. When she was attending
junior high school she had the idea of working in foreign lands.
As she opened the map, she noticed that Brazil was the farthest
country from Japan, and so she desired to go to that country.
Instead she went to Manchuria.

After World War II she returned to Japan and then decided to
go to Brazil. One American missionary gave her $200. With that
she came to Brazil in 1953 on her own. First she went to
Marilia where she taught Japanese to the Japanese children of

that city and where she started a kindergarten. In 1955 she
moved to Maringa, Parana, where there was a Methodist missionary
who invited her to come and work there. Initially she did
visitation, and later she started a kindergarten which she has
continued up to the present.

In 1964, when Kozaki, President of the Kyodan, visited her
church, she spoke about the need of a building. He encouraged
her to start a building campaign and also gave her a vision
regarding the future. In 1965 she went to the United States
and was able to raise enough funds to purchase land to begin
construction. In 1969 she began construction and on August 3,
1975, she dedicated a beautiful two-story building, which she
wants to use for the glory of God. Now she has a kindergarten
with 73 children and five teachers, a Japanese language school
with 50 pupils, and a piano class with 15 students. Beside
these she teaches *soroban* (the abacus). She conducts a regular
worship service in which she preaches, usually attended by about
15 people. She also conducts regular Bible studies and prayer
meetings.

In 1962 Sumiko Miyamoto's sister came to help her. In 1970
she received another teacher, and in 1975 one more came to
increase her team.

Miyamoto thinks that the Japanese of Brazil are more
receptive than the Japanese of Japan. She senses that they are
seeking something, though not necessarily the Christian gospel.
But because they are away from old ties, they accept anything
more easily.

As effective methods of evangelism she thinks that visitation
and becoming friends of the people is the best way to win them
for Christ. She feels setting up a school is also a good
method, for some parents have come to Church through the school.
The kindergarten and Japanese language school pupils attend
Sunday school, which has over 20 members (Miyamoto 1975).

THE NON-CHURCH GROUP

The Non-Church movement started in Japan by Kanzo Uchimura
(1861-1930) had some followers among the immigrants who came to
Brazil in the last fifty years. Most of these joined other
fellowships of believers, instead of maintaining their own
group. Only one, Kanichi Sato, remained without joining any
existing church, maintaining his faith by himself. He was a
graduate of the Tokyo Agriculture School and worked in the
Brazilian society as a swimming coach, where he witnessed to his
faith. A few years ago his pupils erected his statue in the
campus of the school of medicine of Sao Paulo. Other leaders in

the Non-Church Group include Shinichiro Murakami, a dentist, who originally fellowshipped and cooperated with many Christian denominations, but later joined the Non-Church Group. The late Sadajiro Mitsui fellowshipped with the Holiness Church and the late Sadao Yano had fellowship with the Salvation Army (Japanese Division) in the early years, but later joined the Non-Church Group. Another early Non-Church leader, Iyetoshi Ebata, lived in the Amazon, but may have been called to be with the Lord in recent years.

Perhaps one of the more important leaders of this movement in Brazil is Yokuin Koji Tamura, who came to Brazil in 1928 as a Holiness missioanry. That same year he began to read the *Seisho no Kenkyu* (Bible study) by Kanzo Uchimura, and began to be nurtured by Uchimura's and his disciples' works. Gradually he was convinced of the veracity of their teaching, and after eight years of ministry in the Holiness Church, he decided on February 16, 1937, to live in the spirit of *Mukyokai* (Non-Church), and left his denomination.

After a short period of rest, Tamura started a Bible study under the name of *Seisho Kenkyu Kai* (Bible Study Meeting). Gradually he got the followers of the Mukyokai faith.* Hachiro Kani, an officer of the Salvation Army, was his first adherent; then the aforementioned Sadao Yano; Takeshi Obara, a Holiness evangelist; and then Yakuji Yoshinaga, a Holiness pastor, followed. After the war, Hisashi Nagata, a directer of the 4H movement; Shojiro Matsuda, an agronomist; and Hisako Ichikawa, the director of the institution for Feeble-Minded People, came from Japan to join them.

The meetings of the Non-Church Group are held in three different homes--those of the Tamuras, the Yoshinagas, and the Obaras. The number of people who meet in each place is about ten. On Christmas, the memorial day of Uchimura and some of his disciples, they have a joint meeting which is attended by thirty, forty, or sometimes more people.

The religious education of Nisei is being done in each home and also at the Japanese language class. Tamura has a Japanese class for Nisei and Sansei, and for students who are at junior high age and up. He also teaches the Bible. Altogether there are between fifty and sixty convinced followers of this faith plus their families (Tamura 1975).

---

* The Mukyokai Group does not believe in the Church as an institution with ceremonies, rituals, and titles. They believe in the Church as the communion of believers (Koinonia) and in theology they are orthodox. They are Biblicists without being fundamentalists.

THE SAO PAULO CHRISTIAN CHURCH

The founder and pastor of this independent church, Motoi Munakata, was born in Taihoku, Taiwan, in 1924. His family was Congregationalist. As a graduate of the Naval Cadets School he joined the Japanese navy with the intention of becoming a Christian Navy officer. But the result of World War II was a big shock to him, and he began to attend church and decided to be a minister. He entered Union Theological Seminary of Tokyo in 1947 and graduated in 1951. After he graduated form the seminary, he went to Matsuzaki to be the pastor of a Kyodan church where he worked for three years. Then he went to Ushita, Hiroshima, to be the pastor there for another three years. In 1957 he came to Brazil to be the pastor of the South-American Christian Church. Both he and his wife were born and reared in Taiwan and so to go to a foreign country was not too difficult for them. They were the first missionaries to be sent to a foreign land by the Kyodan, although they did not receive any financial support. He worked for the South-American Christian Church (Nambei Kyokai) for nine years, and then there was a split because of a divergence between the pastor and a part of his congregation. In 1966 Munakata, with a group who supported him, left the South-American Christian Church and founded the Sao Paulo Christian Church. In nine years the membership has grown from 20 to 65 members. Munakata also runs a kindergarten which has been a good source of support. He was the pioneer in introducing to Brazil this method of church support widely used in Japan. When he started the Sao Paulo Christian Church he bought a relatively small house which functioned equally for a church, kindergarten, and parsonage. Two and a half years ago the membership bought a good size house, the payment of which was completed in July of 1975. It was really a great undertaking for such a small group and it is amazing that they succeeded. The constituency of the church membership is basically Issei, largely *shoshain* (Japanese corporation employees) and post-war immigrants from Japan.

According to Munakata, the Issei are strongly attracted to the new religions of Japan--they have not changed with respect to their receptivity to Christianity, but their nostalgia for the fatherland, Japan, has awakened in them an interest for the new religions whose followers increase each day. Many of these new religions are of the type that could be called *goriyaku shukyo* ("benefits" religions). They are this-worldly and offer solutions for the problems of daily life. They promise benefits for their followers, and *tatari* (curses) for the non-followers, and this appeals to the insecure Japanese. Also these new religions have close ties with Japanese cultural values. Their priests usually are also the teachers of *ohana* (flower arrangement), *ocha* (tea-ceremony), and *odori* (Japanese dancing). By teaching these things they attract many people to their churches very easily.

To the question of whether the Christian Churches should not learn from the new religions regarding their methods of propagation of faith, Munakata answered that to compete with them in matter of benefits resulting from embracing one faith does not make sense. Rather, he said, Christians should detach themselves from this type of utilitarian approach and go back to the original Christianity which stressed following Christ for Himself alone, not for utilitarian motives. Regarding the tie between the new religions and Japanese culture, he thinks the Christian Churches should, like them, be more deeply rooted in the people's culture, but that historically the Christian Churches have almost always opposed Japanese values. He is not sure whether it is possible to reverse this attitude now. He thinks that the more basic issue is a matter of attitude more than that of methodology of evangelism, and that we should disregard numbers and pay more attention to the quality of Christians we convert. He feels that even though we, as Christians, are a small group, we should have people who are really Christians and to do this we have to free ourselves from the idea that only those who are baptized and join the church are saved. If it is necessary for one to become a church member in order to be saved, then evangelism becomes the supreme command, and by all means we have to bring people into church. But if it is not so, we should not bother ourselves too much in converting non-Christians. He had a choir group and has been running a kindergarten but has never thought of them as means of evangelism. Rather he has considered it a service to society. Thus, the matter to him is not methodology but theology. His theology absolves him of evangelistic responsibility. Two-thirds of his family support comes from the kindergarten and one-third comes from church offerings (Munakata 1975).

THE SEVENTH DAY ADVENTIST CHURCH

The work of the Adventist Church in Brazil goes back to a date prior to the foundation of Instituto Adventista de Ensino in Sao Paulo in 1915. During the period of a little over one-half century, its ministry has expanded to include the areas of education, assistance, hospitals, publication, and evangelism.

Although there were some Adventist believers in the prior years, the Japanese Church was not organized until 1965 when the pastor Tossaku Kanada, now retired, took the initiative.

There is one Japanese Adventist church on 88 Tagua Street, Sao Paulo, and another in Londrina, which is the base for the entire northern section of the state of Parana. The third church is located in Belem, Para, and it is the base for the northern region of Brazil. The Church of Londrina began in 1968, and that of Belem was started in 1972. These churches are attended by members and *interessandos* (those who are interested).

There are seven ministers who exercise the following functions:

Tossaku Kanada	Retired
Kiyotaka Shirai	Associate director of the department of the Sao Paulo association SDAC
Kiyoshi Hosokawa	District pastor in Itarare, S.P.
Shitiro Takatori	Teacher at the Instituto Adventista de Ensino, S.P.
Kojiro Matsunami	Pastor in Belem, Paraguay
Kiwao Mori	Pastor in Londrina, Parana
Yozabro Bando	Pastor in Sao Paulo.

The Japanese Seventh Day Adventist Church is an integral part of the World Seventh Day Adventist Church. The Japanese Seventh Day Adventist Church in Sao Paulo is a part of the Associacao Paulista (Sao Paulo Associacao) which comprises all of the state of Paulo. The total members of the Japanese Seventh Day Adventist Church in the three states aforementioned are over 120.

Besides the regular weekly meetings at the church on Saturdays, meetings are held weekly on Sundays and Wednesdays in different places by the pastor as well as by laymen. The youth have their monthlh spiritual and social program.

The Church has a beneficent department which provides assistance--material and spiritual--to the families in need. This department works through the denominational assistance and hospital centers which provide food, medicines, medical consultation, and dental treatment totally free of charge.

The Japanese SDAC has a Biannual Congress of the believers residing in Brazil and Paraguay who meet for reports and for studying new plans which they have in common.

The Japanese Division has a plan to build its own church so that they may have a more centralized program to bring greater benefits to the Japanese people. The educational work is a part of this program. As the society in general is changing so rapidly, the Church must have an adequate plan for it (Bando 1975).

THE SOUTH AMERICAN CHRISTIAN CHURCH

The founder of the Igreja Crista Sul-Americana, Tomoichi Aoki, was born in the Prefecture of Yamaguchi, Japan, in 1901 as a son of Hinkichi Aoki. After he graduated from an agriculture school, he went to Meiji University to study theology. After his gradua-tion, he was married to Shizuka Okamoto, who was a teacher at the Jiyu Gakuen of the well-known educator, Motoko Hani.

In 1931 he came to Brazil under the invitation of Midori Kobayashi, a Congregational missionary, who was the head of the Missao Japonesa do Brazil (Brazil Japanese Mission). His work was to be the pastor of the Sao Paulo Church, which was a part of the Missao Japonesa do Brasil. After a while, a misunder-standing developed between Kobayashi, who was a Congregationalist, and Aoki, who was a Presbyterian. Thus, on August 12, 1934, Aoki started a new church, the Igreja Crista Sul-Americana. Like Monobe of the Holiness Church and Tanaka of the Salvation Army, Aoki's missionary work was short. A victim of tuberculosis, he died on December 8, 1935, only one and a half years after he had founded the South-American Christian Church. His wife, an educator, had gone to Japan in the beginning of 1935 to raise funds to start a school after the Jiyu Gakuen pattern. Receiving news of the illness of her husband, she returned to Brazil barely in time to see him alive. He died one week after her arrival. The Christian mission among the Japanese in Brazil suffered very high casualties in its early years. Four out of the five pioneer missionaries suffered premature deaths (Takiya 1974). Because of this, for over twenty years this independent church was led by laymen until, in 1957, it received a pastor from Japan, Motoi Munakata. Since 1966, however, it has again been without a pastor most of the time. In 1975 it called a new pastor from the United States, Shojiro Akagi. Its membership was 64 in 1974 (Mizuki 1974).

THE SOUTHERN BAPTIST CHURCH

The Japanese work of the Southern Baptist Church among Japanese was started by Nobuyoshi Togami. It functions as a department of the first Baptist church of Londrina, Parana, but the plan is to organize as a church soon. Togami is supported by the Southern Baptist Convention of Japan, coming as a missionary in 1966. The church (the Japanese department) has 35 members (Federacao 1973:13; Sakai 1975). According to Sakai, who is a school teacher and lay leader in that church, the Sunday school numbered 80 pupils when it was only for Japanese, but when it was integrated with Brazilian children, the number of Japanese fell drastically (Sakai 1975).

THE UNEVANGELIZED FIELDS MISSION

The Japanese work under this Mission was started in the Belem area of the Amazon basin in 1956 by Ken Kunihiro. "He did tract distribution in all the Japanese colonies, in the radius of about 70 kms. of Belem." His main work was in Tomeacu, where he built a congregation of 20 adults and a small church building. In 1961 he left UFM and went with his brother, Hideo, to Campinas to start the Hosana Evangelical Mission. "With no worker among the Japanese with the same vision, the church gradually started to fall apart. A Japanese pastor with a ultra-fundamentalist theological background was called from Japan to take over, but the work got smaller and smaller. He was so independent that he finally began his own work which has been a start-and-fail situation to the present day" (Yamada 1976).

The Igreja Crista Evangelica da Amazonia (The Church founded by UFM) has five preaching points: Tapana, Icoroaci, Belem, Vigia, and Tome Acu. There are three National leaders: Y. Saito, Shin Esashika, and Isamu Ito. There are five missionaries working among the Japanese in this area: Hitoshi and Kathy Yamada, Ann Uchida, Evenlyn Sakata, and Elaine Ige. Ann Uchida has been working in Manaus since March, and Evelyn Sakata is working in Vigia. Altogether the Igreja Crista Evangelica de Amazonia has about 60 members. The work in Castanhal was turned over to the Holiness Church in 1975 and all the members were transferred to the same. The pastor, Takeo Kikuchi, was sent by the Holiness Church (Yamada 1976).

THE ROMAN CATHOLIC CHURCH

The Catholic work among Japanese was started between 1915 and 1918 by a Benedictine priest. But the true catechization began with Father Guido Deo Toro (Jesuit) in 1926 at the Sao Jacinto Church. He baptized thousands of Japanese and their children. His work extended as far as Belem do Para, where he died at almost ninety years of age. He worked for forty years for the catechization of the Japanese. Brother Bonifacio and Father Nakamura were also outstanding in the work of catechizing the Japanese.

Sixty percent of the Japanese have declared themselves as Catholics, but whether this figure is accurate or not is doubtful. Of those who are baptized, 10 to 20 percent may be counted as practicing Catholics.

There are 36 priests and 40 nuns who are working among Japanese under the following religious orders:

Franciscans	5
Jesuits	15
Redemptorists	2
Secular	10
Other	4
TOTAL	36
Nuns	40

(Takeuchi 1974)

B.

Statistics

JAPANESE IMMIGRANTS ENTERING BRAZIL BY YEAR

Year	Number	Year	Number	Year	Number
1908	830	1931	5,632	1954	3,119
1909	31	1932	11,678	1955	4,051
1910	948	1933	24,494	1956	4,912
1911	28	1934	21,930	1957	6,147
1912	2,909	1935	9,611	1958	6,586
1913	7,122	1936	3,306	1959	7,123
1914	3,675	1937	4,557	1960	7,746
1915	65	1938	2,524	1961	6,824
1916	165	1939	1,414	1962	3,257
1917	3,899	1940	1,268	1963	2,124
1918	5,599	1941	1,548	1964	1,138
1919	3,022	1942	-----	1965	903
1920	1,013	1943	-----	1966	937
1921	840	1944	-----	1967	1,070
1922	1,225	1945	-----	1968	597
1923	895	1946	6	1969	496
1924	2,673	1947	1	1970	435
1925	6,330	1948	1	1971	452
1926	8,407	1949	4	1972	352
1927	9,084	1950	33	1973	492
1928	11,169	1951	106		
1929	16,648	1952	261		
1930	14,076	1953	1,923	TOTAL	249,716

Source: Up to 1941 - Hehl Neiva 1945:127: from 1942 to 1973 - Fundacao IBGE - Instituto Brazileiro de Estatistica, *Anuario Estatistico do Brasil*, 1942-1973: see also Consulado Geral do Japao 1974:6.

DISTRIBUTION OF THE JAPANESE POPULATION BY STATE

Brazil

Brasilia	2,575	Pernambuco	494
Sao Paulo	535,356	Paraiba	12
Parana	133,368	R. G. do Norte	37
Santa Catarina	798	Ceara	35
R. G. do Sul	1,627	Piaui	10
Mato Grosso	13,855	Maranhao	214
Goias	2,703	Para	6,561
Minas Gerais	4,799	Amapa	128
Rio de Janeiro	5,356	Amazonas	1,452
Guanabara	2,163	Roraima	53
Espirito Santo	123	Acre	33
Bahia	1,042	Rondonia	75
Sergipe	13		
Alagoas	30	TOTAL	712,900

Source: Consulado Geral do Japao 1974:7.

United States

Northeast District	38,978	*North-middle District*	42,354
Massachusetts	4,394	Ohio	5,555
Connecticut	1,621	Illinois	17,299
New York	20,351	Indiana	2,279
New Jersey	5,681	Wisconsin	2,648
Pennsylvania	5,461	Minnesota	2,603
		Missouri	2,382
Southern District	30,917	*West District*	479,041
Maryland	3,733	California	213,380
Virginia	3,500	Hawaii	217,307
North Carolina	2,104	Washington	20,335
Florida	4,090	Colorado	7,831
Texas	6,537	Oregon	6,843
		Utah	4,713
		TOTAL	591,290

Source: U.S. Department of Commerce - Bureau of the Census
          1972:   Table 60.

Appendices

COMMUNICANT MEMBERSHIP OF THE EPISCOPAL CHURCH

Brazil

Year	Communicants	Year	Communicants
1928	128	1951	815
1929	179	1952	860
1930	183	1953	971
1931	234	1954	916
1932	269	1955	1,002
1933	269	1956	1,043
1934	303	1957	1,036
1935	350	1958	1,050
1936	385	1959	903
1937	402	1960	947
1938	461	1961	1,046
1939	485	1962	1,155
1940	515	1963	1,087
1941	671	1964	1,077
1942	593	1965	871
1943	643	1966	787
1944	623	1967	---
1945	661	1968	861
1946	682	1969	---
1947	668	1970	785
1948	762	1971	840
1949	729	1972	730
1950	775	1973	826

United States

Year	Communicants	Year	Communicants
1945	257	1956	785
1946	355	1957	834
1947	301	1958	908
1948	400	1959	982
1949	453	1960	1,026
1950	451	1961	1,114
1951	---	1962	902
1952	490	1963	927
1953	553	1964	860
1954	626	1965	909
1955	702	1966	933

Source: *Atas e Outros Documentos da Igreja Episcopal Brasileira*, 1928-1973 (Porto Alegre: Imprensa Episcopal); *The Episcopal Church Annual*, 1945-1966.

COMMUNICANT MEMBERSHIP OF THE
FREE METHODIST CHURCH

Brazil

Year	Communicants	Year	Communicants
1953	920	1964	1,385
1954	397	1965	-----
1955	517	1966	1,440
1956	642	1967	1,484
1957	784	1968	1,439
1958	878	1969	1,600
1959	1,091	1970	1,636
1960	1,081	1971	1,601
1961	1,109	1972	1,449
1962	1,198	1973	1,564
1963	1,337	1974	1,653

United States

Year	Communicants	Year	Communicants
1952	382	1964	766
1953	418	1965	800
1954	486	1966	829
1955	568	1967	849
1956	600	1968	882
1957	617	1969	906
1958	667	1970	937
1959	703	1971	1,052
1960	693	1972	1,024
1961	695	1973	1,027
1962	727	1974	1,114
1963	735	1975	1,136

Source: *Relatorio Estatistico da Igreia Metodista Livre do
        Brasil*, 1953-1974. *Year Book*, 1952-1969: *Year Book*,
        Vol. II, 1970-1975 (Winona Lake, Indiana: The Free
        Methodist Publishing House).

COMMUNICANT MEMBERSHIP OF THE HOLINESS CHURCH

Brazil

Year	Communicants	Year	Communicants
1958	746	1967	1,106
1959	775	1968	1,081
1960	797	1969	1,164
1961	862	1970	1,233
1962	948	1971	1,154
1963	962	1972	1,207
1964	990	1973	1,229
1965	1,018	1974	1,282
1966	1,087		

United States

Year	Communicants	Year	Communicants
1952	525	1963	1,325
1953	585	1964	1,363
1954	722	1965	1,401
1955	775	1966	1,409
1956	783	1967	1,374
1957	822	1968	1,463
1958	952	1969	1,556
1959	1,030	1970	1,596
1960	950	1971	1,604
1961	1,075	1972	1,701
1962	1,191	1973	1,714

Source: Questionnaire, Mizuki 1974:
Statistical Report: Local Church, Treasurer and Secretary Report, 1952-1973.

JAPANESE PROTESTANT COMMUNICANT MEMBERS
BY DENOMINATION

Brazil

1.	The Alianca Christian Church	50
2.	The Assemblies of God	230
3.	The Christian and Missionary Alliance	82
4.	The Episcopal Church	826
5.	The Free Methodist Church	1,653
6.	The Holiness Church	1,282
7.	The Hosana Evangelical Mission	112
8.	The Lutheran Church	82
9.	The Non-Church Group	50
10.	The Sao Paulo Christian Church	65
11.	The Seventh Day Adventist Church	120
12.	The South-American Christian Church	64
13.	The Southern Baptist Church	35
14.	The Unevangelized Fields Missions	60

TOTAL   4,731

Source: 1. Kamizawa 1975; 2. Takemura 1976; 3. Federacao Evangelica Japonesa do Brasil 1973; 4. Atas do Vl Concilio
Sul-Central da Igreja Episcopal do Brasil 1974; 5. Relatorio Estatistico da Igreja Metodista Livre do Brasil -
Concilio Nikkei 1974; 6. Mizuki 1974; 7. H. Kunihiro
1975; 8. Arai 1975; 9. Tamura 1975; 10. Munakata 1975;
11. Bando 1975; 12. Mizuki 1974; 13. Sakai 1975;
14. Yamada 1976.

C.

Directory of
Japanese Churches in Brazil

This is an alphabetical listing of the Japanese Churches in
Brazil. Where available, dates of foundation are given.

1. Igreja Crista Alianca, 1a. Alianca, C.P. 2, Mirandopolis,
   Estado de Sao Paulo 16800, Brasil, 1928.

THE ASSEMBLIES OF GOD

2. Igreja Japonesa da Assembleia de Deus, Rua Galvao Bueno,
   701 fundo, Sao Paulo, Brasil, 1964.

3. Igreja Japonesa da Assembleia de Deus de A.E. Carvalho,
   Penha, Sao Paulo, Brasil.

THE CHRISTIAN AND MISSIONARY ALLIANCE

4. Igreja Alianca de Brasilia, Nucleo Bandeirante, Caixa
   postal 80202, Brasilia - D.F. 7000, Brasil, 1960.

5. Igreja Alianca da Liberdade, Rua Galvao Bueno, 401-A
   Liberdade, Sao Paulo, Brasil, 1972.

6. Igreja Alianca de Rudge Ramos, Sao Bernardo do Campo,
   Estado de Sao Paulo, Brasil, 1966.

7. Igreja Crista Sul-Americana (Independent), Rua Bela Flor,
   220, Vila Mariana, Sao Paulo 0412-, Brasil, 1934.

THE EPISCOPAL CHURCH

8. Igreja da Ascensao, Rua Marechal Deodoro, 285, C.P. 47,
    Getulina, Estado de Sao Paulo 16450, Brasil, 1923.

9. Igreja do Calvario, Caixa postal 30179, Butanta, Sao Paulo
    01501, Brasil, 1963.

10. Igreja do Cristo Rei, Caixa postal 64, Registro, Estado de
    Sao Paulo 11900, Brasil, 1923.

11. Igreja Santo Andre, Rua Alagoas, 435, C.P. 13, Pereira
    Barreto, Estado de Sao Paulo 15370, Brasil, 1930.

12. Igreja Santo Estevao, Rua Hemilho Magalhaes, 86, Aracatuba,
    Estado de Sao Paulo 16100, Brasil, 1927.

13. Igreja Sao Joao, Rua Corope, 108, Pinheiros, C.P. 11136,
    Sao Paulo, Brasil, 1923.

14. Igreja Sao Lucas, Avenida Antonia, Caixa postal 1333,
    Londrina, Parana 86100, Brasil, 1943.

THE FREE METHODIST CHURCH

15. Igreja Metodista Livre de Apucarana, Av. Munhoz da Rocha,
    480, Caixa Postal 349, Apucarana, Brasil, 1955.

16. Igreja Metodista Livre de Barretos, Rua Vinte e Quatro,
    1743, Barretos, Estado de Sao Paulo 14780, Brasil, 1955.

17. Igreja Metodista Livre de Campinas, Rua Antonio Joaquim
    Viana, 65, Caixa postal 1575, Campinas 13100, Estado de
    Sao Paulo, Brasil, 1970.

18. Igreja Metodista Livre de Campos do Jordao, Rua Rangel
    Pestana, 192, Caixa postal 220, Campos do Jordao,
    Estado de Sao Paulo, Brasil, 1955.

19. Igreja Metodista Livre de Embura, Rua Herculano de Freitas,
    226, Santo Amaro, Sao Paulo 04743, Brasil, 1939.

20. Igreja Metodista Livre de Itapevi, Estacao Itapevi, E.F.S.,
    Estado de Sao Paulo 06650, Brasil, 1954.

21. Igreja Metodista Livre de Lins, Av. Duque de Caxias, 511,
    Lins, Estado de Sao Paulo 16400, Estado de Sao Paulo,
    Brasil, 1951.

22. Igreja Metodista Livre de Londrina, Rua Hugo Cabral, 328,
    Caixa postal 854, Londrina, Parana 86100, Brazil, 1968.

23. Igreja Metodista Livre de Marilia, Rua Arco Verde, 372, Caixa postal 347, Marilia, Estado de Sao Paulo 17500, Brasil, 1949.

24. Igreja Metodista Livre de Pinheiros, Rua Morato Coelho, 781, Pinheiros, Sao Paulo 05417, Brasil, 1964.

25. Igreja Metodista Livre Santo Estevao, Av. Alda, 821 Caixa postal 328, Diadema, Sao Paulo 09900, Brasil, 1964.

26. Igreja Metodista Livre de Sao Jose dos Campos, Rua Nassau, 52, Sao Jose dos Campos, Estado de Sao Paulo 12200, Brasil, 1962.

27. Igreja Metodista Livre da Saude, Rua Veriano Pereira, 40, Caixa postal 161, Sao Paulo 01000, Brasil, 1936.

28. Igreja Metodista Livre da Zona Leste, Rua Abernesia, 36, Vila Carrao, Caixa postal 16202, Sao Paulo 03400, Brasil, 1964.

29. Igreja Metodista Livre de Zona Norte, Rua Durate de Azevedo, 692, Santana, Sao Paulo, Brasil, 1962.

THE EVANGELICAL HOLINESS CHURCH

30. Igreja Evangelica Holiness de Adamantina, Rua Euclides da Cunha, 308, Caixa postal 239, Adamantina, Estado de Sao Paulo 17800, Brasil, 1953.

31. Igreja Evangelica Holiness de Aracatuba, Praca Ruy Barbosa, Aracatuba, Estado de Sao Paulo 16100, Brasil.

32. Igreja Evangelica Holiness de Bauru, Av. Rodrigues Alves, 1326, Bauru, Estado de Sao Paulo 17100, Brasil, 1953.

33. Igreja Evangelica Holiness de Bastos, Rua Presidente Vargas, 592, Caixa postal 228, Bastos, Estado de Sao Paulo 17690, Brasil, 1932.

34. Igreja Evangelica Holiness de Bosque, Rua Guiratinga, 980, Bosque de Saude, Caixa postal 3919, Sao Paulo 01000, Brasil, 1926.

35. Igreja Evangelica Holiness de campo Grande, Rau Andre de Barros, 161, Caixa postal 347, Campo Grande, Mato Grosso 79100, Brasil, 1971.

36. Igreja Evangelica Holiness de Casa Verde, Rua Jose de Oliveira, 399, Casa Verde, Caixa postal 736, 02512 Sao Paulo, Brasil, 1950.

Appendices

37. Igreja Evangelica Holiness de Castanhal, Rua Coronel Leal
    BNH II, 68745 Castanhal, Para, Brasil.

38. Igreja Evangelica Holiness de Curitiba, Travessa Angelo
    Pizzeta, Bairro Cristo Rei, Caixa postal 6717, Curitiba,
    Parana 80000, Brasil, 1952.

39. Igreja Evangelica Holiness de Getuba, Caragatatuba, Estado
    de Sao Paulo 11660, Brasil, 1964.

40. Igreja Evangelica Holiness de Guararapes, Rua Benjamin
    Constant, 325, Caixa postal 137, Guararapes, Estado de
    Sao Paulo 16700, Brasil, 1932.

41. Igreja Evangelica Holiness de Itaquera, Caixa postal 4126,
    Sao Paulo 01000, Brasil, 1951.

42. Igreja Evangelica Holiness da Liberdade, Rua Barao de
    Iguape, 614, Liberdade, Sao Paulo 01000, Brasil, 1958.

43. Igreja Evangelica Holiness de Londrina, Rua Teresina, 81,
    Caixa postal 465, Londrina, Estado de Parana 96100,
    Brasil, 1942.

44. Igreja Evangelica Holiness de Maringa, Rua Antonio Carneil,
    765, Caixa postal 1052, Maringa, Parana 87100, Brasil,
    1953.

45. Igreja Evangelica Holiness de Paraguacu Paulista, Rua Barao
    do Rio Branco, 513, Caixa postal 324, Paraguacu Paulista,
    Estado de Sao Paulo 18700, Brasil, 1969.

46. Igreja Evangelica Holiness de Pompeia, Rua Jose Moraes, 83,
    Caixa postal 87, Pompeia, Estado de Sao Paulo 17580,
    Brasil, 1942.

47. Igreja Evangelica Holiness de Presidente Prudente, Rua
    Joaquim Nabuco, 947, Caixa postal 137, Presidente
    Prudente, Estado de Sao Paulo 19100, Brasil, 1938.

48. Igreja Evangelica Holiness de Presidente Venceslau, Rua
    Rui Barbosa, 150, Caixa postal 368, Presidente Venceslau,
    Estado de Sao Paulo 19400, Brasil, 1968.

49. Igreja Evangelica Holiness de Santo Andre, Rua Padre
    Vieira, 288, Santo Andre, Estado de Sao Paulo 09000,
    Brasil, 1970.

50. Igreja Evangelica Holiness de Tupa, Rua Piratinins, 45,
    Caixa postal 20, Estado de Sao Paulo 17600, Brasil, 1956.

THE HOSANA EVANGELICAL MISSION

51. Missao Evangelica Hosana de Campinas, Caixa postal 631, Campinas, Estado de Sao Paulo 13100, Brasil.

52. Missao Evangelica Hosana de Bauru, Caixa postal 593, Bauru, Estado de Sao Paulo 17100, Brasil.

53. Missao Evangelica Hosana de Urai, Urai, Parana, Brasil.

THE LUTHERAN CHURCH

54. Igreja Evangelica Luterana de Cianorte, Va. Sao Paulo, Caixa postal 28, Cianorte, Parana 87200, Brasil, 1964.

THE METHODIST CHURCH

55. Segunda Igreja Metodista de Maringa, Caixa postal 366, Maringa, Parana 09720, Brasil, 1955.

THE NON-CHURCH GROUP

56. Sao Paulo Seisho Kenkyu-Kai, Caixa postal 4368, Sao Paulo, Brasil.

THE SEVENTH DAY ADVENTIST CHURCH

57. Igreja Adventista Japonesa, Rua Tagua, 88, Liberdade, Sao Paulo, Brasil.

THE SOUTHERN BAPTIST CHURCH

58. Igreja Batista de Londrina, Va. Parana, Caixa postal 945, Londrina, Parana 86100, Brasil, 1966.

THE UNEVANGELIZED FIELDS MISSIONS

59. Igreja Crista Evangelica da Amazonia, Caixa postal 243, 66000 Belem, Para, Brasil.

THE UNITED CHURCH OF CHRIST IN JAPAN

60. Igreja Crista de Sao Paulo, Rua Cruz e Souza, 44, Aclimacao, Sao Paulo 01531, Brasil, 1967.

Glossary

Arrobas - old measure of weight approximately equivalent to 33 pounds.

Bairro - city district.

Bicho - animal, bug, insect.

Cabeleireira - hairdresser.

Caboclo - Brazilian of mixed Indian and white blood.

Colono - tenant farmer.

Comadre - godmother in relation to the godchild's parents; child's mother in relation to the godparents.

Compadre - godfather in relation to the godchild's parents; child's father in relation to the godparents.

Compadresco - the relationship between a godfather and the child's parents.

Culture - education, erudition.

Emporio - grocery store.

Fazenda - plantation, ranch.

Fazendeiro - rancher.

Feirante - seller at an open-air market.

Interessados - interested.

Nordestinos - Northeasterners.

Padrinho - godfather.

Pecador - sinner.

Quitanda - greengrocery.

Rei - Brazilian monetary unit used until 1940; at the first decade of this century 2000 reis were equivalent to $1.00.

Terra roxa - purple soil.

Tinturaria - dry cleaner.

JAPANESE

Buraku - village, a part of *mura*.

Fuki - a butter bur.

Fukuinshi - a preacher of the gospel.

Gobo - a burdock.

Gokuraku-jodo - land of perfect bliss, Paradise.

Goriyaku - benefit.

Goriyaku-shukyo - religion of benefit.

Gosei - fifty generation.

Hadaka-ikkan - nothing.

Issei - first generation (the immigrants).

Kachigumi - victorists.

Kaori - fragrance.

Konnyaku - devil's tongue.

Kosei-kazoku - an artificial family to meet the requirements of the Sao Paulo State government.

Makegumi - defeatists.

Mura - village.

Mura-hachibu - ostracism.

Myoga - zingiber mioga.

Ninshoku-undo - clarification campaign.

Nira - a leek.

Nisei - second generation, children of immigrants born in the country of adoption.

Ocha - tea ceremony.

Odori - dance.

Ogiri - obligation.

Ohana - flower arrangement.

Ponkan - a shaddock.

Rakkyo - a scallion.

Sansei - third generation.

Seinen-kai - youth association.

Shindo-Remmei - a league of loyal subjects (a group of terrorists organized by victorists to eliminate defeatists).

Shisho - a beefsteak plant.

Shoshain - Japanese corporation's employees.

Soroban - an abacus.

Tariki-hongan - salvation by faith.

Tatari - curse.

Udo - an asparagus.

Yonsei - fourth generation.

Yurei-kai-in - ghost member (inactive member).

Bibliography

Alianca Kirisuto Kyokai
  1935 *Alianca Kirisuto Kyokai Kaisoku*, Lussanvira, S.P.

Allen, Roland
  1962 *The Spontaneous Expansion of the Church*.   Grand Rapids,
       William B. Eerdmans Publishing Company.

  1962 *Missionary Methods: St. Paul's or Ours?*   Grand Rapids,
       William B. Eerdmans Publishing Company.

Ando, Zempati, and Wakisaka, Katsunori
  1971 "Sinopse Historica da Imigracao Japonesa no Brasil" in
       Centro de Estudos Nipo-Brasileiros.

Ando, Zampati
  1973 "Cooperativismo Nascente" in H. Saito and T. Maeyama.

Associaco Rikkokai do Brasil
  1963 *Burajiru Rikkokai 40 Nen Shi*.   Tokyo, Teikoku Shoin.

Azevedo, Fernando de
  1963 *A Cultura Brasileira; introducao ao estudo da cultura no
       Brasil*.   Brasilia, Universidade de Brasilia.

Azevedo, Thales de
  1963 *Social Change in Brazil*.   Gainesville, Florida, Univer-
       sity of Florida Press.

Basabe, Fernando M.
    1968 *Religious Attitudes of Japanese Men: A Sociological
        Survey*. Tokyo, Sophia University.

Barros Basto, Fernando Lazaro de
    1970 *Sintese da Historia da Imigracao no Brasil*. Rio de
        Janeiro.

Benjamin, Paul
    1972 *The Growing Congregation*. Lincoln, Ill., Lincoln
        Christian College Press.

Beyerhaus, Peter
    1971 *Missions: Which Way? Humanizing or Redemption*. Grand
        Rapids, Zondervan Publishing House.

    1972 *Shaken Foundations: Theological Foundations for Mission*.
        Grand Rapids, Zondervan Publishing House.

Blauw, Johannes
    1966 *A Natureza Missionaria da Igreja*. Sao Paulo, ASTE.
        (Translated into Portuguese by Jovelino Pereira Ramos).

Boschman, Paul W.
    1964 *Church Growth in Miyazaki Prefecture*. Eugene, Oregon.
        Institute of Church Growth. (Mimeographed).

Botelho de Miranda, Mario
    1948 *Shindo Remmei: terrorismo e extorsao*. Sao Paulo, Edicao
        Saraiva.

Braga, Erasmo, and Grubb, Kenneth G.
    1932 *The Republic of Brazil, A Survey of the Religious
        Situation*. London, World Dominion Press.

Braun, Neil
    1971 *Laity Mobilized: Reflections on Church Growth in Japan
        and Other Lands*. Grand Rapids, William B. Eerdmans
        Publishing Company.

Bright, John
    1953 *The Kingdom of God*. Nashville, Abingdon Press.

Buarque de Holanda, Sergio
    1936 *Raizes do Brasil*. Rio de Janeiro, Jose Olimpio.

Burajiru Jiho
    1936 "Burajiru Dendo," Sao Paulo, October 26, 1936.

Centro de Estudos Nipo-Brasileiros
1971 *O Japones em Sao Paulo e no Brasil.* Sao Paulo, Centro
      de Estudos Nipo-Brasileiros.

Cintra, Jose Tiago
1971 *La Migracion Japonesa en Brasil* (1908-1959). Mexico,
      Colegio de Mexico, Centro de Estudos Orientales.

Comissao de Recenseamento
1964 *The Japanese Immigrant in Brazil*, 2 vols. Tokyo, The
      University of Tokyo Press

Congar, Marie Joseph
1957 *Lay People in the Church: A Study for a Theology of
      Laity.* Westminster, MD, Newman Press. (Translated by
      Donald Attwater).

Consulado Geral do Japao
1974 *Emigracao Japonesa no Brasil.* Sao Paulo, Consulado
      Geral do Japao. (Mimeographed).

1974 *Agricultura - Atividade Preferida.* Sao Paulo, Con-
      sulado Geral do Japao. (Mimeographed).

1974 *Mobilidade e Assimilacao de Imigrantes Japoneses.* Sao
      Paulo, Consulado Geral do Japao. (Mimeographed).

Cornell, John B.
1970 *Assimilative Strategies of Nisei in the Interior of
      Brazil.* Paper prepared for the Annual Meetings of the
      American Anthropological Association. San Diego, CA,
      November 20, 1970. (Mimeographed).

Crabtree, A. R.
1937 *Historia dos Batistas do Brasil.* 2 vols. Rio de
      Janeiro, Casa Publicadora Batista.

Cruzeiro, O.
1970 *Japao.* Rio de Janeiro, September 22, 1970.

Davis, J. Marle
1943 *How the Church Grows in Brazil.* New York City,
      International Missionary Council.

Dale, Kenneth J.
1975 *Circle of Harmony.* South Pasadena, William Carey
      Library.

Demoor, David Alexander
"Japanese Colonization and Immigration in the Amazon
Basin." An unpublished M.A. thesis, University of
California at Los Angeles.

Diegues, Manuel
1952 Etnias e Culturas no Brazil. Rio de Janeiro,
Ministerio da Educacao e Saude.

1955 Estudos de Relacoes de Cultura no Brasil. Rio de
Janeiro, Ministerio da Educacao e Cultura, Servico de
Documentacao.

1964 O Brasil e os Brasileiros; Ensaio sobre Alguns Aspectos
das Caracteristicas Humanas das Populacoes Brasileiras.
Sao Paulo, Martins.

1964 Imigracao, Urbanizacao e Industrializacao; Estudo
Sobre Alguns Aspectos da Contribuicao Cultural do
Imigrante no Brasil.

Edwards, Fred E.
1971 The Role of the Faith Mission: A Brazilian Case Study.
South Pasadena, William Carey Library.

Episcopal Church, The
1945 - 1965 The Episcopal Church Annual.

Embaixada do Japao no Brasil
1973 Estudo Comparativo do Desenvolvimento Economico do
Brasil e do Japao. Brasilia, Embaixada do Japao no
Brasil.

Federacao Evangelica Japonesa do Brasil
1973 Burajiru Hojin Kirisuto-Kyo Remmei Kamei Kyokai Sho-
zai-chi narabi Bokushi Meibo. Sao Paulo, Federacao
Evangelica Japonesa do Brasil.

1974 Os Passos da Missao. Sao Paulo, Federacao Evangelica
Japonesa do Brasil.

Ford, Leighton
1966 The Christian Persuader: A New Look at Evangelism
Today. New York, Harper & Row, Publishers.

Free Methodist Church, The
1952 - 1975 Year Book. Winona Lake, Indiana. The Free
Methodist Publishing House.

Free Methodist Church of Brazil, The
1953-1975 *Relatorio Estatistico da Igreia Metodista Livre do Brasil - Concilio Nikkei.*

1956 *Jiyu Mesojisuto Burajiru Senkyo Niju Shunen Kinen-go.*

Gaimusho Daijin Kampoho Ryoji Iju-bu
1971 *Nippon Imin ga Burajiru Nambu no Nogyo Kaihatsu ni oyoboshita Eikyo ni Kansuru Kenkyu.*

Gerber, Vergil
1973 *God's Way to Keep a Church Going and Growing.* South Pasadena, William Carey Library.

Gomes da Rocha, Joao
1944 *Lembrancas do Passado*, 3 vols. Rio de Janeiro, Centro Brasileiro de Publicacao.

Goso, Kingo
1958 *Densuke Katsuide Burajiru bura bura ki.* Tokyo, Matsuzawa Shoten.

Greenway, Roger S.
1973 *An Urban Strategy for Latin America.* Grand Rapids, Baker Book House.

Hahn, Ferdinand
1965 *Mission in the New Testament.* Naperville, Ill., Alec R. Allenson, Inc.

Handa, Tomoo
1970 *Imin no Seikatsu no Rekishi: Burajiru Nikkei-jin no ayunda Michi.* Tokyo, Ie no Hikari Kyokai.

Hardoy, Jorge Enrique
1969 *La Urbanizacion en America Latina.* Buenos Aires, Editorial del Instituto.

Hasegawa, Nyozekan
1965 *The Japanese Character: A Cultural Profile.* Tokyo, Kodansha International Ltd. (Translated by John Bester).

Hehl Heiva, Artur
1945 *O Problema Imigratorio Brasileiro.* Rio De Janeiro, Imprensa Nacional.

Hiyane, Yasusada
1949 *Nippon Kirisuto-Kyo Shi.* Tokyo, Kyobunkan.

1951 *Nippon Shukyo Shi.* Tokyo, Kyobunkan.

Horikoshi, Yoshiichi
    1975 "Hokubei Nikkei-jin Kirisuto-kyo Senkyo Hyakunen-sai
          Mukaete," Rafu Shimpo, January 1, 1975.

Instituto Brasileiro de Geografia e Estatistica (IBGE)
    1942 - 1973 *Anuario Estatistico do Brasil.* Fundacao IBGE.

Ianni, Otavio
    1966 *Racas e Classes Sociais no Brasil.* Rio de Janeiro,
          Civilizacao Brasileira.

Ito, Yasoji
    1970 "Shinden no Kaitaku" in Ito Yasoji Sensei Tsuioku
          Kinen Jikko Iinkai.

Ito Yasoji Sensei Tsuioku Jikko Iinkai
    1970 *Zaihaku Hojin Kaitaku Dendo-sha no Shogai.* Sao Paulo,
          Paulista Bijutsu Insatsu Kabushiki Kaisha.

Igreja Evangelica Holiness do Brasil
    1955 *Minami Jujisei.* Sao Paulo, Igreja Evangelica Holiness
          do Brasil.

Igreja Episcopal Brasileira
    1928 - 1974 Atas e Outros Documentos da Igreja Episcopal
          Brasileira. Pelotas, Rio Grande do Sul, Imprensa
          Episcopal.

Izumi, Seiichi
    1973 "Estrutura Psicologica da Colonia Japonesa" in H.
          Saito and T. Maeyama.

Jeremias, Joachin Jesus
    1956 *Jesus et les Paiens.* Neuchatel, Delachaux & Niestle
          S. A.

Journal of Social Issues, The
    1973 Vol. 29, No. 22.

Kelley, Dean M.
    1972 *Why Conservative Churches are Growing.* New York.
          Harper & Row, Publishers.

Kennedy, D. James
    1973 *Evangelism Explosion: The Coral Ridge Program for Lay
          Witness.* Wheaton, Ill., Tyndale House Publishers.

Kishi, Bambi Y.
    1974 "A Description of O.M.S. Holiness Church of America." A
          term paper, Fuller School of World Mission, Pasadena.

Kikumura, Akemi, and Kitano, Harry H. L.
    1973   "Interracial Marriage: A Picture of the Japanese
           Americans," The Journal of Social Issues, Vol. 29,
           No. 2, 1973.

Kirisuto Shimbunsha
    1969 - 1973   *Kirisuto-Kyo Nenkan.*   Tokyo, Kirisuto Shimbunsha.

Kitagawa, Daisuke
           Burajiru Nikkei Colonia ni Okeru Chosa Hokokusho.   Sao
           Paulo (a mimeographed report).

Kishimoto, Koichi
    1947   *Nambei no Senya ni Koritsushite.*   Sao Paulo, Koyasha.

Kraemer, Hendrik
    1958   *A Theology of the Laity.*   Philadelphia, Westminster
           Press.

Latourette, Kenneth Scott
    1953   *A History of Christianity.*   New York, Harper & Row,
           Publishers.

Lamson, Byron
    1951   *Lights in the World: Free Methodist Mission at Work.*
           Winona Lake, Indiana, General Missionary Board.

Ladd, George Eldon
    1964   *Jesus and the Kingdom.*   New York. Harper and Row,
           Publishers.

Leonard, Emile G.
    1963   *O Protestantismo Brasileiro: Estudo de Eclesiologia
           e Historia Social.*   Sao Paulo, Associacao de Seminarios
           Teologicos Evangelicos (ASTE).

Liao, David C. F.
    1972   *The Unresponsive: Resistant or Neglected?*   Chicago
           Moody Press.

Loftin, Marion Theo
    1952   "The Japanese in Brazil: a study in immigration and
           Acculturation." An unpublished Ph.D. dissertation,
           Vanderbilt University. (m/f used).

Maeyama, Takashi
    1971   "Religiao, Parentesco e as Classes Medias dos Japonesses
           no Brasil Urbano" in H. Saito and T. Maeyama (ed.).

200 | Bibliography

Below:

1970   *Ancestor, Emperor, and the Fruit of Love: Religious Attitudes of the Japanese in Brazil.* Cornell University. (Mimeographed).

Mattaki, Ai
1937   *Burajiru Tsushin.* Osaka, April 10, 1937.

McGavran, Donald Anderson
1955   *Bridges of God: A Study in the Strategy of Missions.* New York, Friendship Press.

1957   *How Churches Grow: The New Frontiers of Mission.* London, World Dominion Press.

1970   *Understanding Church Growth.* Grand Rapids, William B. Eerdmans Publishing Company.

McGavran, Donald Anderson, ed.
1972   *Crucial Issues in Missions Tomorrow*, Chicago, Moody Press.

McGavran, Donald A., and Arn, Win
1974   *How to Grow a Church.* Glendale, Calif., Regal Book Division, G/L Publications.

1974   "The Homogeneous Unit in Mission Theory." School of Missions, Pasadena (a mimeographed report).

Mizuki, John
1974   Questionnaires.

1975   Questionnaires.

Monbeig, Pierre
1952   *Pionniers et Planteurs de Sao Paulo.* Paris, A. Colin.

Nakane, Chie
1970   *Japanese Society.* Berkeley, University of California Press.

Nishizumi, Masayoshi
1937   "Burajiru Tsushin," *Mattaki Ai.* April 10, 1937.

1947   "Diary" in S. Ono (ed.).

Nogueira Martins, Ruy
1971   "O Japones no Comercio e Industria" in Centro de Estudos Nipo-Brasileiros.

Normano, Joao Frederico
1943 *The Japanese in South America: an introductory survey with special reference to Peru.* New York, The John Day Co.

Oliveira, Botelho
1925 *A Imigracao Japonesa.* Rio de Janeiro, Tipografia Coelho.

O.M.S. Holiness Church of America
1952-1972 Statistical Report: Local Church, Treasurer and Secretary Report.

Ono, Sukeichi, ed.
1947 *Waga Yuku Michi.* Sao Paulo.

Paulista Shimbun
1972 "Kyo no Wadai," Sao Paulo, May 18, 1972.

Rafu Shimpo
1975 "Hokubei Nikkei-jin Kirisuto-kyo Senkyo Hyakunen-sai Mukaete," Los Angeles, January 1, 1975.

Read, William R.
1965 *New Patterns of Church Growth.* Grand Rapids, William Eerdmans Publishing Company.

Read, W. R., Monterroso, V. M., and Johnson, H. A.
1969 *Latin American Church Growth.* Grand Rapids, William Eerdmans Publishing Company.

Read, William R., and Ineson, Frank A.
1973 *Brazil 1980: The Protestant Handbook.* Monrovia, Calif., Missions Advanced Research and Communications Center.

Ribeiro, Rene
1956 *Religiao e Relacoes Raciais.* Rio de Janeiro, Servico de documentacao, Ministerio de educacao e culture.

Richards, Lawrence
1972 *A New Face for the Church.* Grand Rapids, Zondervan Publishing House.

Rocha Nogueira, Arlinda
1971 "O Inicio da Imigracao Niponica para a Lavoura Cafeeira Paulista" in Centro de Estudos Nipo Brasileiros.

Saito, Hiroshi
1961 *O Japones no Brasil.* Sao Paulo, Editora Sociologia.

1964   *O Cooperativismo e a Comunidade: Caso da Cooperativa Agrícola de Cotia.*   Sao Paulo, Editora Sociologia e Politica.

1973   "Contribuicao de Japoneses na Horticultura de Sao Paulo" in H. Saito and T. Maeyama (ed.).

1974   *Atarashi Burajiru.*   Tokyo, The Simul Press.

Saito, Hiroshi, and Maeyama, Takashi, ed.
1973   *Assimilacao e Integracao dos Japoneses no Brasil.*
Sao Paulo, Editora da Universidade de Sao Paulo.

Schurig Vieira, Francisca Isabel
1967   "A Absorcao de Japoneses em Marilia."   An unpublished Ph.D. dissertation, University of Sao Paulo. (m/f used.)

Shimidu, Amelia
1973   "Assimilacao dos Universitarios Nisseis" in H. Saito and T. Maeyama (ed.).

Smith, Thomas Lynn
1961   *Latin American Population Studies.*   Gainesville, University of Florida Press.

1970   *Studies of Latin American Societies.*   Garden City, New York, Anchor Books.

1972   *Brazil: people and institutions.*   Benton Rouge, Louisiana State University Press.

Staniford, Philip Stroud
1973   *Pioneers in the tropics: the political organization of Japanese in an immigrants community in Brazil.*
London, Athlosu Press.

Suehiro, James E.
1972   *Yorokobi no Izumi.*   Los Angeles, Los Angeles Holiness Church.

Suzuki, Daisetz Teitaro
1959   *Zen and Japanese Culture.*   New York, Pantheon Books.

Suzuki, Nanju
1968   *Burajiru Nippon Imin no Kusawake.*   Sao Paulo.

1969   *Uzumoreyuku Takujin no Ashiato.*   Sao Paulo, Paulista Bijutsu Insatsu Kabushiki Kaisha.

Suzuki, Teiiti
    1969 *The Japanese Immigrant in Brazil.* Tokyo, University
          of Tokyo Press.

    1971 "Mobilidade Geografica de Imigrantes Japoneses" in
          Centro de Estudos Nipo-Brasileiros.

Takiya, Gisuke
    1974 "Kaitaku Senkyosha-tachi no Ashiato" in Federacao
          Evangelica Japonesa do Brasil.

Tinker, John N.
    1973 "Intermarriage and Ethnic Boundaries in the Japanese
          American Case," The Journal of Social Issues, Vol. 29,
          No. 2, 1973.

Thomas, William M. M.
    1939 "Diario Episcopal" in Igreja Episcopal Brasileira.

Tippett, Alan R.
    1970 *Church Growth and the Word of God.* Grand Rapids,
          William B. Eerdmans Publishing Company.

Tippett, A. R., ed.
    1973 *God, Man and Church Growth.* Grand Rapids, William
          B. Eerdmans Publishing Company.

Toyotome, Masumi
    1974 *Enjoyable Personal Evangelism.* Los Angeles,
          Missionary Strategy Agency.

Tsuchida, Nobuya
    1971 "History of Japanese Immigration to Brazil: 1908 -
          1925." An unpublished M.A. thesis, University of
          California at Los Angeles.

U. S. Department of Commerce Bureau of the Census
    1972 *General Population Characteristics: United States
          Summary.* Washington, Govt. Print. Off.

Wagner, C. Peter
    1971 *Frontiers in Missionary Strategy.* Chicago, Moody
          Press.

    1973 *Look Out! The Pentecostals are Coming.* Carol Stream,
          Ill., Creation House.

    1974 *Stop the World I want to Get on.* Glendale, Calif.,
          A Division of G/L Publications.

1976 *Your Church can Grow: Seven Vital Signs of a Healthy
      Church.* Glendale, Calif., A Division of G/L
      Publications.

Wagner, C. Peter, ed.
1972 *Church/Mission Tension Today.* Chicago, Moody Press.

Wako Shungoro Shi Tsuioku-ki Kanko Iinkai
1966 *Hibi Aratanariki: Aru Takujin no Shogai.* Sao Paulo,
      Insatsu Seihon Kabushiki Kaisha Teikoku Shoin.

Watson, Leslie
1968 "Conserving the Converts in the Japanese Church."
      An unpublished M.A. thesis, Fuller Theological
      Seminary.

Williems, Emilio
1948 *Aspectos da Aculturacao dos Japoneses no Estado de
      Sao Paulo.* Sao Paulo, University of Sao Paulo.

1967 *The Followers of the New Faith: Culture Change and
      the Rise of Protestantism in Brazil and Chile.*
      Nashville, Vanderbilt University Press.

Winter, Ralph D.
1970 *The Twenty-Five Unbelievable Years* 1945-1969. South
      Pasadena, Calif., William Carey Library.

1972 "The Planting of Younger Missions" in C. Peter Wagner
      (ed.).

Yamada, Miyoko
1966 "The Pacific Coast Japanese Conference of the Free
      Methodist Church." An unpublished M.A. thesis, Fuller
      Theological Seminary.

Yamamori, Tetsunao
1974 *Church Growth in Japan: A Study in Development of
      Eight Denominations* 1859-1939. South Pasadena, Calif.,
      William Carey Library.

Yamasaki, Nagafumi
1971 *Akatsuchi ni Maku.* Tokyo, Inochi no Kotoba Sha.

1976 *Mashu no Hikari.* Tokyo, Inochi no Kotoba Sha.

Yamasaki, Washio, and Tiyozaki, Hideo
1970 *Nippon Holiness Kyodan.* Tokyo, Nippon Holiness Kyodan.

Yoneda, Isamu
1959 *Nakada Juji Den.* Tokyo, Nakada Juji Den Kanko Kai.

INTERVIEWS

Arai, Toshiko
    1975 Interview with author, July, 1975.

Haibara, Shigeru
    1975 Interview with author, July, 1975.

Hamada, Keizo
    1975 Interview with author, July, 1975.

Hayashi, Hiroyuki
    1970 Interview with author, July, 1970.

Kajimura, Kinji
    1975 Interview with author, July, 1975.

Kunihiro, Hideo
    1975 Interview with author, July, 1975.

Kunihiro, Ken
    1975 Interview with author, July, 1975.

Mita, Shoh Koh
    1972 Interview with author, July, 1975.

Miyamoto, Sumiko
    1975 Interview with author, July, 1975.

Nagata, Mitsuo
    1975 Interview with author, July, 1975.

Niwa, Akio
    1975 Interview with author, July, 1975,

Ono, Makoto
    1975 Interview with author, July, 1975.

Oshima, Takero
    1975 Interview with author, July, 1975.

Ozawa, Nori
    1975 Interview with author, June, 1975.

Ryckman, Harold
    1976 Interview with author, 1976.

Ryckman, Lucile
    1976 Interview with author, July, 1975.

Sakai
1975   Interview with author, July, 1975.

Sukuma, Samuel
1975   Interview with author, July, 1975.

Sakuma, Taisuke
1975   Interview with author, July, 1975.

Shimizu, Seiichi
1975   Interview with author, July, 1975.

Takemura, Koretora
1976   Interview with Makoto Ono, February, 1976.

Takeuchi, Shigeo
1974   Interview with Makoto Ono, 1974.

Takiya, Gisuke
1975   Interview with author, July, 1975.

Tamura, Koji
1975   Interview with author, July, 1975.

Uchida, Kinzo
1975   Interview with author, July, 1975.

Yamamoto, Shinichi
1975   Interview with author, July, 1975.

Yamasaki, Nagafumi
1975   Interview with author, July, 1975.

Yuba, Shigeru
1963   Interview with Wesley King, November, 1963.

Yuasa, Juro
1975   Interview with author, July, 1975.

LETTERS

Bando, Yosabro
1975   Letter to author, July, 1975.

Haslam, Robert B.
1973   Letter to author, October 16, 1973.

Hosokawa, Sueo
1975   Letter to author, September 15, 1975.

Kamizawa, Hisayoshi
    1975 Letter to author, July, 1975.

King, Wesley
    1963 Letter to Clancy Thompson, November 23, 1963.

    1974 Letter to author, 1974.

Ito, Yasoji
    1929 Letter to John Wilson Wood, May 30, 1929.

    1930 Letter to John Wilson Wood, January 16, 1930.

Ono, Makoto
    1973 Letter to author, October 16, 1973.

Ono, Sukeichi
    1975 Letter to author, December 23, 1975.

Onoda, Mamoru
    1976 Letter to author, 1976.

Otani, Andrew N.
    1976 Letter to author, March 18, 1976.

Ryckman, Harold and Lucile
    1974 Letter to author, February 16, 1974.

Tamura, Koji
    1975 Letter to author, July 13, 1975.

Thompson, Clancy
    1974 Letter to author, March 20, 1974.

Yamamoto, Shinichi
    1974 Letter to author, June 10, 1974.

Yamada, Hitoshi
    1976 Letter to author, January 23, 1976.

Index

About the Author

John Mizuki was born November 14, 1922, in Mairiporan, state of Sao Paulo, Brazil. He received his B.A. in philosophy from the University of Sao Paulo, and his Th.B. from the Independent Presbyterian Seminary. He entered the Christian ministry in 1950 and worked as a pastor for three years in Lins and Sao Paulo.

In 1953, he came to the United States, where he attended Asbury Theological Seminary and Princeton Theological Seminary, receiving from both institutions the M.Th. degree.

In 1955 he married the former Miyoko Morimoto and returned to Brazil. He has four children, Paul (22), Steven (20), Ruy (18), and Priscila (14).

After returning to Brazil, he taught at the Free Methodist Seminary for twelve years, of which six years he served as the dean. He also pastored the Free Methodist Church of Mirandopolis, Sao Paulo, for eight years. He served as a member of the administrative board of the Evangelical Confederation of Brazil and of the Brazilian Bible Society.

In 1967, he came to the United States, and ever since has been serving as a pastor of the Glendale Japanese Free Methodist Church in California. From 1969 to 1973 he attended California State University at Northridge, where he did graduate work in sociology. In the fall of 1973 he was enrolled at Fuller School of World Mission, where he earned his Doctor of Missiology degree in 1977.

BOOKS BY THE
WILLIAM CAREY LIBRARY

GENERAL

American Missions in Bicentennial Perspective edited by R. Pierce Beaver, $8.95 paper, 448 pp.

The Birth of Missions in America by Charles L. Chaney, $7.95 paper, 352 pp.

Education of Missionaries' Children: The Neglected Dimension of World Mission by D. Bruce Lockerbie, $1.95 paper, 76 pp.

Evangelicals Face the Future edited by Donald E. Hoke, $6.95 paper, 184 pp.

The Holdeman People: The Church in Christ, Mennonite, 1859-1969 by Clarence Hiebert, $17.95 cloth, 688 pp.

On the Move with the Master: A Daily Devotional Guide on World Mission by Duain W. Vierow, $4.95 paper, 176 pp.

The Radical Nature of Christianity: Church Growth Eyes Look at the Supernatural Mission of the Christian and the Church by Waldo J. Werning (Mandate Press), $5.85 paper, 224 pp.

Social Action vs. Evangelism: An Essay on the Contemporary Crisis by William J. Richardson, $1.95x paper, 64 pp.

STRATEGY OF MISSION

Church Growth and Christian Mission by Donald A. McGavran, $4.95x paper, 256 pp.

Church Growth and Group Conversion by Donald A. McGavran et al., $2.45 paper, 128 pp.

Committed Communities: Fresh Streams for World Missions by Charles J. Mellis, $3.95 paper, 160 pp.

The Conciliar-Evangelical Debate: The Crucial Documents, 1964-1976 edited by Donald McGavran, $8.95 paper, 400 pp.

Crucial Dimensions in World Evangelization edited by Arthur F. Glasser et al., $7.95x paper, 480 pp.

Evangelical Missions Tomorrow edited by Wade T. Coggins and Edwin L. Frizen, Jr., $5.95 paper, 208 pp.

Everything You Need to Grow a Messianic Synagogue by Phillip E. Goble, $2.45 paper, 176 pp.

Here's How: Health Education by Extension by Ronald and Edith Seaton, $3.45 paper, 144 pp.

The Indigenous Church and the Missionary by Melvin L. Hodges, $2.95 paper, 108 pp.

A Manual for Church Growth Surveys by Ebbie C. Smith, $3.95 paper, 144 pp.

Mission: A Practical Approach to Church-Sponsored Mission Work by Daniel C. Hardin, $4.95x paper, 264 pp.

Readings in Third World Missions: A Collection of Essential Documents edited by Marlin L. Nelson, $6.95x paper, 304 pp.

AREA AND CASE STUDIES

Aspects of Pacific Ethnohistory by Alan R. Tippett, $3.95 paper, 216 pp.

A Century of Growth: The Kachin Baptist Church of Burma by Herman Tegenfeldt, $9.95 cloth, 540 pp.

Christian Mission to Muslims - The Record: Anglican and Reformed Approaches in India and the Near East, 1800-1938 by Lyle L. Vander Werff, $8.95 paper, 384 pp.

Church Growth in Burundi by Donald Hohensee, $4.95 paper, 160 pp.

Church Growth in Japan by Tetsunao Yamamori, $4.95 paper, 184 pp.

Church Planting in Uganda: A Comparative Study by Gailyn Van Rheenen, $4.95 paper, 192 pp.

Circle of Harmony: A Case Study in Popular Japanese Buddhism by Kenneth J. Dale, $4.95 paper, 238 pp.

The Deep-Sea Canoe: The Story of Third World Missionaries in the South Pacific by Alan R. Tippett, $3.45x paper, 144 pp.

Frontier Peoples of Central Nigeria and a Strategy for Outreach by Gerald O. Swank, $5.95 paper, 192 pp.

The Growth Crisis in the American Church: A Presbyterian Case Study by Foster H. Shannon, $4.95 paper, 176 pp.

The How and Why of Third World Missions: An Asian Case Study by Marlin L. Nelson, $6.95 paper, 256 pp.

I Will Build My Church: Ten Case Studies of Church Growth in Taiwan edited by Allen J. Swanson, $4.95 paper, 177 pp.

Indonesian Revival: Why Two Million Came to Christ by Avery T. Willis, Jr., $6.95 paper, 288 pp.

Industrialization: Brazil's Catalyst for Church Growth by C.W. Gates, $1.95 paper, 96 pp.

The Navajos Are Coming to Jesus by Thomas Dolaghan and David Scates, $5.95 paper, 192 pp.

New Move Forward in Europe: Growth Patterns of German-Speaking Baptists by William L. Wagner, $8.95 paper, 368 pp.

People Movements in the Punjab by Margaret and Frederick Stock, $8.95 paper, 388 pp.

Profile for Victory: New Proposals for Missions in Zambia by Max Ward Randall, $3.95 cloth, 224 pp.

The Protestant Movement in Bolivia by C. Peter Wagner, $3.95 paper, 264 pp.

Protestants in Modern Spain: The Struggle for Religious Pluralism by Dale G. Vought, $3.45 paper, 168 pp.

The Religious Dimension in Hispanic Los Angeles by Clifton L. Holland, $9.95 paper, 550 pp.

The Role of the Faith Mission: A Brazilian Case Study by Fred Edwards, $3.45 paper, 176 pp.

La Serpiente y la Paloma (La Iglesia Apostolica de la Fe en Jesuchristo de Mexico) by Manual J. Gaxiola, $2.95 paper, 194 pp.

Solomon Islands Christianity: A Study in Growth and Obstruction by Alan R. Tippett, $5.95x paper, 432 pp.

Taiwan: Mainline Versus Independent Church Growth by Allen J. Swanson, $3.95 paper, 300 pp.

Tonga Christianity by Stanford Shewmaker, $3.45 paper, 164 pp.

Toward Continuous Mission: Strategizing for the Evangelization of Bolivia by W. Douglas Smith, $4.95 paper, 208 pp.

Treasure Island: Church Growth Among Taiwan's Urban Minnan Chinese by Robert J. Bolton, $6.95 paper, 416 pp.

Understanding Latin Americans by Eugene A. Nida, $3.95 paper, 176 pp.

A Yankee Reformer in Chile: The Life and Works of David Trumbull by Irven Paul, $3.95 paper, 172 pp.

APPLIED ANTHROPOLOGY

Becoming Bilingual: A Guide to Language Learning by Donald Larson and William A. Smalley, $5.95x paper, 426 pp.

Christopaganism or Indigenous Christianity? edited by Tetsunao Yamamori and Charles R. Taber, $5.95 paper, 242 pp.

The Church and Cultures: Applied Anthropology for the Religious Worker by Louis J. Luzbetak, $5.95x paper, 448 pp.

Culture and Human Values: Christian Intervention in Anthropological Perspective (writings of Jacob Loewen) edited by William A. Smalley, $5.95x paper, 466 pp.

Customs and Cultures: Anthropology for Christian Missions by Eugene A. Nida, $3.95 paper, 322 pp.

Manual of Articulatory Phonetics by William A. Smalley, $5.95x paper, 522 pp.

Message and Mission: The Communication of the Christian Faith by Eugene A. Nida, $3.95x paper, 254 pp.

Readings in Missionary Anthropology edited by William A. Smalley, $5.95x paper, 384 pp.

Tips on Taping: Language Recording in the Social Sciences by Wayne and Lonna Dickerson, $4.95x paper, 208 pp.

THEOLOGICAL EDUCATION BY EXTENSION

Principios del Crecimiento de la Iglesia by Wayne C. Weld and Donald A. McGavran, $3.95 paper, 448 pp.

The World Directory of Theological Education by Extension by Wayne C. Weld, $5.95x paper, 416 pp., *1976 Supplement only*, $1.95x, 64 pp.

Writing for Theological Education by Extension by Lois McKinney, $1.45x paper, 64 pp.

REFERENCE

An American Directory of Schools and Colleges Offering Missionary Courses edited by Glenn Schwartz, $5.95x paper, 266 pp.

Bibliography for Cross-Cultural Workers, edited by Alan R. Tippett, $4.95 paper, 256 pp.

Church Growth Bulletin, Second Consolidated Volume (Sept. 1969-July 1975) edited by Donald McGavran, $7.95x paper, 512 pp.

Evangelical Missions Quarterly Vols. 7-9, $8.95x cloth, 330 pp.

The Means of World Evangelization: Missiological Education at the Fuller School of World Mission edited by Alvin Martin, $9.95 paper, 544 pp.

Protestantism in Latin America: A Bibliographical Guide edited by John H. Sinclair, $8.95x paper, 448 pp.

The World Directory of Mission-Related Educational Institutions edited by Ted Ward and Raymond Buker, Sr., $19.95x cloth, 906 pp.

POPULARIZING MISSION

Defeat of the Bird God by C. Peter Wagner, $4.95 paper, 256 pp.

The Night Cometh: Two Wealthy Evangelicals Face the Nation by Rebecca J. Winter, $2.95 paper, 96 pp.

The Task Before Us (audiovisual) by the Navigators, $29.95, 137 slides

The 25 Unbelievable Years: 1945-1969 by Ralph D. Winter, $2.95 paper, 128 pp.

The Word-Carrying Giant: The Growth of the American Bible Society by Creighton Lacy, $5.95 paper, 320 pp.

BOOKLETS

The Grounds for a New Thrust in World Mission by Ralph D. Winter, $.75 booklet, 32 pp.

The New Macedonia: A Revolutionary New Era in Missions Begins (Lausanne paper and address) by Ralph D. Winter, $ .75 booklet, 32 pp.

1980 and That Certain Elite by Ralph D. Winter, $ .35x booklet, 16 pp.

Penetrating the Last Frontiers by Ralph D. Winter, $1.00 booklet, 32 pp.

The Two Structures of God's Redemptive Mission by Ralph D. Winter, $ .35 booklet, 16 pp.

The World Christian Movement: 1950-1975 by Ralph D. Winter, $ .75 booklet, 32 pp.

HOW TO ORDER

Send orders directly to William Carey Library, 1705 N. Sierra Bonita Avenue, Pasadena, California 91104 (USA). Please allow four to six weeks for delivery in the U.S.

William Carey Library